FALL ASLEEP FOR GOOD

Justin Helzer stood behind Selina Bishop with a hammer, waiting for her to turn her back on him, but she never did.

Then Justin's brother, Taylor, put Rohypnol, the date rape drug, into Selina's wineglass, hoping she would fall asleep for good. She noticed something floating on the surface of her wine, however, and refused to drink.

"Oh, let me get you a clean glass," Taylor quickly said.

Next, Taylor lured Selina into his bedroom. A half hour went by and Taylor came out of the bedroom, complaining, "She's not falling asleep. I'm going to have her go into the family room and I'll give her a back rub."

Selina came out of the bedroom and Taylor spread a blanket on the family room's floor. He had Selina lie down on it and had her face the windows, away from the center of the room. Her head was turned away from Justin, who was standing nearby. She had no idea he had a hammer in his hand.

After fifteen minutes of Taylor massaging Selina's back and shoulders, Justin moved forward and raised the hammer.

UNHOLY SACRIFICE

ROBERT SCOTT

PINNACLE BOOKS
Kensington Publishing Corp.
http://www.kensingtonbooks.com

PINNACLE BOOKS are published by

Kensington Publishing Corp.
850 Third Avenue
New York, NY 10022

All Kensington Titles, Imprints, and Distributed Lines are available at special quantity discounts for bulk purchases for sales promotions, premiums, fund-raising, and educational or institutional use. Special book excerpts or customized printings can also be created to fit specific needs. For details, write or phone the office of the Kensington special sales manager: Kensington Publishing Corp., 850 Third Avenue, New York, NY 10022, attn: Special Sales Department. Phone: 1-800-221-2647.

Pinnacle and the P logo Reg. U.S. Pat. & TM Off.

ISBN: 0-7860-1683-3

First Printing: September 2005
10 9 8 7 6 5 4 3 2 1

Printed in the United States of America

This book is dedicated to Ivan, Annette, Selina, Jennifer, James and Ray.

Acknowledgments

Many people helped me in the creation of this book. I'd like to thank Don Wilson, Chris Darden, Ray and Mabel Carberry, Juley Salkeld, Roger Riddle and Rosanne Lusk Urban, J. Lawrence, D. Golden, G. Tardelli and B. Tweed. I'd also like to thank Tom Moyer, Mike Harkelroad, Howard Newman, the entire staff of Department Four and Criminal Court clerks. Once again, I appreciate all the help of my editor Michaela Hamilton and literary agent Damaris Rowland.

Taylor Helzer wasn't the Second Coming of Christ, he was the Second Coming of Manson.
                    —Olga Land, Jennifer Villarin's sister
                    and Selina Bishop's aunt

PROLOGUE

California Delta, August 7, 2000.

A skier crashed over the waves, rocking down the North Fork of the Mokelumne River on a large personal watercraft. Spray from the wake danced into a clear blue sky, sparkling like diamonds in the bright sunlight. The Mokelumne River ran down from the forested western slopes of the Sierra Nevada range, crossed the fertile Central Valley and exited into a thousand-mile labyrinth of waterways in the Sacramento/San Joaquin Delta.

Behind the personal watercraft, man-made levees enclosed the river, and the landscape appeared not so much like Louisiana, but like the Netherlands. In fact, it was a little bit of Holland right in the heart of California, minus the quaint windmills. All the other superlatives applied, however. Incredibly rich soils produced an abundance of crops, including tomatoes, asparagus, corn, sunflowers, almonds, pears and an array of others. The soil was so rich, in fact, made up of decomposed tules, that if it was set alight, it would burn for days, if not weeks.

And not unlike Holland, whenever a levee broke, the water came crashing in, to reclaim an island—not with salt water, but freshwater, to make it a haven for bass, crawdads, catfish and scores of other fish and marine life. It was these fish and the recreation potential that annually brought a legion of outdoor enthusiasts to the California Delta. The twisting rivers and sloughs were a watery haven for fast speedboats and personal watercrafts, sedate houseboats and sailboats, and intrepid windsurfers. In fact, the junction of the Sacramento and San Joaquin Rivers was one of the best windsurfing areas in the world. It drew enthusiasts from as far away as Europe and Australia.

These miles of often-mysterious waterways had also lured one of the twentieth-century's great mystery writers to its shores—Erle Stanley Gardner, the creator of countless Perry Mason mysteries. Spending part of each year at Bethel Island, the prolific Gardner wrote dozens of courtroom dramas that eventually sold millions of copies and turned into the popular Perry Mason television series, with its star Raymond Burr.

In his leisure time, Gardner spent days out on the Delta, exploring its channels and sleepy towns. He wrote of one area, The Meadows, in his book *Gypsy Days on the Delta:* "This is a really beautiful part of the Delta country, uninhabited islands bordered with huge trees, the waters fairly well sheltered, the scenery a yachtsman's delight."

The Delta was indeed a sort of pastoral Arcadia, and had witnessed one of the most colorful and romantic scenes in California history. In 1832, the French Canadians, of the Hudson Bay Company, and Native Americans worked together as trappers along the sloughs of the Delta. Captain Michel Laframboise presided over an encampment on the eastern shores of the region. Miss A. J. Allison wrote of the encampment and its inhabitants: "They formed themselves in Indian file, led by Mr. Laframboise, the chief of the party. Next to him rode his wife, a native woman, upon her pony, quite picturesquely clad. She wore a man's hat with long black feathers fastened in the front and drooping behind her gracefully. Her short dress was a rich broadcloth, leggings beautifully embroidered with gay beads and fringed with tiny bells, whose musical tinkling could be heard at several hundred yards distance. The trampling of the fast-walking horses, the silvery tinkling bells, the rich handsome dress and fine appearance of the riders, whose numbers amounted to sixty or seventy, had a quite imposing appearance."

This Arcadian scene in the Delta was soon to vanish, however. The richly clad cavalcade of trappers brought not only prosperity to the region, they brought smallpox and other diseases. A few years later, trapper Ewing Young wrote of the Delta Indians: "The poor creatures knew no remedy. They resorted to their charms and flocked to sweat houses and there, in groups of several hundreds, would dance frantically around a blazing fire and thus while dancing around, the malady would seize them and they would fall down in agonies of death till the sweat houses could contain no more. So impregnated was the atmosphere with the effluvia of decomposing and putrifying bodies that it was almost impossible to navigate the rivers."

In the year 2000, almost 170 years after the plague years of the 1830s, the California Delta waterways would once again become rivers of death. An event would occur that would eclipse Perry Mason's most sensational cases. It would beggar description, becoming more ghastly and more bizarre, until it took on an air of nightmarish unreality. The trigger of the event was floating just beneath the murky waters of the North Fork of the Mokelumne River, like a sea mine, ready to explode upon an unsuspecting world.

On a big loop of the Mokelumne, near the Lighthouse Resort and Rancho Marina, Steven Sibert, a skier, slowed down when he caught sight of a dark object bobbing in the water ahead. At first glance, it appeared to be only a clump of floating vegetation, not an uncommon sight in the area. Large drifts of water hyacinth sometimes broke loose and floated on the waters. When Steven Sibert came closer, however, he saw that the object was not vegetation. It was a duffel bag.

Surprised and curious, Steven Sibert opened the duffel bag and stared at it in horror. Within its sodden interior were dismembered human body parts.

Steven Sibert had no way of knowing at the time that the body parts weren't from some gangland slaying—they were much more bizarre and unbelievable than that. The victims in the duffel bag had been struck down by a man who proclaimed himself to be a prophet of God. He believed he had been given a commandment by God to declare war on Satan and usher in the millenial reign of Jesus Christ's Second Coming.

The young prophet had taken the name Jordan, as if aware that he was crossing over the river into a wilderness of his own devising. He was at war with the established order of the Mormon Church, at war with the United States government, and at war with Satan and all his minions. In his quest for righteousness, he had two disciples to help him in his grandiose plans to transform America. If America had to be transformed by blood sacrifice, then he was willing to take whatever measures he deemed necessary.

The young man may have called himself Jordan, but in reality he was thirty-year-old Glenn Taylor Helzer. He had been a devout Mormon, National Guardsman, successful stockbroker, prophet and now murderer.

As Steven Sibert gazed down on the severed body parts, he witnessed the fruits of Glenn Taylor Helzer's unholy sacrifices.

CHAPTER 1

The Golden Child and Aspect

Taylor Helzer's father, Gerry, was a devout Mormon and an insurance salesman. In time, he would also become an expert white-water raft guide and operator. Taylor's mother, Carma, was also a devout Mormon, housewife and sometimes physical therapist. They led a typical, middle-class Mormon life of church, family and responsible living. The family moved often through various states, which included Texas and Georgia. The family eventually settled down in the small town of Pacheco, California, about thirty miles from San Francisco, in Contra Costa County. Contra Costa was a mix of rolling hills, vibrant cities and industrial complexes. It was a place where intrepid mountain man Joseph Walker decided to settle down, as well as world-famous naturalist John Muir. His home in Martinez became a magnet for the environmental movement, as well as a splendid working farm and orchard.

Glenn Taylor Helzer was born on July 26, 1970, and from the beginning, he was the beloved son in the

Helzer household. Taylor was bright, charming and good-looking, and it seemed that life for everyone began to revolve around him. Even from an early age, he could quote scripture from the Book of Mormon with great presence of mind and a gift for memorization. One of the local bishops of the church predicted great things for Taylor.

Even though his first name was Glenn, it wasn't long before almost everyone began calling him Taylor. One of his cousins, Charney Hoffman, had many things to say about Taylor in the years to come. Of Taylor's youth, Hoffman said, "We lived with them for some time when I was young in Georgia. As we got a little bit older, we continued to meet. I stayed in touch with Taylor. I absolutely loved him. He was very influential in my life and lots of other people's lives. He was never, never judgmental toward my family, though my family is definitely not an example of how the Latter-Day Saints church would like people to live.

"Taylor was very accepting, regardless of the fact that's not always the case with people who are very religious. But Taylor always sought to foster a lot of love and understanding in all of his relationships.

"I remember going to Marriott's Great America and somebody said something to make me think they were stupid. I remember being sarcastic to that person. And Taylor stopped me. He had insight to know that I was being cruel to somebody else because somebody had been cruel to me. He said, 'Wait a second, do you understand that you probably hurt that person's feelings?'

"Taylor was always the light in a group. You were always having fun as long as Taylor was there because he brought people together."

Justin Helzer was born on February 12, 1972, and became the middle child after a daughter, Heather, was born to the Helzers. Justin was shy and polite. He seemed awkward compared to his dynamic and charismatic brother, Taylor. Justin was forever in Taylor's shadow, even at an early age. Whereas Taylor seemed to have countless friends in school, both male and female, Justin had almost none. He was painfully shy around girls and tried not to stick out in class. This became somewhat difficult as he grew in height, towering over his classmates by the time he was in junior high school.

When the Helzer children were teenagers, they went to live for a while with their grandfather, Doyle Sorenson, who was Carma's father. Doyle was very religious and some thought him to be on the fringes of the Mormon faith.

On one occasion, Doyle claimed that he had seen Jesus Christ in his front yard. It wasn't just a vision, he said. Jesus was there in the flesh, and Doyle went outside to talk with him. The vision was not of a short duration—Doyle later claimed that Jesus was there for hours. Taylor was very taken with his grandfather Doyle. He admired his piety and spirituality.

Taylor had problems living up to these ideals, however. He felt guilty after sinning, especially if he masturbated. Consumed with guilt, he tried committing suicide at one point. Years later, a psychiatrist, Dr. Douglas Tucker, said, "Taylor as early as fourteen was experiencing ideas that were unusual and inappropriate. He was receiving inaudible messages by the age of fourteen. Taylor was told he had the gift of revelation, but he didn't know if the messages he was receiving were from God or Satan."

In Concord, California, in 1985, a girl named Ann met Taylor Helzer at Ygnacio Valley High School. Even though Taylor didn't play sports and wasn't involved in student government, Ann realized that almost everyone at Ygnacio Valley High knew Taylor. He was dynamic and personable. "There was something charismatic about him," she said later. "You noticed him." For a time after high school, Ann and Taylor went their separate ways, but she would not forget the charismatic young man.

By contrast, Justin ghosted through his high school years. He was pleasant and amiable, but had none of Taylor's flair for self-advertisement. Not that he was without some admirers. Years later, William Smithausen, who was a biology teacher at Ygnacio Valley High, said, "I remember Justin very well. He was one of the tallest kids in class. He had a wonderful smile and was a pleasure to teach. He added humor to the class. Very pleasant and cooperative. Even after teaching more than five thousand kids, I remembered Justin. He was unique."

One thing that made him unique was his absolute docility. He seemed to be always waiting for someone else to direct him, especially his brother.

At the age of seventeen, Taylor decided to join the National Guard. He was underage, however, and his relative Jill Tingey recalled, "They (he and Carma) came down because he was going into the National Guard. Carma and Taylor were there and kept running into red-tape problems. So they were, off and on, at our place for six weeks. Taylor was so sweet and wonderful. My children loved him. He was cooperative and he was helpful. We were doing various projects, gardening and painting the fence and stuff. He was awesome. I wished he was my kid."

Taylor ran into problems in the National Guard in Texas, however. His eyes were opened by the drinking, swearing and chasing after women by his fellow unit members. He even began preaching to them about the errors of their ways. To some, he was a terrible prig, but a few of his fellow recruits listened to what he had to say. If nothing else, Taylor was always very talkative and knew how to persuade some individuals.

After the National Guard, Taylor decided to go on mission. For young Mormon men and women, going on mission is one of the highlights of their lives. They are sent to another area or country, are teamed up with a partner and teach about the Book of Mormon and the LDS Church.

Charney Hoffman recalled Taylor's going-away party. Hoffman said, "The main meeting is actually given to the family members and the departing missionary to deliver some type of message. The message of the meeting from Taylor and from his parents was after other people spoke. And the things people said about Taylor were to the effect of—he had a good effect on them. Taylor, according to what people said, read scriptures with virtually anyone who raised their hand. Most of the people talked about insights that Taylor brought, which is actually unusual. Usually people give their own comments, but in that ward, he had a lot of clout. People were very, very proud of the interaction that they had with Taylor. People were excited to share insights about life, about scripture, about anything. The positive influence that he had in their lives."

When he reached Brazil, Taylor was exuberant about his mission. He wrote in a journal that he needed to work on everything. He said, "I can't disobey the slightest whispering of Spirit." He added that he needed to follow through on everything that the Spirit told him.

One time on a plane trip in Brazil, there were members of a rock-and-roll band sitting across from him. Taylor smiled at them, but they did not smile back. He felt that they were cold and dead. He wrote later, "I hope I will remember that it is not fame or money that make people happy."

A person who knew Taylor very well on his mission in Brazil was a young man named Jonathon Taylor. Jonathon left home for his mission at the age of nineteen in 1990. He recalled, "I served my mission in Brazil, specifically the Brazilian Mission, which was where the headquarters of the mission territory was located. Although the territory of the mission was quite large, it included a number of different territories, Brazilian states and larger cities. I served in many of those areas.

"When I arrived, I felt equal parts excited and overwhelmed. Excited simply because I was anxious to serve on a mission—I had certainly been trained in the language—but nervous because you're a little bit out of your element. It's a new experience and you're a long way from home.

"I met Taylor Helzer on my second day in the country. I met him in a small rural city about sixty miles outside the mission headquarters in a town called Oxidental. There were four missionaries assigned to that area. We all lived in a very small house.

"Missionaries are given the title of elder, or if she's a female, they're given the title of sister. So I was Elder Taylor to him, and he was Elder Helzer to me. When I first met Taylor, he was energetic, passionate and seemed to really relish the mission experience. He also struck me as very intelligent. I liked him immediately. He spoke the language relatively well for somebody who had been in the country only as long as he had been. He was on his mission a few months longer than I had been, so we struck up a close friendship relatively quickly.

"He was excited and passionate about the work. He seemed to work very, very hard at it. I enjoyed working with him. He was not my official companion initially, but he kind of became my de facto companion. You always work in twos. His companion was about ready to go home, and my companion was a friend of his companion. They were both Brazilian and spent a lot of time together. So Helzer and I became de facto companions.

"I very much enjoyed working with him—he seemed to have a genuine care for the people. And I certainly learned some things from him. I felt that he was particularly effective in teaching. People seemed to like him, and he had a very, very capable manner about him.

"Scripture and religious doctrine was of interest to me, and it was also of great interest to Helzer. We would spend a lot of time studying scripture and that's not atypical of a missionary. Helzer was more skilled at it than most. I think that's one of the reasons we became good friends."

There was almost a mania in Taylor's reading and interpreting of scripture, however. Sometimes he would stay up all night reading scripture from the Book of Mormon and dwelling upon what was written there. He would go off on tangents, trying to discern thoughts beyond the surface meaning. It led him into some strange interpretations of scripture.

Taylor had a hard time sleeping at night. He would write in his journal, hour after hour. Some of the main topics were about the Last Days, faith, miracles and his future family. He said, "I have been feeling the fruits of Spirit. It is impossible to turn my mind off. I have never felt the spirit of the Holy Ghost so strongly before."

Jonathon Taylor started to notice a change in Taylor Helzer's demeanor. He said later, "The changes in Taylor were fairly abrupt. Probably three-and-a-half to four months into our six months together. Some of the conclusions and beliefs he began to draw—he'd state them more emphatically. Our relationship became a bit more strained. We would end up butting heads on issues, where I would state, 'You know, Helzer, I think you're taking that a little too far. You're lacking certain pieces of information in order to make that conclusion.'

"He sensed he had been given additional inspiration to kind of understand how these things connected. It also carried over into our teaching. When we would teach together, he began to teach these things he was studying. And the church has a very set curriculum that you're supposed to teach people who are interested in hearing about church doctrines.

"Helzer dwelled upon certain cataclysmic events in the Latter Days. These were of particular interest to him. He would talk about his opinion that there would be the elimination of technology. He thought technology would be rendered useless in the Last Days, and the church or religious leadership would really fall into groups that would be led by warrior prophets, who would defend the people and their faith."

Taylor Helzer envisioned a sort of Mad Max world with bands of people led by warrior priests. They would adopt a fortress mentality. They would practice survivalist skills and fight against the forces of darkness. The landscape would be a mixture of Book of Revelations, chaos and Lord of the Rings–type setting.

Jonathon Taylor said, "I struggled with that concept. And he started to take [those ideas] to our mission president. Helzer started to debate scripture with the mission president. Taylor would come out from those meetings and say, 'Well, you know I brought up such and such, and he doesn't know anything about it.' Taylor just seemed increasingly frustrated with our mission president. He started to view the president as not a spiritual leader.

"Then Helzer started to read writings of other church

leaders of a higher level, and I would say it was a similar reaction. If there were things that he didn't feel were accurate or if he didn't agree with them, he kind of dismissed them by saying the church leaders either knew the truth and weren't revealing it, or they didn't know the truth and therefore he was not accountable to them. Maybe there were others more qualified to be in their position.

"We parted as friends, and he was moved to a different location in the mission. I saw him probably three or four months later. He immediately wanted to start talking about some of these doctrinal issues, saying he had received additional thoughts and inspiration."

In the end, Taylor Helzer came home from his mission, very disillusioned that others would not see things his way. He not only felt this way about the mission in Brazil, he was beginning to feel that way about the top leadership of the Mormon Church in Salt Lake City.

Charney Hoffman noticed the change in Taylor when he arrived home. Charney said later, "Taylor believed that because of the story of Adam and Eve in the Bible, he believed that the paradigm of good and evil was something brought to us or given to us by the Devil. One needed to reject the false paradigm in order to be saved. A kind of Buddhist-type take on Judeo-Christianity.

"In talking to him, he would become very upset, very irritated, if you didn't agree with his perspective. It was hard for him to communicate with people who couldn't see things the way he saw them. To anybody else, it would look really weird."

Despite all his struggles with faith and doctrine, Taylor did find time for romance. He ran into Ann, whom he'd known in Ygnacio Valley High School, at a movie theater, one month after he returned from his mission. He liked her and thought she was very pretty, but she was not a Mormon. Taylor discussed this problem with his cousin Charney Hoffman. Hoffman said years later, "We talked for a long time. He told me how he was making the decision whether or not he ought to marry Ann. That kind of spiritual quest. He wanted to make sure that marrying her made sense in terms of his overall spiritual goals.

"We spent a long time talking about these things in his personal life. He actually didn't even want to date Ann until she actually converted to his religion. He felt that it would be inconsistent with his spiritual life. So he persuaded her to learn about the LDS Church, and eventually she joined. They had their first date when she was baptized into the Church."

Even as Taylor dated Ann, there was a substrata of angst occurring in his life. Like many of the other members of his family, Taylor believed that one day modern society would break down. Charney explained later, "We went on a survival campout. A bunch of people in our family got together. The purpose from the survival meeting was based on the idea that one day there would be apocalyptic disasters requiring people to fend for themselves without the benefits of modern technology. People would have to build their own forts and live off the land.

"In our family, there are a lot of people who have a very apocalyptic perspective on life in general. A little survival concept was consistent with my extended family's general belief that one day in this great cosmic battle between good and evil they would be required to survive on their own."

It was no wonder that Taylor, and even to a larger degree, Justin, began to adopt ideas from right-wing survivalist James "Bo" Gritz. Bo Gritz was a highly decorated Green Berct who had served in the Vietnam War.

After the war, he led commando-style missions into Southeast Asia searching for American POWs. Gritz also adopted a stance of anti–big-government ideals, stating, "Tyranny always wears the badge of authority."

In 1992, he ran for president of the United States on the Populist ticket, with the slogan "God, Guns and Gritz." He also taught survival classes in the western mountains. By the late 1990s Gritz imbued these classes with an apocalyptic Christian rhetoric. He founded the Center for Action—Fellowship of Eternal Warriors. On his Web site, he stated, "Contact me if you feel God has called you to be a spiritual warrior for these last days."

It's not apparent if Taylor or Justin Helzer ever contacted Bo Gritz, but they certainly would adopt the phrase "spiritual warrior" as part of their lexicon.

Despite survivalist tendencies and visions of apocalypse, Taylor and Ann were married in April 1993, a fact that disturbed Justin greatly. He was away on mission at the time and knew nothing of the upcoming marriage of Ann and Taylor. Ann said later, "Justin was hurt that Taylor never consulted him about getting married. He felt it was such a major decision. Justin couldn't understand why Taylor wouldn't wait the mere six months remaining of his mission, before getting married."

The wedding took place at the Oakland Mormon Temple, but because non-Mormons were not allowed inside the temple, a ring exchange also took place in Walnut Creek.

Perhaps Taylor should have consulted Justin about the marriage. According to Ann, the marriage began to unravel right from the beginning. In fact, things were so bad that she and Taylor went in for marriage counseling soon after the honeymoon.

The counseling apparently didn't do much good. According to Ann, she and Taylor constantly argued.

Everything had to be his way. He could never admit that he was wrong. She said, "Taylor had an unrealistic view of the world. He had never been able to watch television at his parents' home. So in our home for the first time he could watch cable television. He would stay up all night and then have to be at work by six A.M. He couldn't pull himself away. He said, 'There's so much great stuff on.'

"He would also stop into arcades after work and forget to come home for dinner. He even said, 'I want to try everything.'"

The one thing he wanted more than anything else was sex like he saw on porno videos. He begged his wife for the things he saw, he cajoled her and pestered her constantly. But Ann was not comfortable doing some of the things depicted on the videos.

Even the births of two daughters did not help. Now there were even more things to argue about, especially about their upbringing.

Ann had some very perceptive insights about Taylor's role in the extended Helzer family. She said later, "Taylor had a strong personality. He appeared to run the family. He was held up on a pedestal— especially by his mother, Carma. But everyone in the Helzer family looked up to Taylor. He was the Golden Child."

Ann seemed to think that Carma, not Gerry, ran the Helzer family. Gerry was just a "laid-back nice guy," in her estimation. Carma was more forceful and driven. Ann said, "Carma took the lead. She also communicated quite a bit with me and Taylor during our marriage."

If Taylor was the "Golden Child," in the Helzer family, Justin was almost a ghost. He lived in the shadow of his dominant brother. One time Justin even admitted, "I'm just an aspect to her." Carma seemed to shower all her devotion on Taylor. Later, she would even admit to this, saying that she should have spent more time with Justin. Yet even she could not seem to get enough of basking in Taylor's glow. He was a dynamo of energy and ideas.

Strangely enough, it was the births of Taylor and Ann's daughters that brought Justin much closer to Ann. She said, "Justin was loving and sweet. He definitely made time for the girls. He'd read books to the girls and would spend two hours with them when he came to visit. My kids thought Justin was the neatest person around. He was their favorite uncle."

Ann recounted one more interesting fact—she trusted Justin more with her girls than she did Taylor. Taylor was too self-absorbed; everything had to revolve around him.

Ann's uncle happened to work for Morgan Stanley/Dean Witter, and he agreed in 1993 to show Taylor the ropes within the company, even though Taylor had taken only one semester of college classes. In some ways, Taylor was tailor-made for Dean Witter. He had a charming personality, drive, ambition and talent for salesmanship. He wasn't afraid to dive into cold calls, something most salesman and brokers hated. Taylor had a natural gift of gab and selling ability. In May 1993, he joined the Morgan Stanley/Dean Witter branch in Walnut Creek. His sister, Heather, already worked there as a secretary. She remembered that year as being particularly good. Taylor seemed to be getting on track at last.

George Calhoun, a salesman at Dean Witter, possessed a hearty manner and good cheer. He rose in Dean Witter eventually to become a branch manager. In 1993, Calhoun noted, Taylor Helzer was hired into his office as a financial adviser trainee. Calhoun could see the potential that Taylor possessed. He said later,

"Taylor was a rising star. He was somebody who could meet people with money and bring them in. He was very outgoing. Very friendly. Always upbeat.

"He would come in and say things like, 'George, I love this job! This is a great job. I'm thrilled!'

"I was aware of his Mormon upbringing. He was a clean and wholesome guy."

Taylor did well at the office branch and was hired full-time. His list of clients eventually grew to around two hundred people. These were people who had funds that ranged anywhere from a few thousand dollars up to nearly a million dollars. Taylor seemed to be genuinely interested in helping them manage their money.

Then in late 1996, George Calhoun started to notice a change in Taylor. Calhoun said, "Taylor started smoking cigarettes and going out to nightclubs—two very un-Mormon-like activities. He let his hair grow long. He became more unkempt and less reliable."

Calhoun tried to talk with Taylor and bring him back on track. Taylor just smiled and said he could go out nightclubbing and handle his office duties as well. Yet as time went on, it seemed that Taylor was more interested in nightclubbing than he was in performing his duties.

Another person acquainted with the dynamics of the Helzer family was Dane Williams. In 1987, when he was nineteen years old, he joined the LDS Church and went to some of their dances. He also spent a lot of time at the Helzer household and went river rafting with them almost every summer.

Of Taylor he said, "I was very influenced by Taylor. The way he carried himself. His knowledge of scripture."

About Justin, Williams said, "He was sincere and compassionate. From what I was able to see, Taylor seemed to look out for his brother. I thought they were inseparable. The river-rafting trips were a huge bond. I don't recollect them fighting. Not even a cross word."

On these raft trips, usually on the American River in the foothills of the Sierra Nevada range, Gerry would lead the group and Taylor often was the leader on a particular raft. These rafts could hold up to six people, and Gerry and Taylor became experts in white-water navigation. They took friends and family along on trips. On one occasion, they even took a family of Taylor's clients along. They were an elderly couple, Ivan and Annette Stineman, and their daughter, Nancy, and her boyfriend. Justin would sometimes help on the raft trips, but he was always second fiddle to Taylor.

Dane Williams said of Justin, "He kind of did everything his brother did. Taylor went into the National Guard. Then Justin joined the National Guard. Taylor worked for an asphalt company, and then Justin did."

Justin's National Guard stint came during the Gulf War years. He became a military policeman (MP) and spent his time in Germany. One person who knew Justin then was Nicolai Nenad. Nicolai was a fellow MP. He said later, "Justin was a polite guy. No cursing. No drinking. He was always an 'Opie.'" (This was a reference to Ron Howard's open and naive character on *The Andy Griffith Show*).

"There was never any back talk from him. In some ways, he was too nice to be an MP. You could put money right on the top of a bunk. He wouldn't take it. He trusted everybody.

"He was brought up not to see a naked body. So one day, me and the other MPs played a trick on him. We took a soldier's manual and put nudie girl photos between the pages. Somebody asked him if this was the schematic of an M16 rifle. He looked at the photos and covered his eyes.

"He didn't want to talk about pornography or anything like that, but we didn't treat him like an outcast or anything. He was easy to tease, but he got along."

One thing Justin learned about as an MP was how to handle weapons. He carried a military-style 9mm pistol with him when he was on duty. He was a good marksman.

When Justin got home from his stint in the National Guard, he was still an Opie—open, trusting and naive. He began to take some classes at Diablo Valley College in Pleasant Hill, and Emily White was a fellow student there. She had a class with Justin called Institution of Religions. It was basically a world-religions class. Justin was so taken with the pretty brunette that he asked her out on a date. She recalled of their first date, "It was to a religious concert. It turned out to be a cool date."

They went out a few more times and Emily recalled, "Justin was always happy. Always a smile on his face. There was an innocence about him. Tender."

Justin was heartbroken when Emily transferred to Brigham Young University in Utah. He wrote her poems. He wrote her love letters. But she did not return to California.

Diablo Valley College math teacher Tom Mowry also remembered Justin. He thought Justin was a hard worker and good at homework, but not on exams. Mowry agreed to spend extra time with Justin and help him prepare for exams. Justin went into his office several times a week and clearly wanted to learn. The sessions paid off. Justin took the class a second time and passed with a B grade.

Mowry recalled, "He was an all-around nice guy. In fact, he was a sweet guy."

It took Justin six years to get a two-year degree at Diablo Valley College, but when he did get his Associates of Arts degree, he did it with a 3.5 average.

* * *

If Ann and Taylor's marriage was a struggle from the very beginning, by the summer of 1996 it was sliding toward a precipice. Taylor wanted to test the "sinning side of life." He began smoking cigarettes and drinking alcohol, two un-Mormon pastimes. Ann said that in 1996 Taylor really took to alcohol. Then in 1997 he began experimenting with drugs. He smoked marijuana, tried cocaine, mushrooms and ecstasy.

Ann said, "He felt he had missed out in his teen years, so he wanted to try everything that everyone else got to do. He started staying out all night at nightclubs. He began to resemble a fifteen-year-old with his attire. He was all over the board. He went off the deep end!"

There were times that Taylor wouldn't even come home for several weeks on end. Ann no longer trusted him with her daughters. She wouldn't let Taylor take them out of the house.

Another friend of the Helzers, Christina Kelly, began to notice Taylor's strange behavior as well. Kelly had first met Carma in 1992 when she went to a health club for an injury to her back. Carma attended to Kelly during therapy rehabilitation. Kelly met Taylor at the health club and liked him almost immediately.

Kelly began going on raft trips with the Helzers, and Taylor would often guide the rafts through white water. He was strong and good-looking. Kelly said of him, "He was gentle and loving and attended the LDS Church regularly."

Then, by 1996, she noticed a dramatic difference in Taylor. He started questioning the doctrines of the Mormon Church. She had a conversation with him about this and he told her, "I've been betrayed by the church. I got married, went on a mission, and it wasn't meant to be. I did everything I was supposed to do. I can no longer be a member of the church."

Even longtime friend Dane Williams noticed the dramatic change in Taylor. He said, "Taylor was becoming weird. I felt sad that a close friend made some bad choices. He was smoking, experimenting with drugs and morality issues. I had looked up to him. Now I didn't want to be around him."

Soon Ann began to notice another troubling development. Justin was starting to emulate Taylor's behavior. She said, "Justin was a follower. He lacked self-confidence. He would never stand up to or argue with Taylor."

To top it all off, Carma Helzer had taken a self-help course in Utah called Impact. She was so enthralled by what was taught there, she recommended it to both Taylor and Justin. Unfortunately, with their precarious mental states, Impact was to have disastrous results for them and everyone around them.

CHAPTER 2

In To Me See

Various people in the Helzer family and their friends would go through Impact, or a similar program like it, at different times in the 1990s. Carma Helzer was the first of her immediate family to attend, followed by Gerry, Justin, Heather and Taylor. Some of the most telling statements about Impact would come later from Charney Hoffman and others.

Charney Hoffman said, "The staffers at Impact basically enforced the group. You go, and if you protest something that's happening, you have a bunch of staffers that come up and try to help you get with the program. They all work with the facilitator who is extremely totalitarian. Very authoritarian.

"All in all, the staffers do the facilitator's bidding. If anybody doesn't look like they're getting with the program, they teach that person to hate themselves until they learn to love themselves. Impact was very emotionally manipulative. I know a lot of people who snapped because of going through it."

Jill Tingey, Carma's cousin, said of her experience in Impact, "The thing that I remember that I didn't like—it was very abrasive. I think the philosophy was to break down the old beliefs or things that don't work, and rebuild. But that breakdown was abrasive and it seemed like abuse to me. I'm not a shy person, but I kind of crawled inside myself, and I didn't want that to happen to me. I didn't want any of them tearing on me. There were a lot of good things—individualization and thinking deeply. But some of it was really in your face."

A friend of Carma Helzer's named Jeanette Carter was introduced to a program like Impact called Harmony. She said later, "It was all about overcoming obstacles in one's life. Places where people were stuck. It broke down the barriers.

"It was a positive way of communicating with my children. I was often angry at my kids. I wanted to be like Carma. It cost two hundred eighty dollars for the first level, which was called Quest. Quest stood for who you really were in life. It was a way to find the center of your life. The first level was four consecutive days and started at six A.M. on a Wednesday and went all day.

"Quest was led by a man named Dion. Dion asked everybody questions about their lives. This happened in front of a dozen other people. Dion was the facilitator. He challenged you. It was very intense. People were crying and getting sick. Dion was professional and authoritative. His voice was commanding.

"I hated the first two days. Then I started to feel differently on the third day. It was more loving, but still tough. I started to feel a difference in myself. It changed me."

Carter did admit that some people hated Harmony all the way through the course. One particular instance was brutal. Carter said, "You play a game and pretend you are on a ship with other people and it was going to sink. You pleaded for your life. You told them why you wanted to be saved. Only three people could be saved in a lifeboat. Everybody had three Popsicle sticks. You gave some to the people you wanted to save. Most people kept one Popsicle stick for themselves."

Even though Carter could have saved a Popsicle stick for herself, she gave all of hers away. In essence, she drowned while saving others. It is not recorded if Taylor and Justin tried to save themselves in the game of lifeboat. One thing is certain, Taylor loved the idea of certainty and dynamic forcefulness that the facilitator had. He wanted to become a facilitator himself one day. One of the most prevalent ideas of Impact and Harmony was that there was no right or wrong—just what works. "Right" and "wrong" were supposedly belief systems that often retarded a person's self-awareness. Both Impact and Harmony stressed the dynamics of self, not groups or social interaction. This only reinforced Taylor's already considerable vision of himself as a leader who had an important message for others around him.

One thing Charney Hoffman did notice about Taylor as things disintegrated in his marriage, "He seemed more interested than ever in showing people how the Latter-Day Saints had deviated from the path that was previously held. Taylor was very zealous to point out differences between what the church had taught in the early days with what the church had been teaching in more recent times.

"I remember pointing out that several people within the church disagreed with his interpretation of things, his perspective. He said in so many words that he no longer cared what the leaders of the church said. His reason was because they simply had parted from the path originally set forth by the founders of the church. When I started to disagree with him, he seemed to become very upset if I didn't see things the way he did."

Taylor was disappointed with the way things had turned out with Ann as well. He began to believe that the Latter-Day Saints Church had lied to him. He believed he had followed all their rules and still was not happy in his job, his marriage or his life. It didn't dawn on him that he might be wrong in his appreciation of their doctrine. Instead, they must be wrong and it was his purpose in life to bring them back to the way the founders had anticipated that they go. Everyone always said he had drive, charisma, charm and a dynamic personality. He was just about to prove that with an impressionable young woman who had moved to the area from southern California.

Keri Furman was one of those girls who was a beauty from the day she was born, in 1976. Keri, however, grew up in a troubled home in southern California. She later said of her childhood, "I was a latchkey kid. When I was eleven, I cooked for myself and cleaned the house for my dad, who worked two jobs to support my brother and me."

Keri's mother had left the family when Keri was young. It forced her to grow up with a very independent streak. She also indicated that the person she was growing up with was not her real father, but rather a stepfather. She said later, "I was naive when I was young. I grew up very badly with a stepfamily." Anxious to get out of the house, she graduated early and was on her own by the age of seventeen.

To support herself, Keri began selling perfume in southern California. Looking for a change of scene, she moved north to the Bay Area, selling perfume and working in a veterinarian's office. She said later that she was in a bad relationship with a man older than herself. She indicated that it was an abusive relationship. She recalled, "I didn't know how to show my feelings then."

In 1998, Keri began working as a waitress at the Peppermill Restaurant in Concord. One evening, a tall, handsome young man sat down and she served him. He was Taylor Helzer. Keri thought he looked adorable. They began chatting and really hit it off.

After the meal was over, instead of leaving a tip, he left his credit card on the table and told her to buy something nice with it. She was blown away by the gesture. No one had ever done anything like that for her.

Keri said later, "He was different. Enticing. I wanted to know more about him. I didn't use the credit card, but I called his number from a business card he left. He came into the restaurant again the very next night.

"He was exciting. Very straightforward. He would say what was on his mind. He was loving and kind. It felt good being around him."

Taylor and Keri developed a relationship, even though he was still married to Ann. Keri eventually moved into an apartment on Victory Lane with Taylor. A man named Tyler Bergland lived nearby and met Taylor on the apartment grounds. Bergland said, "He was very charismatic. Very open. He could get people to open up. He could get you to explore things in different ways."

After the apartment on Victory Lane, Taylor and Keri rented a house, along with Justin and housemates Olivia Embry and Brandon Davids, on Oak Grove. Within this house, they were free to do as they pleased, which over time became free to do as Taylor pleased.

By this time, the Mormon Church was not a big factor in Taylor's life and Keri only went there once with him.

She said of the experience, "I really didn't care about it. I was in a youth group when I attended a Christian church when I was younger. Being a Mormon wasn't for me."

Of that early period with Taylor, Keri recalled, "He gave me more confidence. In the beginning, he was very loving. He would hug me for half an hour. 'Why are you so free?' I would wonder. I wanted to be a better person. He made a lot of people feel that way. It was special just to know him.

"He made me feel pretty. And I had been in an abusive relationship before Taylor with a different boyfriend."

Keri said of Justin, "He was sweet and kind. He had a loving environment with his brother. I didn't grow up in a happy home. They gave each other hugs, though Taylor was domineering. I saw them fight only once. It was a wrestling match in the front yard. It was like boys wrestling."

Keri may have thought of the residence on Oak Grove as a loving household, but a cloud came over that residence when Taylor sought to quit his job at Dean Witter. He began to ask friends how he could scam the company by feigning mental illness. He wanted to get disability and not have to work anymore.

Charney Hoffman said later, "Taylor didn't say he was not really mentally disabled, but that was kind of what he implied in the idea that he was going on disability. He asked me to promise not to tell anybody what he was doing. I never promised not to tell anybody, just reassured him by telling him that I had no reason to tell anybody. He seemed to accept that as a commitment that I wouldn't.

"I remember him ranting and raving how the welfare system was messed up. He asked me to trust him that by doing what he was doing, he would be able to ultimately fix the system. Maybe I asked him how. It didn't make a lot of sense at the time. It seemed nutty."

Taylor also told Tyler Bergland at one point that he was faking mental illness to scam the system. Bergland recalled, "Taylor said he didn't want to work anymore. He'd like to scam the system. He said he'd practiced acting crazy and they'd have to pay him. I never saw him crazy, though."

Taylor made Keri confirm his mental distress with Dean Witter. He wouldn't shower or shave for a few days before going to see a psychiatrist. And once in the office, he would babble on about wild ideas and experiences. Keri said that she went along with him to several sessions. She recalled, "I had to drive him to a hospital once. When he got there, he hid in the bushes outside. Some big guys had to come outside and get him. I thought he was faking everything, including the sessions (with the psychiatrists)."

Taylor had decided that just being a stockbroker was too ordinary a life. After going through Impact and Harmony, he had his own plans for America and his place in it. The plans were very nebulous in the beginning—unformed thoughts and schemes that percolated in Taylor's mind without solid foundation.

To get Keri on his wavelength, Taylor insisted that she go to Harmony in Sacramento. He drove her there without her knowing where she was really going. Keri later said of the experience, "I thought it would make me a better person. That it would change my life. I did become a woman after going through it. I got in touch with myself and my femininity. Able to accept love."

What happened next depends on statements that Keri made at future dates. And the circumstances vary. In one version, she said that she and Olivia were looking at a *Playboy* magazine. Half-jokingly, they dared each other to pose nude for *Playboy*. Keri told Taylor what they were talking about and he said, "Go for it!"

In another version, it was Taylor who came up with the idea and talked her into doing it. Whatever happened, the truth of the matter was that Keri was concerned about the size of her breasts and wanted breast enhancement. The problem was that neither she nor Taylor had the money for this. Each breast enhancement would cost $5,000 per procedure. (Another source would speak of each breast enhancement costing $2,500, for a total of $5,000.)

Eventually Keri went to Taylor's dad, Gerry, and got a loan to cover half the cost. She had to come up with money elsewhere for the other half. When the operation was completed, Keri's figure became 34D-26-33.

With her new body, Keri posed nude as Olivia took photos of her in the backyard of the Oak Grove residence. Keri then sent the photos to *Playboy*. A while later, *Playboy* was impressed with Keri and they had a professional photographer photograph Keri in the nude. Some of the photos that eventually made it into *Playboy* were of her in-line skating in short shorts wearing a pink top. Another was of her crouching down near a fence with an Irish setter. Another had her posing with a straw hat, see-through pink blouse and tiny pink shorts.

The rest of the photos were the most revealing of all. Keri wore lingerie pulled aside to show her breasts and pubic area, or she wore nothing at all, except for gold-colored sandals. The *Playboy* article described her as a cross between Pamela Anderson and Claudia Schiffer. Keri said that she liked to think of her new self as a version of Marilyn Monroe. She described Marilyn as being sweet and friendly with everyone, male or female. Of the new her, Keri said that she always wandered around with a huge smile on her face and people wondered what she was so happy about. She responded that she was happy to be alive and had a lot more going for her than she did before.

One thing she wrote about in *Playboy*—and it's not certain if she was talking about Taylor or another boyfriend—was a memorable occasion. Keri said that her boyfriend woke her up early one morning and told her he was going to give her a surprise. He told her to go back to sleep and he'd wake her up when he was ready. An hour and a half later, he blindfolded her and led her into the bathroom. Sade was playing on the radio. When he took her blindfold off, the Jacuzzi was filled with milk and little flower-shaped candles. He told her that Cleopatra had milk baths every day and she deserved one as well. Then he bathed her with milk and shaved her legs.

One thing more was added to Keri Furman's new persona—she called herself Kerissa Fare in the *Playboy* article.

Not everything was milk and honey at Taylor's house, however. Even though four other people lived in the house on Oak Grove Road and Taylor didn't even work, it was decidedly "his house." Keri said later, "Everybody had to do what he wanted to do. You lived by his rules. Because he went to Harmony, I had to go there, and Olivia and Brandon as well. No one was ever on his level. If you didn't agree with him, then you 'just didn't get it.' I was putty in his hands. He was coming up with a lot of schemes. Taylor ran the house. Everyone had to live by his rules."

Whereas Taylor made everyone adhere to his rules and was very vocal about it, Keri said that Justin was quiet and sweet at the Oak Grove home. She said, "Justin was so innocent. He'd be excited by the smallest things. A song he loved. A piece of jewelry. Justin had few material things. He appreciated everything he had.

"He ate organic foods. He was compulsive about his food and health. He wouldn't even try a cookie from a store. He did yoga and meditation in his bedroom. A lot of times, he was either in his bedroom or at work. He never had a girlfriend when I was there.

"Justin was totally nonviolent. One time I was going to kill a bug. He said, 'No, take it outside.' He wouldn't kill a fly."

Taylor introduced Keri to the rave scene. By this time, he was using and selling ecstasy at the raves. According to Keri, she didn't take any drugs at that point. She claimed that she didn't even take aspirin. But one day she had a terrible headache and Taylor gave her something. A while later, he asked her, "How do you feel?"

"I feel great!" she responded.

"That's ecstasy," he said.

From then on, Keri started using ecstasy with Taylor, especially at raves. She liked to dance and ecstasy gave her a feeling of freedom and movement.

At one point, Taylor forced Justin to go to a rave. According to Keri, "Taylor told Justin to watch him deal drugs. Justin didn't want to do it, but he did it. It was our daily lives to be directed by Taylor. Taylor told him how to think, walk, talk and hold his head up. How to dress. He told Justin, 'Don't be flashy with jewelry.'"

The rave scene wasn't Justin's scene, however. He preferred dressing all in black and attending Goth clubs. He went alone several times and took Taylor and Keri once. She thought it was vampirish and kind of weird. Goth clubs were not for her or Taylor.

Everyone was working and paying rent at Oak Grove except for Taylor—even though, according to Keri, Taylor was receiving substantial checks for his disability. Taylor told the others it was important he kept his money to invest in the schemes he was coming up with. At first, these schemes were somewhat along the line of Harmony. He told Keri he wanted to start a counseling group for couples to be able to communicate better. He would be the facilitator and help their relationships. He didn't want to use his real name for this, so she toyed around with the idea and made up some business cards for him with the name Jordan Taylor. The cards basically asked people if they wanted better relationships, better sex and more joy in their lives.

Taylor continued to sell drugs at the raves, especially ecstasy, to help fund his ideas. As time went on, his ideas started to gel toward a plan he called In To Me See. When spoken quickly, this phrase sounded like "Intimacy." As his ideas for In To Me See became more grandiose, he talked Keri into dancing nude at a club in San Francisco called the Gold Club. She agreed, and as she danced and gyrated before men on the stage, she received money from them. Later, she would claim she could make between $500 and $1,000 a night at the Gold Club.

Even with this good income, Taylor wanted more and more money for In To Me See. And his plans for Keri's involvement became more bizarre. According to Christina Kelly, she had a conversation with Keri about this. Keri supposedly told Kelly that Taylor wanted her to have private sessions with men, dance for them and then have whatever sex they wanted with them. According to Christina, Taylor became very upset when Keri supposedly gave one man oral sex, but did not charge him for it.

In To Me See changed and grew and began to focus around something that Taylor called the Twelve Principles of Magic. He went so far as to print these principles on the back of a psychedelic poster. He hung this poster on a wall in the house on Oak Grove for all to see.

In a paraphrased version of the twelve principles, they read:

1. He was already perfect, so he could do no wrong.
2. There was no such thing as right or wrong.
3. He was all powerful and the creator of everything in his life.
4. Life was always right and he embraced all the results of it.
5. All the results of life, he created for himself.
6. He believed nothing, and perceived the world without fear.
7. His perceptions were always right.
8. Unconditional, fearless love was the most profound in the universe.
9. Spirit knew everything.
10. He gave total control by losing control.
11. What goes around, comes around.
12. There was a higher person than himself—Jesus Christ, the Son of the Father.

At some point In To Me See faded away and Taylor began to talk of Transform America, or Impact America. The terms became almost interchangeable as he used one term with a certain person and the other term with another. It was to be a very powerful institution with himself as its leader. He said he needed three core people to run Transform America. By now, the number three was almost sacred to Taylor. It had echoes of the Trinity, the three Wise Men and other connotations. Taylor wanted Justin and Keri to be among his *three core people*—people he could trust implicitly to carry out his orders.

Taylor kept explaining to Keri that there was no such thing as right or wrong. He didn't like those terms she said. She recalled, "He explained that there was only good and evil, not right and wrong."

Taylor began a remorseless crusade in his scheme to implement Transform America. Whether from too many drugs, or an actual onset of insanity, he became absolutely manic on the subject. He would talk to Keri and the others about it ad nauseam. When they didn't understand what he was saying or disagreed with him, he would become irate.

Keri recalled, "If you didn't go along with him, he'd talk to you for hours. It was always, 'You shouldn't think of things like that, you should think of things this way.' Taylor was in control of everything. He was relentless. He was on drugs. If you disagreed, he'd say, 'You're stuck in your stuff. You aren't on my level.' And if you disagreed, you were evil.

"I'd beat myself up because I didn't see things his way. I'd finally say, 'Okay. I get it,' even if I didn't, just to make him stop.

"For the first time in my life, I really felt special and loved. I was afraid I would lose that if I disagreed with him."

To try and make money for Impact America, Taylor came up with an idea called the Feline Club. He pushed Keri into helping him on the project. The club was supposed to be a place where rich men could meet beautiful women. It was to be an escort club, but only for rich yuppies. In essence, it would be a high-class prostitution club. Olivia and Keri were supposed to oversee the girls and the club and make suggestions to make it better.

Some of Taylor's ideas about the place included free drugs on platters for anyone who wanted them. One idea was that it would cost a man $300 to be with a beautiful girl and not have sex with her. It would cost $500 or more to have sex with the girl.

Keri said later, "People would come over and say our house was weird." Just how weird it had become can be ascertained by comments from Brandon's girlfriend, Sarah Brents. Sarah, in her own way, was just as beautiful a blonde as Keri. Sarah stayed over at Oak Grove on several occasions and agreed with most other people that "Taylor was outgoing, vibrant and confident. He would walk into a room and draw attention to himself."

She said of Justin, "He was a nice person. He seemed polite and together."

Sarah saw a different side to Taylor one day when she asked him what he did for a living. He told her he was on disability. Then as Keri walked by, Taylor slapped her on her derriere and said, "This is my meal ticket."

According to Sarah, Taylor used ecstasy, pot, meth, GHB and Special K (a cat tranquilizer used as an illegal drug). She said that Keri used ecstasy and pot. The only person in the household that didn't seem to use drugs very often was Justin. Sarah made no mention of Brandon or Olivia.

Sarah was told at some point that Taylor made money by selling drugs at raves. She was asked to go to some Goth clubs by Justin, but she said, "I wasn't into that."

About the sexual nature of the house on Oak Grove, Sarah related later, "Justin, one time, watched Keri and Taylor having sex. It was all right, because Taylor said it was okay."

Sarah also knew about Keri posing nude for *Playboy*, but nothing freaked her out more at the Oak Grove home than Justin's eating habits. She said, "He would make large smacking sounds. He would get it all over his face. It was almost animalistic. One night I went into the kitchen and Justin was down on all fours, eating from a plate on the floor. I was scared. I went back to Brandon's room."

Of Justin's sex life, Sarah said, "Well, he didn't have one. He told me he'd had sex with a girl once in his twenties. And that was it."

Sarah's initial impression of Justin in the beginning was mainly positive, though she did acknowledge several quirks that he had, especially when it came to food. But her impression of him as a nice guy changed dramatically after she broke up with Brandon. It's not apparent if Brandon left Oak Grove about that time, but Sarah continued to go there. Knowing that Sarah had broken up with Brandon, Justin asked her if they could go out sometime. She told him she didn't think of him that way. She only thought of him as a friend. In response, he said, "I've only been friends with you to see if I could fuck you!"

Sarah was startled. She had never seen Justin in this light. But she was even more startled one day when he told her he had a new piercing and asked if she wanted to see it. Before she could answer, he pulled down his pants and revealed his penis. Sarah said later that he did not have a piercing there. His whole intent seemed to have been to flash her.

The entire household on Oak Grove was by now revolving around Taylor's schemes. Taylor determined that he needed lots of money to implement Transform America, or as he was calling it more often now, Impact America. One of Taylor's get-rich-quick schemes was the manufacturing of meth. Keri came home from work one day to find a meth lab set up in the garage. She was incensed. She said later, "I was mad. That was my home too! I didn't want that there."

In the long run, it didn't matter what Keri wanted. Taylor ruled the roost at Oak Grove. He gathered all the ingredients to make meth, except red phosphorus. There is some indication that he eventually got the red phosphorus, but the drug operation apparently never amounted to much. Taylor seemed to be left in the roll of a distributor, not manufacturer.

Another person who didn't like Taylor with drugs was his cousin Charney Hoffman. He said later, "Taylor was very belligerent when he was wasted. I remember driving with him one time and he criticized my driving. He said he was wasted and he could drive better than me. My brother grabbed his face as hard as he could, squeezed his face and all Taylor could do was put his hands up. He used to be articulate, polite and a joy to be around. Instead of him being able to talk his way out of a situation, that situation blew out of control."

Christina Kelly said of this period, "I remember one rave in Santa Cruz where Taylor was selling ecstasy. We all used it. Justin reacted badly to it and got violently ill and threw up. I didn't find the experience that great either. But then it started to kick in. At the rave, I enjoyed it. I felt good sometimes and other times I was nauseous."

The Feline Club idea was dropped around this time by Taylor and a new plan emerged where he would get young girls from Mexico. He told Keri that they were to go down to Mexico, get the young girls and set them up in the house on Oak Grove. They would basically turn them into sex slaves. Taylor said he would train them in how to pleasure a man. And Keri was to keep an eye on them.

There was a half-baked plan to have the young girls pose as sandwich-delivery girls from a deli who would take sandwiches into a Dean Witter office. They would make friends with young rich yuppie stockbrokers and eventually invite them over for sex. Taylor would take pictures of them on the sly. Then after they had sex, the girls would threaten to sue Dean Witter for $50 million, because they would only be fourteen or fifteen years old. According to the plan, Dean Witter would settle for $20 million, and Taylor would even give the blackmailed stockbrokers a million, so they wouldn't commit suicide.

Taylor and Keri eventually did go down to Mexico, but not to get young women as sex slaves, but rather to buy Rohypnol, the date-rape drug. Keri said later, "I didn't want to do a lot of things he told me to do. But I'd go ahead and say okay, and then I'd do them."

She even heard Taylor starting to talk about some scheme called Brazil. He only let her in on a very limited amount of what he was cooking up about Brazil. But by this time, Taylor was losing faith that Keri would ever be his third-core person. He became more suspicious of her and would often talk to Justin alone. He began to shut Keri out of his plans. She only heard the name Brazil mentioned and not much else about it.

Taylor became even more irate with Keri when she stopped dancing at the Gold Club. The money she made there was supposed to help fund Impact America. But Keri was beginning to be just as frustrated with Taylor as he was with her. She said later, "I realized at some point that he was just a parasite."

Keri even tried to warn Justin not to become involved in Taylor's schemes. They seemed to cost everyone money except Taylor, but Justin responded, "Oh, no! Taylor knows how to make money. He'll pay me back."

It was not only Taylor's insistence on illegal schemes, but his insistence that he was divinely inspired that made Keri nervous. Taylor kept telling everyone in the household, "I'm on my life's mission to impact America. It's my calling from God! My mission is to spread love to everybody."

Just what this vision of love was to be, Taylor let a woman named Jessyka Chompff know. She said later, "Impact America was to be a self-realization course. To learn more about yourself. Another term came up for it as well—Transform America. He would get things rolling by starting a club. Everyone there would be beautiful and rich. Taylor would be the one who got them together. It would be a kind of porno Fantasy Island. A Disneyland of sex.

"Taylor would market sex and drugs. But it sounded unrealistic to me. I thought, 'Why would rich men need him to find beautiful women for them?'

"It was hard to listen to all this stuff. I thought he would be in over his head. I didn't think he could be a drug kingpin."

Keri was also having her doubts about Taylor and his wild schemes. She wanted to get on with a modeling career that had nothing to do with sex clubs, principles of magic or Impact America. She went down to Los Angeles to have more professional photos taken. She said of Taylor's schemes, "I didn't understand a lot of it. It didn't feel right in my heart. I wanted out."

By the end of 1999, Taylor was ready to toss her out of his inner circle anyway. It was now very apparent that Keri was not going to be his third-core person. He would need another—someone who would truly believe in him and his visions. Someone who would accept him as a prophet. Someone who knew in her heart and soul that he was divinely inspired by God. He didn't have to look any farther than the Third Ward of the Latter-Day Saints Church in Walnut Creek.

CHAPTER 3

In the Company of Angels

Dawn Godman was the single parent of a six-year-old son. She was born in Amador County, California, in the Gold Rush country. She lived in the backwoods with her family, at 3,500 feet in elevation. It was about forty-five minutes to the nearest town. The area around her home was filled with oaks and pine trees. She learned how to shoot a pistol and rifle at a young age, and was a real country girl.

Of her family life, Dawn said later, "When I was about nine or ten, my dad came down with chronic asthma. He almost died a couple of times. Mom had to provide for the family. Dad changed dramatically. You never knew what he'd do after that. Dad would be fine one minute, and then a split second later he would get mad.

"Mom spent most of her time focused on Dad, not the kids. I became responsible for the house at ten years old. I wasn't happy as a child. But I wasn't unhappy either. I preferred to spend time by myself. We were out in the country and I spent a lot of time in the forest alone."

At seventeen years of age, Dawn filed for emancipation from her parents. She soon had a boyfriend, Patrick, and they got married while she was still a teenager. A year later, a son was born to them. The marriage did not last, however, and she and Patrick got a divorce.

Dawn attended Sacramento City Junior College and studied nursing. To support herself and her son, Dawn took a job as an attendant in a convalescent home. As part of her work, she took patient's vital statistics, helped feed them and eventually worked her way up to helping in the intensive care unit.

Because of stress at work and having to take care of a son by herself at home, Dawn began taking methamphetamines at the age of twenty-two. She said later, "It ruined my life. I couldn't relax. I couldn't do my job. Getting high was the most important thing in life."

Dawn eventually lost her job and the meth use became so bad by 1996 that her ex-husband filed for and got full custody of her son. She started living in a car or even camping out in the woods. Drug-ridden and desperate, Dawn tried committing suicide with a bunch of painkillers. She said later, "In December 1996, I attempted suicide. It failed. I was in a mental-health ward for three days. I thought about whether I wanted to live or die. I realized that life was important to me because I had a lot of things to pass on to my son.

"I had been raised Pentecostal. I wanted something better for my son, and to get that for him, I needed to feel that for myself. I liked that the Latter-Day Saints took care of its members. I found the values I was raised with, stronger in the Mormon Church."

In 1996, a friend gave Dawn a copy of the Book of Mormon. She eventually read it all and a companion book, *The Pearl of Great Price.* Dawn joined an LDS ward in the foothills, first living in a homeless shelter in Jackson, and then staying at a friend's house. She even stayed a weekend at the house of the president of the local Latter-Day Saints relief society, before moving in with her grandmother in Martinez, in Contra Costa County. Of the LDS, she said, "The Mormon Church provided a community. When growing up, I never belonged in any group. I was always different. I had to fight to go to a dance. My brother always had everything given to him. I had to do everything possible to get a teacher to notice me, even though I was an A and B student. Nothing was ever good enough with my parents. With the LDS, people would really listen to me."

Dawn began to go to church every Sunday at the local Mormon Church. She took the new member lessons and studied them all through 1997 and into 1998, when she finally became a full-fledged member of the LDS. She became such a member in good standing, she was allowed to go inside a temple. Her reaction to the temple was that it was a very sacred place. She said later, "You could feel the spirit of God there. In the Mormon Church, I felt I had a purpose in life. I felt that the Bible was only part of the story. The Book of Mormon described other stories. Those of the Nephites and Lamanites. All of the stories of the Book of Mormon were interesting and I believed it was the truth."

Dawn had her photo taken at the Oakland Mormon Temple with star quarterback Steve Young, of the San Francisco 49ers. She was even allowed to see her son, again on weekends. She was progressing far in her life and looked forward to the day when she could have full custody of her son.

In 1998, Dawn made a fateful decision—she

decided to join the Singles Third Ward in Walnut Creek. As chance would have it, that singles ward had a game night, and the game was a murder-mystery dinner. It was somewhat like the game Clue, except actual people took on the roles of characters in the mystery. Dawn was sitting in a room with others of the ward when Taylor, Justin and a male friend walked in. Most of the other people shunned the trio, because of their odd looks. They certainly didn't fit the clean-cut Mormon stereotype. Both Taylor and Justin wore all-black clothing and Taylor even wore a head scarf. To many, he looked like a nineteenth-century preacher. There was talking and laughter among the other participants, but nobody went over to talk to Taylor, Justin and their friend. No one that is except Dawn Godman.

She said, "My first impression of Taylor and Justin Helzer was that they looked like what I used to look like in my old life. That's why people were avoiding them. I made it a point to talk to them.

"Very quickly I realized that Taylor was very perceptive. He realized that my boy was shunned in the ward. The LDS taught their children to be quiet at meetings. But my son was rambunctious. I had to take him out a lot. That didn't matter to Taylor. My son was all over Taylor. But Taylor gave him attention. He made a deal with him. If he would be quiet until the break, Taylor would play hide-and-seek with him in the church corridor.

"I was amazed that someone would take the time to recognize that my son needed attention. I was grateful for Taylor to be willing to spend time with him. I was motivated to know Taylor. His presence was powerful."

As for Justin, he introduced himself and spoke not another word to Dawn that evening. He was totally in his older brother's shadow.

The next time Dawn met the Helzer brothers was about a week later, at a Sunday meeting at the LDS church. It was a Testimony Sunday service, somewhat akin to the Quaker practice, where anyone in the congregation could get up and speak. Taylor got up in front of the others and began giving his testimony of faith. The story he told concerned being at a card room, the California Grand Casino. He was going to drive to his parents' house, but instead a voice told him to go the other way so that he could help people. He followed the voice's directions and spotted a woman and two small children walking down the road. Believing that they might need a ride, he stopped and asked them if this was the case. They said yes, and Taylor revealed, "The Spirit made me turn around for them." He expounded on the fact that when God put opportunities in your way, you needed to seize them.

Dawn was impressed by Taylor's story. She recalled, "He went out of his way to listen to Spirit and took action to accomplish what Spirit told him to do."

Taylor spoke about the Spirit a lot that day, and the message was particularly appealing to Dawn. In her own personal life, she received and acted upon revelations in daily life. Dawn began going to church services at the Third Ward on a regular basis. She had very little contact with Justin, but talked extensively with Taylor about scripture, revelations and Spirit.

Kelly Lord also remembered Taylor that day very well. She said later, "It was Testimony Sunday, where any member could stand up and give their testimony about the faith and religion. People would talk if they were moved by the spirit of God. God the Father, God the Son and God the Holy Spirit. Most people would get up and say something like, 'I heard the Spirit as a voice.' You wouldn't say, 'The Spirit just told me such and such.'

"Not Taylor, though. He got up and spoke in those exact words."

It was a mesmerizing, powerful, bravura performance. He had much of the congregation spellbound. One person who was not spellbound by it was Bishop Brett Halversen, who was there. He listened for a while to Taylor's revelation and he couldn't make sense of it. It didn't seem to have anything to do with Mormon theology. Halversen said later, "The things he shared were not cogent for me. After two or three minutes, I asked that he be excused for the next person to testify. I shook hands with him after the meeting. There was no acrimony."

After his testimony, some people joined Taylor and Justin in the parking lot for an informal study group. Generally after church services, the members would file off to Bible study or Book of Mormon study classes. There was a tradition of parking-lot meetings, however, for those who wanted to go there and discuss the service in a more informal setting.

Dawn Kirkland knew of the parking-lot meetings that Taylor began, with Justin at his side. Within weeks, Taylor had twenty or more people out listening to him rather than attending regular classes. It began to become a real danger to the established order of the ward.

Taylor was dramatic, forceful and in his element. He spoke with great conviction and passion. He was in command of a growing flock, but his messages were not those of the mainline LDS faith. He spoke of how the mainline church had veered off the path from Joseph Smith's teachings.

Taylor told Kirkland at one point that he had a revelation from God to speak to the group. He asked her, "Do you know what it is not to commit sin? The only sin I've committed in the last month is one time not smiling at a cashier."

Taylor claimed to be living a perfect life without sin. He was spotless. He was beloved of God.

This scared Kirkland. She said, "He was so charismatic, but I saw a great darkness in him and wanted to leave."

She even warned Dawn Godman to stay away from Taylor. Kirkland pulled her aside from one of the parking lot meetings and said, "Take care. I'm concerned about the Helzers. They aren't the right people to be spending time with."

To this, Dawn Godman replied, "But they're my friends."

Kirkland gave up trying to convince Godman to beware of the Helzer brothers. She said later, "Everybody has to make their own choices. I wasn't the boss of her."

Kirkland was in a position of leadership in the Third Ward, however, and she was very concerned by Taylor's messages and his growing flock at the parking-lot meetings. Kirkland finally decided to go see Bishop Halversen and expressed her concern to him. She told him, "I'm worried that people are being led astray."

Kirkland later spoke of Taylor's divergence from doctrine about the nature of Satan. In the Mormon Church, Satan was often referred to as the Adversary. She said, "You can be influenced by the Adversary and his minions." She likened it to a radio. If you tuned in one station, you could receive messages from God, but if you tuned in a different station, you could receive evil.

Kirkland also realized that Taylor was veering from other doctrines of the LDS faith. According to Kirkland, one of the Mormon doctrines was about three Nephites who asked Jesus Christ after his resurrection if they could stay alive as well and follow him to the New World (the Americas). This was allowed to them. But somehow Taylor twisted this around to form his own sacred company of three. He said that he needed three core people to be his apostles. He would never come right out and say he was a prophet of God, but he certainly led others to believe that is what he felt.

Taylor quit the parking-lot meetings, but he wasn't through influencing young women. He talked Kelly Lord into taking a Harmony class in Sacramento. The lead facilitator at that time was Sherry Matheson, who had split off from Impact in Salt Lake City.

Lord had a rough time with the first phase of Harmony, as Jeanette Carter had experienced. Lord said later, "It broke down all your defenses. It left you wide open. I felt confused. I didn't really know how to move forward."

She was taunted and mocked by the facilitator there. Everyone was programed not to give any sympathy to another person. They were supposed to speak truthfully, about themselves and others, even if it hurt.

The second level still confused and upset her as well. She said, "It was more intense."

By the third level, however, she changed her tone. She said, "It was more gentle and safer. A place to find your own beliefs."

When Kelly Lord passed the third level, Taylor gave her a big hug and said, "You're starting to get it." Which meant, she was starting to "get him" and the things he said.

It was around this third-level time that Lord took a trip down to Los Angeles with Justin. Taylor had already warned her not to compare notes with Justin about Impact America. Kelly disobeyed Taylor's command, and on the way down asked Justin what he knew about Impact America. She said later, "He just gave me a blank stare."

Justin was completely loyal to his brother and would not divulge any information that Taylor did not want others to know about.

Despite his loyalty, Kelly said, Taylor belittled Justin more than once in front of others. One incident particularly stood out in her mind. Justin was in the kitchen when Taylor strode up to him with a dirty plastic cup. He berated Justin for the cup being so dirty. Taylor screamed, "See, this is why roommates don't like you!"

Justin was humiliated in front of the others, but he did not say a word to his brother.

At one point, Lord pulled Justin aside and told him, "You need to get away from Taylor."

Justin ignored her.

Lord said later, "All energy went to Taylor. He was always the center of attention. If any attention went to Justin, Taylor would be angry. He wanted it all for himself."

Lord was also starting to get concerned for Dawn Godman. She noticed that Dawn was falling under Taylor's spell. One night, Taylor had Dawn wear a see-through netting top. Lord was astounded. Godman had never worn anything like that before. It was very non-Mormon attire. Lord noticed that Dawn dressed modestly before this, but not after.

"Getting it" was very big with Taylor. If you agreed with him, "you got it." If you didn't agree, "you didn't get it."

At a certain point, Taylor would quit arguing with the person and become completely silent for ten minutes or more. He would turn off his charm. He would leave the person yearning for the bright Taylor Helzer they knew and loved.

A test of loyalty became more and more pronounced with Taylor as the 1990s ended. Kelly Lord said that he started asking her unusual questions. One day at a

Carl's Jr. restaurant, Taylor said, "If I asked you to rob this Carl's Jr. for me, would you be open to that?"

Lord said later, "I was so taken aback, I didn't respond. It was like a loyalty test. Also, it was like, 'Was I at his level of consciousness?'

"Another time he asked me, 'What would you do if you read in the papers that I was in jail for something they said I did.? Would you come get me?'"

"Absolutely," she answered.

"Good," Taylor responded.

She said of Taylor, "He could overwhelm you. It was intoxicating."

Kelly Lord's world was in chaos around Taylor. "He was condescending," she said. "Only he could talk to God directly. One time he told me, 'Do not talk to me. Leave me a message on my message machine. If I find it worthy of a response, I will call you.'

"I thought, 'Oh, that's nice!'"

Even after this snub, she still phoned him back. She recalled, "I had to call back. I was still intrigued by Taylor. His energy was so powerful. And I was not a pushover.

"In truth, he never said he was a prophet of God to me. But he had episodes where he talked to God. He said he heard things through revelation."

On another occasion, Taylor told her, "I'm very clear. If people aren't loyal to me, I'll just kill them."

Lord was incensed and told him to leave.

This test of loyalty was a huge thing with Taylor, and it was making Lord more uneasy and suspicious of his schemes all the time. Once at a seminar in Marin County, at a Hilton Hotel, Lord met Taylor there. Lord was angry with Taylor because she had just found out that he was using and selling drugs. She angrily accused him of this and told him that he was full of crap.

Then she said if he didn't watch himself, he was going to end up like David Koresh at Waco, Texas.

She said, "Taylor was quiet at first and then made himself very big. He got very close to me and said, 'If Kelly gets in my way, she's fucked!'"

Lord said later, "I took this as a threat."

Taylor asked her, "Are you clear about this?"

She answered yes.

Kelly had nothing to do with Taylor for a while after that, but it was hard for her to stay away from him. Months after the incident at the Hilton, she invited him over for dinner. Taylor began spouting all sorts of gibberish again. Then, at one point, he walked out into the rain, lifted his arms toward the heavens and started ranting. She just stood quietly in the background, watching this bizarre performance.

The last straw with Taylor, as far as Kelly Lord was concerned, had to do with a package.

"One time he phoned me and said, 'If I asked you to deliver a package, would you do it?'"

This scared Kelly Lord and she hung up the phone. Later, she called him back and said, "I'm not going to do anything with packages."

Then she related, "He was unhappy. He told me, 'You haven't reached my level.'"

Indeed, she had not. Kelly Lord would admit later, "I still had my own mind. I wouldn't deliver any package that someone just gave me."

If Kelly Lord would not come to his level, then Taylor would have to look elsewhere. It remained to be seen if Dawn Godman still had her own mind. Taylor began to tell Godman that she needed to take a course in Harmony. He expounded on the fact that it would make her a better person, one that understood herself and the world more clearly. Dawn was so swayed by Taylor's exhortations that she went to see the bishop of the area, Bishop Halversen, about monetary support for attending Harmony in Sacramento. Bishop Halversen was very much against this idea. He already knew some of Harmony's philosophy didn't jibe with LDS teachings. But Dawn was determined to go. She said later, "I prayed a lot and was inspired to go to Harmony."

Bishop Halversen told her, "You should pray some more."

Dawn did, and decided that her prayers were guiding her toward Harmony. If someone as charismatic as Taylor said that it would be good for her, then it must be true. She decided to go, and Justin agreed to house-sit her apartment in Martinez while she was gone. Taylor kept her in the dark about what the experience would entail. All he told her was that it would break down people's walls and make them more open to listening to what he had to say.

Of her experience at Harmony, Dawn said, "It was a warehouse in Sacramento, totally sealed off. No windows. Music, lights, the thermostat, everything was controlled by the staff. Initially there were thirty people in the group. A person could not just come and go as they pleased. A person had to even ask permission to go to the bathroom, and a staff member would always escort them there and back.

"A facilitator engaged everyone in conversation. The initial day was one of personal attacks. It put you on edge. I was almost afraid of him. You were constantly, verbally attacked. He'd say things like, 'Oh, you're stuck in that.' You just stand there and take it. You had to stand up all during the attack.

"Our facilitator was Dion. He was six feet tall, blond-haired, nice-looking. He wore a business suit. He had a presence. He was like Taylor. There was no cursing allowed, but everything else was fair game. In one instance, Dion told everyone that a woman had been molested at a young age by her father and brothers. He made her stand. Dion called her a slut. He asked her how many times it happened and how many partners she had. She told everything. This went on for an hour.

"Dion didn't react to anyone's problems. He was cold. No emotion. It was his job to open her up. Everyone had to be willing to open their self up like her. It was all very intense.

"At the sessions, you look into another person's eyes and think of your roles in the past. Get in touch with your inner child. You started judging people and building walls in childhood. With Harmony you got back to being a child. A pure child with no walls. No values. People with walls couldn't understand Taylor.

"For example, a spider crossed my leg as a child. It scared me. So all spiders were bad. But that's not true. Spiders have their place in the world."

Dawn completed two levels of Harmony. The first level was called Quest. The second level was called Summit. Quest, she said, was to open the walls. Summit was to give a person new tools. Taylor told her that Summit was very important. He also said that it would get her to the point where there was no right or wrong. Only results. He claimed, "Since right and wrong is a judgment, it can't be relied on." Taylor gave her an example. He told her that she could be going to the store to get something and have an accident. The accident would leave her paralyzed. But was it wrong to go to the store in the first place? No, he said, she needed something, so she went there. There was no right or wrong in making a decision to go to the store. It had nothing to do with what occurred later.

Dawn said of Harmony, "The goal was to get to a

place of no fixed values. Taylor insisted that everyone close to him had to go through Harmony."

Taylor told Dawn that she would not be required to go through the third level of Harmony. He said she could gain more benefit from listening to him, and reading books that he recommended, than actually being there. The first book that he gave her was *The Celestine Prophecy*. The second book was *Mutant Message Down Under*. Dawn read the books and then discussed chapters with Taylor about the works and her life's experiences.

Dawn said later, "I was bonded to Taylor by then. He gave me something I never had before. It was safe to be with him. It was safe to tell him my daydreams. He'd sit on the couch and just hold me for a long time. He made me feel special. I felt that my life had a purpose. I was where I was supposed to be. I felt incredibly close to God. Taylor believed everything could be filtered through the Twelve Principles of Magic. Spirit knew everything that was going on around you. It could guide you. It was a way to love your life and be in alignment with God."

Dawn also formed her own ideas about the Twelve Principles of Magic. She said later, "I believed we were all perfect and what others saw as defects in us were opportunities for us to grow." She also added, "I believed that Taylor and Jesus Christ were brothers."

Dawn claimed that her relationship changed with her son after Harmony and talking with Taylor. She said, "I saw him (her son) not as a child, but as a person in a small body. I learned to communicate with him. I gave him the emotional support I never gave him before."

By this time, Taylor was "totally charismatic and dynamic" to Dawn. She recalled, "I came to believe that he was a prophet of God. A seer and a revelator. He communicated directly with God and disseminated revelations from God. I thought of the stories listed in the Bible. I thought of Moses, the head of the Israelites. He guided them. The way Taylor guided me.

"A prophet of God is ordained by God. Any individual can receive revelations, but a prophet is raised up by God. Taylor had the insights into the dynamics between people. Everything he said would be true."

As an example, Taylor would talk about the dynamics between two people. Dawn recalled, "I would talk to them and everything Taylor said about them would be true. He had an impressive command of scripture. There was a huge sense of peace being around him. A power from what he was saying. A sense of joy. I understood it to be the spirit of God.

"I'd never met anyone like him before. He wouldn't stumble over words. He could reference scripture to news events. He made you see the impact of a person in the world.

"Taylor could do all of this with Keri and with Justin. Taylor would talk about how Justin needed to do certain things. He'd give him instructions on what scriptures to read. Ways for him to live his life aligned with the Spirit."

Of Taylor's gift for prophecy, Dawn said later, "I believed it all without a shadow of a doubt. I believed as much that Taylor was a prophet as I believed that Jesus was God's son. At one point, Justin and I had a discussion about whether Taylor was a prophet. I prayed about it and realized that he was a prophet and that I should follow him."

Dawn also believed that God's law was higher than man's law. And Taylor told her that Satan had been a useful tool in the world. He said that if not for Satan, Adam and Eve would have never had sex, and the world would have remained unpopulated. Satan had played an important role in the development of the world.

As time went on, Justin also became more talkative with Dawn. He told her about his life in the Mormon Church and about other religions he was reading about as well. He was particularly intrigued by Buddhism and their thoughts on Reincarnation, as well as certain dietary regimens. She could already see that he was eating foods that were healthy and that he enjoyed it. He didn't have a yen for junk food.

At her place in Martinez, Dawn got to know the Helzer brothers a lot better, especially Taylor. She said, "He spent every minute of every day talking to me. He even dropped by work to talk to me. He was like my best friend. I knew he lived with Keri on Oak Grove for a while; then they moved into a condo in Martinez. I didn't know her very well."

By this time, Dawn also had interactions with Justin. She said, "Sometimes I would go shopping with him. I cooked for him once a week. He definitely enjoyed his food. He didn't talk while he ate. He was just too much into his food. After dinner we'd talk about a whole range of things. We'd also spend a lot of time praying. We'd pray about our goals and our daily life. We'd pray that God would guide us."

For the most part, however, Dawn talked and prayed with Taylor. He began telling her about something called Transform America. She recalled, "He talked about how bright people could have a lot of joy. They could live consciously. He wanted to transform America and the world.

"Taylor said he would pick a small town somewhere and tell the city council that a Transform America group in their town would boost tax revenues. People would be happier and make more money. He would send the mayor and councilmen, along with their families, to the group for free. When they went through it, they'd be happy and encourage other townspeople and their constituents to go."

By this means, Taylor hoped that a community would donate one percent of tax revenue to his non-profit organization. He would go from town to town, setting up local chapters of Transform America. Bit by bit, the whole nation would see the benefits such a group brought.

Taylor waxed poetic on his plans. Dawn said later, "Transform America would bring on the perennial reign of Christ. It was a way to shift consciousness in the world. Peace and joy would replace chaos and war."

There was only one problem, as far as Taylor was concerned, he needed money, and lots of it, to start Transform America. He told Dawn, "I'll need at least a million dollars just to get it going." He led her to believe that there was already an organization called Transform America in place, but that it was secret, and that she shouldn't mention the name to others. So Dawn never shared what Taylor was telling her at that time with other people.

By this point, Keri Furman had just about had it with Transform America and Taylor. She said, "There were meetings when I had to leave the room so he could talk to Justin or Dawn in private. He (Taylor) told me, 'Go to your room!'"

Finally Keri had enough of Taylor and his demands and secretive ways. She packed up her belongings and headed for southern California, to be in touch with the Playboy organization there and pursue her modeling career.

Dawn, however, was falling more and more under Taylor's spell. She was working for the Bay Alarm Company at the time, and she told her supervisor, Yolanda Dobbins, "I'm being inspired for a job more in line with what I'm called to do. Me and my friends are going to make a lot of money."

By now, Taylor was not only giving her visions of Transform America, but his plans for In To Me See as well. Of this plan, Dawn said, "It would be a safe place for wealthy businessmen. Safe from reporters. Since CEOs are too well-known for that kind of place, there would be privacy."

One of the prerequisites before a girl was allowed to become part of In To Me See was a questionnaire that Taylor began to devise. Dawn helped him type it up and even added suggestions. She said later, "He'd ask me about how a question should be phrased; then I'd help. But he came up with the ideas."

Taylor wanted only women who lived up to his principles, and, in essence, "got it," as far as he was concerned.

Dawn said, "If the girls wanted to have sex for money, that was okay. It would totally be up to them. Then the money they made, Taylor could invest it for them. He was good at that. It would encourage them to join. As he said, 'You need money to make money.'"

Taylor even floated a bizarre idea by Dawn that concerned fast-food restaurant chains. It would be a scam. They would shoot out windows in various locations to make sure the stock would drop. Then supposedly he would buy into the stock at a low point, and trade it when it rebounded after the shootings stopped. He hoped to make a lot of money this way. This plan never got off the ground.

Mainly, Taylor concentrated on the questionnaires for In To Me See. The questionnaires' thrust was to see whether a girl had a high sense of right and wrong, or was ambivalent on the subject. Taylor planned to hand out the questionnaires to young women at raves while he sold ecstasy. There is some evidence that he actually did this on one occasion.

Dawn, Justin and Taylor all went to a private rave in

San Francisco on New Year's Eve. Of course, there was all the talk at the time of possible Y2K disasters, but nothing of that sort happened.

It's surprising that as suspicious and paranoid as Taylor was, he showed the questionnaire to some people besides Dawn. One of these was Christina Kelly.

Kelly recalled some of the questions on it. She remembered:

Sex before marriage is wrong? T F
I am a powerful sexual person? T F
I am a religious person? T F
I don't do drugs? T F
Lying is wrong? T F
Stealing is wrong? T F

If Taylor was preaching, educating and proselytizing for Impact America and other schemes, Justin was looking inward. He kept a journal of his thoughts and aspirations. In one section, he wrote of creating a world that he desired. He said that his own advice would be his greatest source of wisdom. Then he listed his top three goals for the year:

1. Driver?
2. A sexual lover.
3. Become a druid.

Farther down the list were his hopes to get a degree or a good career.

Justin went into more detail about becoming a good sexual lover. He said that he wanted to express trust, self-expression and passion.

Of becoming a druid, he said that they were possessed with confidence, peace, pleasure and heroism. He admired the game Dungeons & Dragons. According to a cousin, he and Taylor once played the game for twenty-five hours without a break.

In another journal, Justin listed more goals:

1. A degree.
2. Self-awareness.
3. Earn $45,000 a year.
4. Physical strength.
5. Be out of debt.
6. Get a new car that was silver and black.
7. Harmony.
8. Detachment.

In a later section, he wasn't expressing his love for Druidism anymore, but rather an admiration for the teachings of spiritual leader Deepak Chopra. Justin spoke of "love portending," pure consciousness and a field of infinite creativity. Justin proclaimed under this new regime he could accept the present moment as a gift.

Throughout Justin's writings, the urge for detachment kept popping up in his texts. He wanted to detach himself from worldly things. He spoke of detaching himself from "the drama of everyday life." He tried to simplify his already austere world. He wrote of releasing ego, finding courage and finding a relationship with a woman of mutual attraction.

As far as sanctuary went, he said, "I imagine it into existence."

Some of his thoughts were fairly esoteric. He wrote of releasing pure light into the universe and translating food into pure energy. He obsessed about creating the perfect body for himself. He took his meditation and exercises to extremes.

Justin kept coming back to one sad and lonely fact, however. He had no girlfriend and despaired of ever

finding one. He wrote hopefully of sending and receiving eye contact with a beautiful woman. He yearned
for what his brother had in the realm of women. Once
again, he wanted to be like his charismatic brother,
Taylor.

There was a darker side to Justin's journals as well.
He wrote of embracing pain and death. He said that
Spirit saw the value of pain and death. These things
were not to be dreaded. He saw life and death as com-
plementing each other.

Despite still being married to Ann, despite his relationships with Keri and Dawn, Taylor found time to be
around and influence other young women. One of
these women was named Robin Stewart. She met
Taylor at a birthday party and recalled, "We got involved
very quickly. He was very positive all the time. What was
so attractive about him was that he was so positive and
achievement-oriented. He had an attitude like, 'I am
wonderful. Life is wonderful.' He was very, very outgoing. He said he could do anything he set his mind
to."

After a while, however, Stewart began to see some of
Taylor's dark side. She said, "None of his behavior
ever mortified him. I was very antidrug, but he was experimenting with things that were taboo. He was into
pornography and trying sexual things out of the mainstream. I wasn't comfortable with that. He wanted to
experience all of life's experiences and not be afraid
of pain. He wanted to eliminate fear. He thought you
could grow from experiencing pain."

The last straw for Stewart was a rafting trip. She remembered, "It was early summer. The river was very
high. The rest of his family didn't want to do it. But
Taylor was all for it. He guided us on the raft down the

river. Afterward, he told us he'd been partying all night. We had our lives in his hands. It was very upsetting for me."

Another young woman, Elaine Totten, spoke of Taylor in the same manner as Stewart. She said, "He was charming, exciting and full of life." But she also spoke disparagingly of a rafting trip with Taylor. "He was not good at following through. He was always late. I was the one who had to rent the trailer for the raft. He had a boat and no transportation."

Totten, who was Mormon, was also disturbed by Taylor's new philosophies. She said, "He showed me how reincarnation could be supported in the Book of Mormon. He said the Latter-Day Saints had gone down the wrong path after Joseph Smith. He believed all the later presidents of the church were misguided.

"Taylor's whole countenance was no longer radiant. He told me he had communicated with animals. One time he communicated with a fly. He said to the fly, 'If you land on my food, I'll have to kill you.' He said the fly communicated back to him, 'I won't,' then flew away."

Debra McClanahan also knew Taylor, Justin and Dawn. McClanahan lived in an apartment on Ryan Road in Concord and in 1998 had met Dawn at the LDS church in Danville. Justin and Dawn showed up one time in costumes at her apartment. They were going to a Goth club. Both Dawn and Justin were dressed all in black, and Justin wore knee-high boots. This was the first time Debra met Justin. She recalled later, "He was quiet and shy. Dawn did all the talking."

Debra was in no way shocked by Dawn and Justin's attire. In fact, she dressed flamboyantly with long, flowing dresses or skirts and an almost gypsylike appearance. Debra considered herself to be a witch who practiced white magic—in other words, a good witch, or "white witch." She claimed never to have cast evil spells or dabbled in black magic. She took Wicca very seriously and attended meetings.

On a later occasion, Dawn took care of Debra's daughter so she could go out to dances. Dawn eventually introduced Taylor to Debra. Debra said later, "He was charming. He was very nice. It was around Christmastime and he wished me a merry Christmas."

Like Keri Furman, Kelly Lord and Dawn Godman, Debra McClanahan was drawn to Taylor Helzer. Eventually she and Taylor had an affair. Taylor and Debra had been out all night at a rave when he dropped her off at her apartment around five in the morning. Instead of leaving, he got into bed with her and they had sex.

Debra also gave Taylor full-body massages. She believed that massages released energy and were almost spiritual. Debra met Taylor's mom, Carma, who was a massage therapist. They discussed the importance of a good massage. In time Debra gave massages to Justin as well.

Debra was very frank about her sexuality and those around her. She said that when she gave a massage to Taylor or Justin, and they had an erection, she would stimulate them until they ejaculated.

Debra also admitted that she gave Dawn a sexual massage as well. In fact, she related that one night in Concord she and Dawn were at a place called Catfish Charlie's Bar when they hooked up with another person. Debra did not specify if this was a man or a woman. They all went back to Debra's place and had a ménage à trois.

Christina Kelly knew Taylor, Dawn and Justin. She went to raves with Dawn and Taylor and knew that Taylor was making money by selling ecstasy at raves. He eventually told her about In To Me See, but she was under the impression it wouldn't be sexual in nature. She thought it was just for rich men who needed escorts to some function. She said about Taylor, "He could light up a room."

Of Justin, Kelly said, "He was gentle and loving. Not a person who attracted attention."

Then she spoke of one of Justin's strange habits. She noticed that when Justin stayed over his parents' house, he slept in a closet space beneath the stairs. There was a mattress there on the floor. She said, "He was like a little kid. He loved it there."

It was not yet certain who Taylor's third-core person would be for his future plans. He always had his eye on various impressionable young women. One of them was Lina Richardson.

Lina was a very pretty blonde who fell under Taylor's spell. She later said, about him, "Taylor was the sun. He was one of the most intense, charismatic people I ever met. I still can't comprehend his personality, totally.

"When I was around Taylor, he occupied my every sense. He was overwhelming. We were at a tire store once. He spoke to everyone there. Before long, everyone was smiling. They were drawn to him. He had a gift."

One day Taylor visited with Lina at her parents' home. He was so bold as to ask her parents about their sexual habits. Nothing was off-limits for Taylor. As far as Lina's sexual habits went, she told him that she was a virgin. For some reason, known only to himself, Taylor passed this information on to Justin.

One day out of the blue, Lina got a phone call from Justin, whom she barely knew of and had never met in person. He told her that he was amazed that she was still a virgin and he thought it was great. Lina was absolutely stunned that Taylor had passed this information on to his brother. She told Justin, "I can't believe we're having this conversation."

This did not deter Justin. He went on and on about how great he thought it was that she was a virgin. At a loss for words, Lina told him, "Thank you." And thought to herself, *Why the hell are you calling me about this?*

At the end of the conversation with Justin, Lina said, "Can I please talk to Taylor?"

She jumped on Taylor about the situation, but he wasn't shocked at all and couldn't understand why she was upset.

In time, however, Lina learned to like and admire Justin. She recalled, "There was an innocence about Justin. He was one of the gentlest people I ever met. His presence was so small compared to Taylor's.

"Justin was very quiet and extremely focused on small everyday things. One time Taylor and I stopped by Gerry's house. There was a place underneath the staircase for when Justin was there. He slept there in a sleeping bag. He was very happy with the small things. He talked on and on about new juices he had found.

"Justin admired Taylor in everything he did. His brother was God. Justin was the quintessential younger brother."

On one occasion Taylor left Lina with Justin alone in the house. She felt awkward at first, but then Justin made her relax by building a fire. Lina recalled, "I was in a very awkward situation. Yet Justin made me feel comfortable. I had never seen anyone build a fire so slowly or carefully. He brushed all the soot out and brushed the ashes onto a paper. He was slow and meticulous. Then he very carefully built the fire."

After the episode with the fire, Justin asked Lina to go with him to a Goth club. She went along, but the Goth scene was not for her. She said, "Goth clubs were all about death and depression."

The Goth scene certainly fit Justin's view of life; but not Taylor's exuberant manner. Lina said of Justin, "Compared to Taylor, Justin was a shadow."

Lina spoke of Taylor's presence being so overpowering that often she felt ill after having been around him. According to Lina, Taylor wanted to marry her, even though he was still married to Ann. Lina said, "I couldn't understand his vision. It just seemed wrong. I told him the road he was on wasn't the right one."

Lina wanted to know who was in the inner circle he kept talking about. He wouldn't tell her.

One time near the end of their relationship, she told him, "Your energy is dark. It's evil."

After hearing this, according to Lina, Taylor cried. She was obviously not going to be a part of his scheme.

There were always more women in Taylor's life, however. One of these was Jessyka Chompff. She had met Taylor through her boyfriend, Alex. They went together on a trip with Taylor and really hit it off with him.

They hit it off so dramatically, in fact, that Jessyka would confess years later that on her wedding night to Alex, her new husband gave Taylor to her as a wedding present. They all climbed into bed and had sex. Then Alex left Taylor alone with Jessyka so she could enjoy him. According to Jessyka, however, Taylor was impotent, so they just "messed around and did other things."

Strangely enough, Justin did not want to be left out of the mix, as far as Jessyka was concerned. He expressed his love for her. She kissed him a few times on the lips, but that was it. He was so enraptured with her that he wanted to live with her, but things never developed that way.

Dawn Godman's friend Dawn Kirkland interacted with Justin, rather than Taylor. She had been a member of the LDS Church since 1992. She said later that she often prayed for "comfort, and I'd receive a feeling of peace and love." She had dinner at one point with the whole Helzer family at their home and went rafting with them as well. This was when Taylor was living with Ann and out of the picture a bit more. She called Gerry, "Brother Gerry."

She said of Justin, "He was friendly and funny. He cracked jokes all the time." She really liked Justin, but only as a friend, as so many other women did.

As time went on, Taylor began to trust Dawn Godman and Justin with his ideas, the way he never had with Keri. He began to tell them more and more about his plans for Transform America. Dawn remembered that up until the year 2000, she thought that a prototype of Transform America already existed. It wasn't until early 2000 that she realized that Transform America did not yet exist. All of it was still only a daydream of Taylor's.

She said later, "He expressed that Transform America had to start soon because by the time it spread, the world would be close to Christ's return to earth. It was already the Last Days. Prophecies from the Bible were coming true.

"One time in the car, he told me, 'Spirit tells me it's time you got to know everything.'"

They drove up into the Oakland hills and parked at the LDS temple there. Then they got out and sat on the temple grounds. Taylor told her, "This is such a sacred mission, I want the angels to protect us from Satan and his minions. They can't overhear us here."

Then he proceeded to tell her everything about his plans for Transform America. She said later, "I thought what a great opportunity and blessing to be able to be a part of this mission. Taylor said that he needed a core group of three to become a full-fledged prophet of God. He already had Justin. He needed me.

"It was the first time up on the temple grounds that I knew people would have to be killed to implement

Transform America. There was no set number. I believed he had a direct commandment from God to do this. Everything he said came directly from God. I never felt that he was wrong in planning kidnapping and murder. And neither did Justin.

"We felt we were in the company of angels. A sense of being protected. A sense of security like I never felt before. It was as if someone was standing over you. As if you were a child and a person held you in his arms.

"Killing was acceptable to God on certain occasions. There was the story of Solomon and [King] Agog in the Bible."

These stories alluded to the fact that evildoers could be killed to help a nation, especially if a nation was suffering from tyranny.

"Then there's the story of Nephi in the Book of Mormon."

This story referred to a man who was instructed by God to kill a man who abused his power in keeping the Golden Tablets in which the history of the Nephites was written.

"Transform America was a way to bring harmony to the world. It would bring in Christ's millennial reign of peace."

Now all Taylor needed was a fitting person to be sacrificed for his grandiose plans. Someone who would give her life, whether she knew it or not, for his grand scheme. In the end, he chose a young woman who had ties to one of America's living legends of blues. Her name was Selina Bishop and her father was blues legend Elvin Bishop.

CHAPTER 4

Fooled Around and Fell in Love

Elvin Bishop started playing blues guitar as a college student in Chicago in the early 1960s. He said later that he was influenced by the likes of Howlin' Wolf, Muddy Waters and other blues musicians who had traveled up to the Windy City from the Deep South. Bishop joined with singer Paul Butterfield, guitarist Mike Bloomfield and keyboardist Mark Naftalin to form the highly successful Butterfield Blues Band.

One music critic said of Elvin's playing style, "He doesn't just pick and strum, he wrestles with his guitar, strangling the fret board and shaking the whole instrument to pop out every last drop of music."

Bishop eventually went off on his own, but he kept his style of blues, and he sometimes intermixed it with country-and-western elements. He had talent and drive, and one day in California a girl named Jennifer went to one of his shows.

Jennifer Villarin grew up in Salinas, California, as part of a large family. Jenny's big brother was David, who said later that he always stood up for her. "She wasn't a fighter. She was a whiner and a crier when she was little, but I stood up for her," he laughingly recalled.

The family was so expansive and helpful that they took in Robert Asuncion when he was a very small boy. He said of Jenny, "She was sweet and pretty. Somebody I could brag about. I was always close to her. Whenever I'd go away and come back home, it was like I'd never left. She was very loving."

Sister Lydia said, "Jenny was a big mouth as a kid. But we all loved her."

Sister Olga recalled, "Jenny would brush our hair every morning. We gave her a hard time, but we loved her."

Olga recalled the first time that she and Jenny went to see Elvin Bishop play. She said, "We went to see Elvin as he played onstage at the Stanford Amphitheater. It was amazing. Jenny had a fake ID and went back to see Elvin after the show."

In this case, it may have been love at first sight. Before long, Elvin would write his most famous song, "Fooled Around and Fell in Love." The song was about Jenny.

Elvin was very protective of Jenny Villarin. He realized that there were problems in the family when Olga's father (Jenny's stepfather) abused Jenny. According to Olga, her father molested Jenny. Olga said, "Elvin rescued her. He took her out of there on her eighteenth birthday. He saved her from a bad environment.

"We were all happy after we left home. Jenny always tried to protect us. Jenny's first years with Elvin were happy ones. But she was just too young when Selina was born."

Selina Bishop was born on October 17, 1977. Olga said, "We called Selina our 'Little Bean.' She was just like a little kidney bean. She was so cute. She was the one I cottoned to. Selina had such a soft little voice, but she was so sweet."

The Bishop household was not an ordinary one. Elvin and Jenny lived the life of a rock musician. Jenny's niece Jill recalled, "We used to live in Capitola near Santa Cruz. And it wasn't unusual for Elvin and Jenny to show up at two or three in the morning after a show. They'd sit up and talk for hours."

David Villarin said that he traveled with Elvin's band a few times. He recalled, "Elvin led a musician's life. Most of the time he wouldn't get out of bed until three in the afternoon."

It was exciting and romantic for Jenny, but also tiring. She had a young daughter to take care of. Jenny said to niece Jill, "You're my pumpkin. I love you so much. I have this new little sweet pea. But you will always be my pumpkin."

Olga said of Selina as a child, "She was very quiet. She had a tiny, high-pitched voice. You had to listen hard to understand her."

In fact, Selina's voice was so soft, David could often not understand her. He once asked Jenny, "What language is she speaking?"

It was English, though it was very soft English.

David said of Selina, "She was the bright spot of Jenny's life."

Olga agreed. "You can't describe that closeness. Selina was everything to her. Selina was so loving. She'd climb up into your lap to get lots of hugs. She'd try to make you happy if you were sad."

Despite Jenny's love for the child she had by Elvin Bishop, their relationship became more and more difficult as time went on. Finally it ruptured when Selina was three years old, and Elvin and Jenny went their separate ways. Selina, however, retained a love for both parents, and stayed with each of them on different occasions.

Olga said that Selina loved music. "She loved everything from rap to Elvin's music. But she had her own funny ideas about music. She tried playing drums. But she had her own style. That was Selina."

After the split with Elvin Bishop, Jenny and Selina moved around a lot. Their county of choice, however, was Marin County, just north of San Francisco. They both loved the woods and the nearby ocean. They stayed with various friends, and even spent a period of time in a small motor home, basically camped out in the woods. Luckily for them, Marin County was a very laid-back place where things like that were not uncommon.

One place that Selina loved while growing up was a café down the road called the Two Bird Café. Beginning at five years old, she would stop there in the morning, every day before catching the school bus, and get a cup of chocolate. The owner, Tony Micelli, thought she was very sweet and polite.

Jenny made ends meet by working at cleaning houses and taking care of young children. She also developed a keen sense of making quality jewelry that used precious and semiprecious stones. This brought her into direct contact with a man named James Gamble. Over time, James would become a very good friend of hers.

James Gamble was born on April 11, 1946, in Daly City, just south of San Francisco. Jim had a younger brother, Larry, and his father and mother divorced when Jim was nine years old. His mother, Frances, recalled, "Jim was five years older than his brother. He was the leader. It was fun raising two boys."

In his teenage years, Frances said, "Jim was a

straight-A student until he found out that being an A student wasn't considered macho. Then his grades went downhill. Jim thought he was a big shot. He wanted to be good at everything. He was a catcher in baseball and played football in high school. He liked swimming. But he also got a drinking problem early on. He would sneak drinks. He even got in a [car] wreck when he was under the influence of alcohol."

Perhaps to straighten up and fly right, Jim joined the U.S. Air Force in 1963. He attended basic training in Texas, and was then stationed to a field in Illinois. Jim didn't fly planes or jets; instead, he got into the weather bureau. During this period, he married. He and his wife had no children, and they divorced by 1971.

Jim moved back to California, got into electronics and married again. He worked for the Sylvania Company in the earliest days of computers. Two children were born this time—Erin and Ty. Yet even the bond of children did not keep the marriage together. This one fell apart in 1987.

Looking for a change of scene and retiring from electronics, Jim moved from the Bay Area up to Laytonville, north of the "Wine Country." It was a town of about one thousand people set among redwood forests, oaks and hills. In his new surroundings, Jim began to become interested in rocks, gems and lapidary. His speciality was sun stones from Oregon and he even bought a turquoise mine near Mina, Nevada. He loved going to rock and gem shows all around the West and this brought him into contact with Jenny Villarin, who was making jewelry at the time.

They were a good pair. Jim was very gentlemanly and kind; Jenny was sweet and a free spirit. They began a relationship that was more good buddies than a boyfriend/girlfriend relationship. Selina liked Jim a lot as well. They became good friends. Jim treated Selina like he treated everyone, with kindness and consideration.

Jim liked playing cards and socializing. He was well-known for his generous spirit, and often bought rounds of drinks for others, or bought them lunches. Jim always seemed to be looking out for other people.

A woman who knew both Jim and Jenny during this period was Rosanne Lusk Urban. She recalled, "I lived in Lagunitas and Jenny was my best friend. We took to each other immediately. Jenny was generous, kind, sweet and giving. She was very gentle and honest. She held different jobs—worked at an office, cleaned houses, made jewelry. She busted her butt to make ends meet. She was a hard worker."

Jenny met a new boyfriend who wanted to move back to Pennsylvania. Even though she and Selina loved Marin County, they pulled up roots to follow him there. It was not a good move. According to Rosanne, the new boyfriend did not treat them well, especially Jenny. Yet she and Selina stuck it out there for five years.

Selina missed Marin County and her friends so much that she decided to move back to California on her own in 1998. This brought her back into the Villarin family's realm in the Salinas/San Jose area. For a while Selina lived with her aunt Olga and applied for college in Saratoga. She took graphic-arts classes and even made silk screens of her father Elvin Bishop's album covers. She was proud of her dad and got along well with him, even if her mother didn't.

Around this time, Selina was remembered by her cousin Lucia Villarin. Lucia said, "Selina had a tiny voice, but a big heart."

Deciding that was where she wanted to live, she moved back into the area and often stayed with Gloria

LaFranchi and her family. Rosanne Urban said, "I knew when Selina came back, Jenny would be back soon. They were inseparable. They loved each other very much."

Not long after that, Jim Gamble heard through a friend of Jenny's, that she wanted to move back from Pennsylvania, but she didn't have a car or enough money to move. Good friend that he was, Jim dropped everything and drove all the way back to Pennsylvania to help Jenny move. Rosanne Urban said, "He was the type of guy to do that. He was so generous."

These were very happy times for Selina and Jenny back in Marin County. Brother Robert recalled one particular barbecue. "Jenny came up to me, put her arms around me and said, 'I love you.' She didn't do it for any particular reason. It's just the way she was."

On Christmas Day, 1999, Selina wrote in her journal that it was the first time she and her mother had spent Christmas together in three years. She wrote that a person never knew what new experiences life would bring. She said that she'd been particularly happy lately. Then she added that as a treat, they opened presents, ate eggs benedict and drank mimosa. Then while her mom took a nap, she lay in a Jacuzzi tub and it was so relaxing, she nearly fell asleep.

A few days later, she wrote, "January 2, 2000—Well, the world didn't end. The world got through another year, from what I've seen of the news. This New Year was very peaceful. I am on the journey of my life."

Olga could see how happy Selina and Jenny were by the year 2000. She went to visit her a lot of times with her kids. They played in the Miwok Village Park. In one photo that Olga snapped, Selina was inside a giant burned-out redwood log, while her children sat on top of the stump.

Sherrie Lynn, Selina's twelve-year-old cousin, said

that Selina was like a big sister to her that year. She loved it when Selina took her over to Japan Town in San Francisco. It was a treat to go across the Golden Gate Bridge into the city. Japan Town was filled with exotic items and restaurants from that nation.

Sherrie said, "Selina was never one to judge people. She was an all-around great person. It was great to have such a cool aunt."

To get on her feet back in Marin County, Selina took a job as a waitress at the Two Bird Café, the same café where she had sipped chocolate while waiting for the school bus as a child. Two Bird owner Micelli was happy to hire Selina. He said, "She was great. Friendly, responsible and always had a big smile. Just the kind of person you like to have as a waitress."

Jenny and Selina stayed at various times with Jenny's friend Gloria LaFranchi. Jenny and Selina mixed in so well with the family, it was more like being close relations than just friends. They also stayed on occasion with Rosanne Urban. There was mutual admiration between Rosanne and Jenny.

Jenny got a job at the Paper Mill Creek Saloon and also a job at the Nicassio Store. She even worked part-time helping kids at a day camp in the area.

Urban noticed that a different relationship had grown between Selina and her mother after their return from Pennsylvania. She said, "They were more like friends than a mother and daughter. They really liked each other's company. They hung out together."

Rico LaFranchi, Gloria's son, was eighteen in 2000 and he thought of Selina as his sister. They liked hanging out together and going to parties. And by 2000, they also liked attending raves. One rave in particular stood out in Rico LaFranchi's mind. He said later, "In April 2000, there was an underground rave in Guerneville. There were no flyers or anything.

You just called a number about seven P.M. and got directions.

"Selina and I went. It was a small rave, as those things go. It was very peaceful. People dancing and giving each other back rubs. There was ecstasy there."

Rico took some ecstasy at the rave and so did Selina. Of that particular experience, Rico said, "It made me feel happy. I could feel the beat. Relaxed. Everybody was having a good time. There was no violence."

Rico noticed that Selina got her ecstasy from one particular dealer at the rave. Rico said later, "The guy stood out. A lot of people wear colorful clothes at raves, but he was dressed all in black. He was about six foot two, tall and lean, and his hair was tied back in a ponytail."

Selina seemed to be very taken with this ecstasy dealer and she hung out with him for most of the night. When she and Rico left the rave around three in the morning, she told him that the dealer was named Jordan, but that wasn't his real name. He kept that a secret. "Jordan" lived somewhere over in the East Bay. In fact, Jordan was Taylor Helzer.

From that point on, Selina became very enamored of Jordan. One person who realized this was Selina's friend Julia Bernbaum. She'd been a friend of Selina's since the sixth grade. Bernbaum said, "Selina was my best friend. We grew up together. She was usually quiet, but she had a wild side too. She liked going to dances and meeting people. She began seeing this guy named Jordan. She said she knew that wasn't his real name. That added to his mysterious appeal. It made him exciting for her. He wined and dined her. He always seemed to have lots of money. He didn't say where he got it, but she guessed it might have been from drug sales. In fact, Selina started selling ecstasy with him at raves in May. She said she was very into him."

Rosanne recalled, "She talked a lot about her new boyfriend. She was kind of naive. It was kind of like puppy love. She was kind of like a young teenage girl."

Selina spent every chance she could with Jordan. She truly believed that he loved her. Her life seemed to be on a definite upswing. She even decided to get a place of her own in Marin County. According to one source, it was Jordan who pushed her to get her own place. Perhaps he was already thinking that he could eliminate her easier if she lived in her own residence.

Jay and Leora Soladay owned a split-level house on Redwood Drive in Woodacre. They lived on the upper floor, with their one-year-old baby, Ty, and decided to rent out the lower portion of the house in June 2000.

The Soladays placed a sign on the community bulletin board, at the local post office, telling of the rental. There were a few responses, but the Soladays weren't crazy about some of them. Then they noticed a card on the bulletin board from Selina. Her note was cute and pleasant. When they met her in person, they liked her immediately.

Leora said later, "Selina moved in, in mid-June. She was sweet. There was a nice way about her and she was great with Ty. We rented the lower quarters to her for eight hundred dollars a month.

"She'd go up and play with Ty, and we'd sit and chat. Sometimes we chatted about her new boyfriend. She seemed to be very taken with him."

Unfortunately, Selina did not know that Jordan was not taken with her. She was only an instrument in his scheme. He devised an incredible tale for her. He said that he was going to come into a lot of money from a great-uncle and that he didn't want his ex-wife to know about it.

Taylor wanted her to open up five accounts and he

would funnel the money to her to place $125,000 in the accounts. He said that she could keep $5,000 from each account—in other words, $25,000.

This plan changed in some respects over time, but mainly stayed the same. All he needed was her willing compliance. To this end, he did wine and dine her and take her dancing.

On one occasion, he, Selina, Dawn and Justin all went to Ashkenaz, a place in Berkeley, to listen to a reggae band. Dawn pretended to be friends with Selina and was talkative. In the back of her mind, however, Dawn realized that Selina would have to be sacrificed. Dawn said later, "Taylor and I talked about whether or not she (Selina) was the right person for the role. We prayed that God would send the right person. And that person would give up their life for a greater cause.

"I never asked Selina if she was willing to give up her life for the Children of Thunder [as Taylor, Justin, and Dawn now called themselves]. But I was willing to take her life for the Children of Thunder.

"The right person was whoever Spirit led Taylor to. As time went on, that person seemed to be Selina Bishop."

Julia Bernbaum learned of Selina's trip to Ashkenaz with Jordan, "Sky" (Dawn Godman) and "Jason," Jordan's brother. Bernbaum said, "She thought Sky was cool. She babbled on and on about them. She was excited. This was her new crowd. She thought of Jordan as this mystery man. She was intrigued. She said he was charming and dynamic. She was enthralled and a little bit in awe of him."

Selina wrote in a letter that she was "just chillin'" in her new place and very excited about it. She said that she and Julia could use the pool that her new landlords had. She wrote that her place would be "cute" when she got some new furniture.

Selina was especially hopeful that Julia would meet

Jordan. She said that she had never met anyone like him before, and she hoped he would stay with her. Selina cautioned that Jordan would be very busy for the next couple of months on some project. On the bright side, it would give her and Julia more time to hang out together. Selina wrapped it up by saying that she was very proud to have a new home and that she'd never been happier.

CHAPTER 5

Children of Thunder

Taylor Helzer decided that he needed a house to plan everything in private with Justin and Dawn. Since he wasn't working, it was going to be up to Justin and Dawn to foot the bills, but Taylor had them so much under his influence at that that would not be a problem. All he had to do was to get Justin to leave his present residence.

All winter and spring of 2000, Justin had been living in a house on Wren Lane in Concord. He was only renting a room in the house and had other housemates there as well. One of these was Johnette Gray. Gray already knew Justin well because they had started to work for AT&T at the same time in 1999. Since Johnette's own house was in Sacramento, about seventy miles away, and she worked in Concord, she decided to rent a room in Concord during the workweek and go home on days off.

She related about Justin, "He was naive and a slow learner on the job. Very methodical and patient. He addressed everything in a thoughtful way. I accepted him, but noticed he was very unusual.

"When we went to lunch, he had an unusual way of eating. It was loud and he'd chew with his mouth open. He'd chew his food very slowly. He was mainly a vegetarian, but he would eat an occasional burger."

Once Gray was in the house with Justin, she was able to observe his habits more closely. She noticed that he was very regimented in his living and always ate and went to bed at the same time. He didn't watch television and would only listen to a radio in his room once in a while.

Gray also noticed that Justin could be talking about something and then suddenly stop, as if he'd run out of steam. Once, he even told her, "I don't want to talk anymore. Just because I'm in your presence doesn't mean I want someone to talk to me."

Despite these quirks, Gray thought that Justin was "naturally nice and gentle." He talked about spiritual issues once in a while, but he didn't proselytize. It wouldn't have worked with her anyway—she was a confirmed atheist.

Gray also observed how Justin exercised and meditated daily. His exercises were yoga in nature and very physical, almost to the realm of martial arts. When he did these exercises, he grunted and moaned and cursed. Eventually the landlady had to tell him to tone them down.

Justin told Gray that he had been raised Mormon, but now he wasn't so sure about their doctrines. He said that he'd been to a retreat in Sacramento called Harmony and he really liked it. To Gray, it seemed that the retreat wasn't so much religious in nature as it was a self-aware-ness group. Justin showed her a video of Harmony, but Gray was not impressed. She said later of its leader, "The woman looked kind of lost."

The only socializing Justin did while at Wren Lane was to go out once in a while to a Goth club. At those times, he would dress up in black clothes, black boots and black cape. It was his one foray at being hip.

Since Johnette Gray wrote poetry, Justin decided to show her a poem he had written. She read it and said later, "It was very unusual and creepy. Especially the last lines." The poem described bloodletting and the sacrifice of someone on an altar. The sacrifice victim gave his life for the greater good of humanity.

When Johnette was through reading it, she asked Justin, "Did you dream this?"

"No," he answered.

She responded, "Well, it would make a good scary movie."

Justin and Johnette also had another housemate named Michael Henderson. Like Gray, Henderson noticed Justin's strange eating habits and said, "He really got into his food. He was like a little kid. The food would get all over his face. He was unusual. But we got along."

Working on Justin's vulnerabilities and fears, Taylor painted the picture of a world that needed saving. He tapped into Justin's considerable mistrust of the federal government, which had been reinforced by Bo Gritz. According to Taylor, America needed redirection, and they were the ones to do it. But first they needed adequate accommodations. Something set away from prying eyes. They needed a house of their own.

Tom Cheng managed a house that his cousin rented on Saddlewood Court in Concord. This was in a nice suburban part of town near the Mount Diablo foothills. In the spring of 2000, the people who had been living in the rental house for a number of years moved out, and the house was up for rent again. Cheng hired a real estate agent to show the house and several people looked at it. One of those people was Justin Helzer.

Justin was duly impressed with the house. It seemed to fit the parameters that Taylor had laid down—in a quiet neighborhood, where they would not be conspicuous behind closed doors.

Justin went to look at it a second time and brought his sister Sky, who was actually Dawn Godman. Justin met at the house with Tom Cheng and Justin seemed like a "nice guy" to Cheng. Cheng showed Justin around the house and they did a walk-through. They both agreed to what shape the house was in and noted all the defects.

An agreement was written that only Justin would be the one living in the house with no other people there. Cheng asked why Justin needed so much space, since he was going to be living on his own. Justin answered that he needed one bedroom for exercise, one bedroom for meditation and one bedroom for sleeping. Justin never mentioned that Taylor and Dawn would be moving into the house as well.

A rental agreement was signed by Justin on April 29, 2000. The rent would be $1,650 a month. He made an initial deposit of $3,650 to move in. Justin paid Cheng with a cashier's check.

Despite the fact that only Justin was supposed to live at the house on Saddlewood Court, Dawn and Taylor soon moved in with him. The residence would not only be a living space for them—it would be the launching pad for all of Taylor's schemes.

Dawn later explained, "There would be three insiders. This was because when Christ went to the New World in the Book of Mormon, three disciples asked to remain with him until the Second Coming. There was a parallel story in the Bible. In the Book of John in the Bible, John requested of Jesus that he stay until the Second Coming. John's father was called Thunder.

"I took on the name Sky, Taylor took on the name Jordan and Justin took on the name Jason.

"The *J* letters were significant. Both of the original Sons of Thunder's names (John and James) started with the letter *J*. In the first inception of Taylor's plans, there was a kidnapping plan to kidnap five people. We would get their stock portfolio information. These would be placed into another person's account and then it would be funneled to Taylor. The five people would have to be killed and then the person who opened the account would have to be killed as well."

By this time, Taylor, Justin and Dawn knew that the account holder would be Selina Bishop. They still weren't sure who the people who owned stocks and mutual funds would be.

"Our meetings began in earnest at Saddlewood," Dawn said. "Taylor told Justin he needed a gun. It was understood why he needed the gun."

On May 5, 2000, Michael Raymond was working at Hogan's Sporting Goods in Concord. A tall, blond-haired young man with a ponytail came into the store asking to see some handguns. The handguns were kept in the back of Hogan's and Raymond took the young man back there to view a display case. The young man was Justin Helzer.

Justin told Raymond that he had used a 9mm Beretta pistol as an MP in the military and liked them. Raymond gave him one of the guns from the display case to look at, and Justin handled it. It was a semiautomatic Beretta 92.

Justin liked the gun and decided to purchase it. He showed his driver's license and military discharge papers. The driver's license had his old address printed on it. The total cost for the purchase came to $550.

While he was at it, Justin bought a box of .22 shells and .762 Russian ammo that would work in an

AK-47 assault rifle. He also bought some 12-gauge shotgun shells. Justin gave the clerk his old address on Wren Avenue as his place of residence.

On June 6, a person calling herself Sky Anderson bought a Craftsman, Model 315, reciprocating saw and blades at a Sears store. She paid $117.42 in cash for the items. Later, she went online with eBay and purchased a Stun Master taser. It could produce up to a hundred thousand volts and drop a person to the floor instantly. Dawn paid $79.95 in all for two tasers. She used a false name and a PO box for the place where the tasers were to be delivered.

In June, Selina Bishop was at a mall and had some photos taken at a machine there. Some of them were meant for Jordan. Selina told Bernbaum that Jordan was cooking up some scheme and was going to get a whole lot of money. She said that Jordan didn't want to share any of the money with his ex-wife, so he was going to funnel the money into an account that Selina would set up in her name. She seemed to think that Jordan was going to receive $200,000, and that he would give her half. Later, this was modified to $100,000, and she would get $20,000.

Selina told friend Jordan Miller a slightly different version of this. According to Miller, "Selina was very much in love with Jordan. He told her that he was getting an inheritance from his great-uncle and the money would allow them to live together. He needed to hide this from his ex-wife. It was about one hundred twenty-five thousand and she would get twenty-five thousand, if she helped him in his scheme.

"My boyfriend, Jess, and I weren't happy about this scheme. But she said she was so happy with him. We didn't want to burst her bubble. After all the struggles in her life, we were happy for her.

"I wanted to see a photo of this Jordan, but he wouldn't let her take one of him. He said he was protecting her from his drug ring. We were supposed to meet him at a bar in San Francisco, but I had to work and he was always changing his plans.

"I did hear one of his messages on her phone machine, and it was full of love. But she was upset because she couldn't go over his house. He did buy her a cell phone so he could call her anytime."

On July 2, 2000, Dawn bought three ski masks at Copeland's Sports in Concord. She then bought three pairs of water-ski gloves. Dawn had to return later, however, because two of the gloves were too small for Justin and Taylor. They needed extra-large gloves for their hands. Clerk Elizabeth Hand on that occasion recalled Dawn at her counter with a man in the background. The man was probably either Taylor or Justin.

Dawn also bought some weights for a weight set. They eventually were to be used for the weight they could add to a bag, not for exercise. These cost $49. Dawn paid for all of this with cash.

Pagers were purchased for the Children of Thunder so they could keep in touch with each other. These were purchased at Double Header Pagers. And a voice mail service was opened up for Dawn, Taylor and Justin. All three members of Children of Thunder had cell phones as well, but Justin rarely used his.

On July 10, Dawn adopted a young Rottweiler at the Contra Costa County Animal Services Center. The dog was named Jake. Later that day, Taylor adopted a Border collie and named him Blackie. A third dog, an Australian shepherd, was adopted by Justin and named Taser.

They also adopted a fourth dog, a large mastiff, but

due to its massive 180 pounds, and aggressiveness, the animal control center required that the dog be spayed and neutered. The operation was done, but neither Taylor nor Justin nor Dawn ever picked up the mastiff.

The dogs were part of Taylor's scheme—he wanted to see if the dogs would eat human remains if they were chopped up and fed to them. Dawn began to build a dog run in the backyard of the Saddlewood residence. She hammered and nailed and used the reciprocating saw. Neighbor Kaye Shaman was aware of a lot of construction and a lot of noise coming from the backyard of her neighbor's house.

The meetings of the Children of Thunder were on a daily basis now at Saddlewood. All of them would sit down in a circle and open each meeting with a prayer. Then Taylor would give out his ideas. Dawn said later, "We'd talk about if an idea was a valid one or not. Whether it would work and how expensive it might be. When Taylor talked, I believed that Spirit was talking through him.

"We believed as Children of Thunder we were declaring war on Satan. This was so Satan wouldn't get the opportunity to be loosed upon the earth. Evil was Satan and his minions. He was the opposite of God. God is pure joy. But Satan was the balance. Such as light and dark. Joy and sadness. Satan was the balance of God.

"Justin even once declared, 'Satan got a bad rap.'"

Taylor's role as a prophet was also taking on one more unforeseen and incredible aspect. Dawn recalled, "Taylor believed that the Latter-Day Saints had gone astray. It was twisted. He didn't agree with some of their principles anymore. I would think and pray about what Taylor said and then decide. Justin didn't say what he felt."

According to Dawn, there was a scheme Taylor called Brazil, where Brazilian orphans would be adopted by them. The children would be brought back to the United States and molded into assassins who only followed orders from Taylor. They would be sent on a mission to kidnap the Twelve Apostles of the LDS Church, its president and his two counselors. These men would be forced to contact the media and say that the United States government was behind the kidnapping. Chaos would be created across the United States, especially in Utah. In the midst of the chaos, Taylor would be seen as a unifying force in the Mormon Church. He would be appointed by the kidnapped president of the church, on television, to become the new president of the Mormon faith. Taylor as president, and his counselors, Justin and Dawn, would form the new hierarchy and choose twelve new apostles. The old apostles would be killed, as well as the old president and his two counselors. Such things had to be done, Taylor insisted, to save the world.

Brazil, however, was for the future. Children of Thunder project was to take place within weeks. Taylor relied a lot on Dawn because of her organizational skills. He didn't believe that Justin had what it took in that capacity. Taylor would constantly test both Dawn and Justin to see if they would follow his orders, no matter how outrageous. Dawn said, "Justin didn't challenge Taylor on any of his plans. Once war was declared on Satan, Justin was on board."

It was determined as time went on that the dogs wouldn't work as a means of disposing human body parts. Taylor, Dawn and Justin had bought soup bones and meat from a deli and tried feeding it to the dogs, but they just wouldn't eat enough. Blackie and Taser were released at an unknown location near Bay Point, never to be seen again. Jake, however, was retained.

Taylor had a hard time giving up his plan to feed some human flesh to the Rottweiler.

Taylor allowed very few visitors to the Saddlewood residence during the inception of Children of Thunder. One of those allowed to come there was Debra McClanahan. She said later, "Taylor allowed me there, but he didn't fully trust me. I had to complete four things before Taylor said that he would trust me. The first three things were to take all three levels of Harmony. He would tell me what the fourth was later."

Taylor did open up to her, however, about some of his ideas. He asked her if a great man could become a prophet.

"President Hinckley is a prophet," she responded.

Taylor said, "He's just a man, after all."

Debra recalled, "Taylor never said to me that he was a prophet, and I didn't think that he was. But I was led to believe that the others thought he might be a prophet. Dawn certainly believed it.

"I did think that Taylor was a seer and a revelator. Someone who has foresight and can see into the bigger picture. He was being spoken to by Spirit. He would just listen as if in a trance. You couldn't talk when he was in such a state. After the Spirit spoke, he'd point directly at Dawn and say, 'Get this.' He wanted to point out how important it was."

To get closer to Taylor, Debra McClanahan took the first two levels of Harmony in July 2000. The third level was scheduled for September 2000. Taylor let her in on a variation of the schemes he was planning. According to Debra, one scheme was that Taylor would select three young, beautiful, underage girls and take them on a cruise, one by one. Each cruise would be at least five days in duration. He'd teach them everything they needed to know about sex and how to please a man. He'd set them up in an apartment and have a caretaker watch over them and cater to their needs.

In a variation of the plan Dean Witter, the girls would start to work in a sandwich shop and deliver sandwiches and lunch items to stockbrokers at Dean Witter. The girls would come on to young men in the company and take them back to the apartment. They would supply the men with Viagra and ecstasy and have sex with them.

Once they gained the men's trust, they would "pull sheets." In effect, they were going to take photos of blue sheets spread all over a bed, so that they could blackmail the brokers. The stocks would fall; the girls would threaten the stockbrokers with blackmail. The girls would also get attorneys to threaten Dean Witter with lawsuits of up to $50 million. Taylor estimated that Dean Witter would settle for $20 million, and he and the girls would accept. The girls would get some money, the lawyer would get some money and Taylor would take the lion's share. He'd even give a million dollars apiece to the stockbrokers, who had been blackmailed, so they wouldn't commit suicide.

Of all of this, Debra said, "Oh, wow!" She also added later, "I thought it was just wild talk."

Debra came up with a wild idea of her own, however. She told Taylor she would meet someone who made adult films and ask $2,000 for being in a movie. She thought she could make $6,000 to $8,000 a week by this means.

Taylor had an unexpected reply, though, especially for someone who had pushed Keri Furman into dancing nude and posing for *Playboy*. He told Debra, "If you think that's what you want to do, okay. But is that what you want to be known for?"

Debra discussed the adult-film idea with Justin. He was more enthused about it than Taylor. Justin told her he'd like to film a man and a woman having sex on the hood of a car during rush hour. Justin didn't say he wanted to be in the movie, but he definitely wanted to film it. He told Debra, "It would be fun."

Debra related that one time after "intimacy" with Taylor, he put a folder on the bed. It contained a photo of women in lingerie and a questionnaire. She saw that it contained two pages of true and false questions. The questions contained such things as:

There is no difference between right and wrong? T F
There is no such thing as good and evil? T F
Stealing is wrong? T F It depends
Breaking the law is wrong? T F It depends
Murder is wrong? T F It depends

Taylor asked her if she had any problems with the questionnaire. She told him that she didn't.

Taylor and Dawn wouldn't let Debra McClanahan in on everything that was happening with Children of Thunder. Debra said of Saddlewood, "They'd often speak to each other in code in my presence."

Just how touchy Taylor could be, Debra found out one evening at Saddlewood while they were all playing a game of Risk. Dawn got up from the table and it was Debra's turn. Justin took two cards that he neglected to take during his turn and Taylor told him, "You can't take two cards. If you do, I'm not playing anymore."

Justin took his two cards and that was it as far as Taylor was concerned. He got up from the table and refused to play anymore.

There is evidence, though sketchy at best, that Taylor, Dawn and Selina went out on a personal water-craft at Lake Berryessa, and a receipt from that area seems to prove that they did. According to Dawn, "Taylor's thoughts were that Selina should have some fun before she was killed."

Taylor wanted a safe kept over at Debra McClanahan's apartment. Debra said, "Dawn had a portable clothes washer and wanted to sell it, but I didn't have enough money at the time to buy it. Dawn told me I could have the washer if a safe was stored in my apartment."

"But you have to leave it in the front room," Dawn said.

Debra replied, "No, we can leave it in my daughter's room.

"I didn't feel good about having that safe in my house. Taylor and Dawn brought it over with the washing machine. Eventually I put the safe in my bedroom in the walk-in closet."

Debra became aware at some point that Taylor was storing drugs in the safe. These were the drugs he sold at raves. One day Dawn was getting into the safe and Debra's daughter found a small package of drugs that was left out. Debra was incensed about this, since her daughter could have found the drugs and unwittingly swallowed them. She told Dawn and was very angry. Dawn said that it would never happen again.

Justin knew about the contents of the safe as well. On two occasions, he got the safe, pulled some things out of it and returned it to Debra's closet.

Interestingly enough, Taylor told Debra McClanahan about Brazil, even though he didn't trust her in some other areas. According to her, he said, "It's important to get a plan into action with a board of twelve directors. [He] would set it up as an orphanage of these Brazilian children and all of them would have to go through Harmony. They would all have to owe allegiance to [him]. Justin and Dawn would be below [him] in the hierarchy. And [I] would work for Justin."

As Children of Thunder moved along, Taylor was becoming more and more manic. He used a lot of meth during this time and talked, on and on, at great length. He also had a short fuse. Once while playing canasta at Saddlewood, Debra discarded a queen, and Dawn said in an offhand remark, "I knew she was going to do that."

Taylor shouted at her, "That's a lie! No you didn't!"

Obviously there was to be only one seer and prophet at Saddlewood Court.

Another time Debra McClanahan was lying on a bed next to Taylor watching a videotape on philosophy. She spoke up during the video and he became very angry because it interrupted his train of thought. He rewound the tape and made her watch the whole thing again from the beginning.

Debra said later, "He would often get upset and angry. He would get up and walk out of a room if you didn't see things his way. He'd say we didn't 'get it.'"

Unexpectedly, Mike Henderson, Justin's old housemate, was allowed to come to Saddlewood Court by Taylor during the days leading up to the Days of Thunder. Henderson arrived about seven-thirty one evening and had a meal of calzones with Taylor, Justin and Dawn. Henderson said that Taylor was dressed up at the time in a shiny dark outfit and Dawn was dressed up like a gypsy. Only Justin wore regular clothes.

Dawn told Henderson that she was a practicing witch and Taylor said he was a warlock. Then Taylor tried to impress him with a mind-reading trick. Henderson was not terribly impressed, but said later of it, "Hey, whatever floats your boat."

Taylor wrote in a journal that he was starting a coven. He was inspired to do it so "that the weak may become strong." He said he would advertise it in a newspaper. It was to be open to all and would honor darkness and light. In a prophetic line, he wrote, "All those who are afraid, let them run now."

He said the coven would not be about money—it would be about mastering fear. The coven would be filled with ritual, the ritual of darkness and light. There would be a meeting in the daytime and one at night, to honor darkness and light. Then in a side note, he wrote, "Keri is the Lamb, I am What Is." [Taylor still kept in touch with Keri by phone.]

In another note, he wrote about Spirit and nature. He said that free agency was not a gift from God, but a law of the universe, adding that mankind was all sparks from the same fire. He stressed that no one was a victim of God, and no one was a victim of their mortal nature. He spoke of forces that constantly tugged on us to and fro, and the most difficult thing was to "go the other way." The farther one went in one direction, the stronger polar force in the opposite direction. He said that so many people wandered around sideways and wondered why they felt so dead. As for him, he said that he got to move Now on his Father's straight and narrow.

The chart he drew on the next page was anything but straight and narrow. It was a circle called the Medicine Circle. To the east was water and trust and faith. To the south, fire, wisdom, clarity and sight. To the west was earth and strength. And to the north was wind and the straight and narrow.

One thing was a constant in the house on Saddlewood, a need for more and more money to implement Taylor's grandiose plans. Taylor told Justin to take out another loan, and Justin dutifully complied. On July 21, 2000, Justin went in to a Washington Mutual Savings branch in Concord and applied for a $5,000 loan. A loan specialist there, Steve Trahain, looked at Justin's credit report and noted that Justin already had a debt of nearly $30,000 in various loans and credit card debts. Trahain turned down Justin's application for yet another loan.

Taylor tried his luck at getting money from Jeanette Carter. He phoned her in Bay Point and said that he was onto a hot stock deal. If she would let him invest $5,000, he told her he would double her money in two weeks. Carter could hear Justin's voice in the background saying, "Yes, he'd double it for you."

According to Dawn Godman, much later, if Jeanette Carter had given Taylor the $5,000, the Children of Thunder would have been called off. Just how long Children of Thunder would have been called off, however, is anybody's guess. Five thousand dollars was a drop in the bucket when Taylor kept saying it would take at least a million dollars to implement his largest schemes.

Jeanette Carter declined to give Taylor the money, but she did allow him to come out to her five-acre property and fire his pistol. This was probably the 9mm Beretta that Justin had purchased for him. Taylor told Carter, "I have big plans."

Next door to the Children of Thunder on Saddlewood Court, Kaye Shaman was getting fed up with the dog's noise. It seemed to be a vicious dog that would jump at the fence when anybody was around. One day the dog got loose from the yard and was roaming the sidewalk. Shaman became so upset, she phoned Tom Cheng, who knew her through his previous tenants.

Shaman's phone call alerted Cheng to the fact that there were three people living in the rental home on Saddlewood, rather than just one. And they had a dog to boot, which was not part of the contract. Cheng drove by the residence one evening to investigate, but it was getting late and he didn't knock on the door or look into the backyard. At the time, he had no idea that he was on the Eve of the Children of Thunder.

Taylor, Dawn and Justin got into their premission mode. Taylor had originally picked a target day of Saturday, because most people on his list would be home, but he later changed this to a Sunday. Dawn said of the final plans, "It was Taylor's call to make. It would be based on old records of stock portfolios and areas that would be safest for us. Based on whether people had a close neighbor or lived close to a freeway. Whether they had a normal routine.

"Taylor wanted the targets to be elderly people, people who'd already lived a long life. He planned to use enough Rohypnol on them so they would just stop breathing."

Just in case, though, both Taylor and Justin would carry briefcases with pistols, tasers, handcuffs, leg irons and a small blowtorch. The plan was set for the following afternoon of Sunday, July 30, 2000. Taylor's former client Bob White, of Walnut Creek, was on the top of the list due to his having the largest portfolio, and also the fact that he lived alone.

CHAPTER 6

Days of Thunder

On the morning of July 30, 2000, all three members of Children of Thunder sat in a circle in the home on Saddlewood and prayed. Then they declared war on Satan to the Universe.

In the afternoon, Dawn Godman showed up at Debra McClanahan's apartment on Ryan Road in Concord. It was a hot day and Debra and her daughter were out by the pool, along with several other people. One of those persons was Alexandra Price, who had known Debra and her daughter for eight months. She saw them at least once a week around the pool area. Price was sitting with Debra and the kids at the pool when a blond heavyset young woman showed up. The arrival of this blonde stuck in Price's mind because someone in the pool said the word "fuck," and Debra explained to her young daughter in very graphic and sexual terms what the word meant. Price was taken aback by this.

Price noticed that the blond woman wore a bright large dress that was almost like a mumu. The woman talked with Debra for a short while and then borrowed some keys from Debra. As she turned to go, the blonde said to Debra, "I love you."

Price may not have known what was going on, but Dawn Godman certainly did. She told McClanahan at one point, "You're not going to see Taylor. You're to buy four adult tickets for *X-Men* at the movie theater in Pittsburg."

If McClanahan's car broke down on the way there, she was to take a cab to the movie theater. She was to see the 8:00 P.M. show. After that, she was to buy four meals at a restaurant and keep the receipt. All of this was to be an alibi for Taylor, Justin and Dawn.

Dawn went into Debra's apartment and left a $100 bill for the tickets and dinners. Debra surmised it was because Taylor was going to make a drug deal, and she needed to create an alibi for him. She had no idea it was for something much more heinous than that and would include murder.

Later that evening, Debra McClanahan did take her daughter to the movie theater in Pittsburg, and bought four adult tickets rather than just an adult ticket and a child's ticket. They watched *X-Men*, as instructed, and then went to Denny's restaurant in Antioch after the movie. Debra bought four meals in all and kept the receipts.

Even as she did it, she related later, "I was wondering what was going on. What have I done? I knew I was creating an alibi. But I didn't know why."

Miles away in Concord, the Day of Thunder was in progress.

Around 1:00 P.M., Dawn bought some handcuffs and leg irons at Not Too Naughty, an adult bookstore in Pleasant Hill. Melissa Mahan, the store clerk, thought it was somewhat strange that Dawn bought a pair of handcuffs that didn't have a key. Once a person had their hands cuffed, it would be almost impossible to extricate them.

At 4:36 P.M., Mike Walla was working at his store, Cork and Bottle, when a large blond woman walked in and bought a $50 bottle of wine and a $15 bottle of wine, along with two cigars. These weren't for Dawn, Taylor and Justin. They were a stage prop for Taylor's scheme that he planned to use at Bob White's house.

Back at Saddlewood Court, Taylor went over the flowchart with Dawn and Justin of what was to occur later that evening. On the top of the list of potential victims was Bob White. The trio discussed the idea that they would kill up to five people at Bob White's house if they had to. Then they made sure that the guns and knives were ready for use. Taylor talked of contingency plans in case something went wrong.

Bob White had been one of Taylor's wealthier clients at Dean Witter and lived in an ideal location for a kidnapping. His house was near an empty lot and there were no close neighbors. When all was ready, Justin and Taylor drove over to Walnut Creek in the Saturn, while Dawn followed behind in Justin's pickup.

Dressed in business suits and carrying briefcases, Taylor and Justin walked from Taylor's black Saturn up to White's door as Dawn kept watch from Justin's pickup. Taylor intended to use the story, when greeting White, that he had recently made a lot of money for a neighbor of White's. Taylor would say he was in the area and wanted to celebrate with White. Thus, the bottles of wine and cigars. Once he and Justin were inside the door, any killing would depend upon whether other people were in the house. They would keep Bob White alive long enough to sign over some checks and put them in Selina Bishop's name. Then he would be killed.

In the pickup truck, Dawn had handcuffs and a bucket. The bucket was in case the Helzers had to urinate. If so, they would use the bucket. They didn't want to leave any telltale DNA evidence in Bob White's house.

In the end, however, all the precautions were for naught. Bob White wasn't home, and for a very good reason. Unbeknownst to Taylor, Bob White, who was the pilot of a private jet, was thousands of miles away in San Antonio, Texas.

Disappointed, Justin and Taylor went back to the pickup and discussed what to do next with Dawn. They discussed calling things off for the rest of the day, but Taylor was for pressing on. The next targets, number two on his list of former clients, were Ivan and Annette Stineman, and unfortunately for them, they were home that day.

Ivan and Annette Stineman were born in the Midwest and moved to California with their parents in the 1930s. They met each other in southern California during World War II and fell in love. Ivan was serving in the coast guard. They were married in 1945 and started a family in Pico Rivera in southern California. Daughter Nancy came first, followed by Judy.

Nancy recalled that her father was a quiet man. "He was a thinker. Even though he was caring, he wasn't the huggy type. But I always knew he loved me. He liked to putter around the house and the yard in his spare time. He was also a good carpenter and an all-around handyman."

Of her mother, Nancy said, "Mom was the stronger one. They made a good team."

Judy recalled, "Our parents were always interested in our lives. They made sure we did our homework. They watched over us and cared how we did."

All of the family loved animals when the girls were growing up. They had cats, dogs and birds. They even had chipmunks and a monkey. To top it off, they all bought horses so they could go horseback riding together in the area.

Nancy and Judy especially loved camping. They would take off in the family station wagon, and she and her sister would sleep in the back. Outdoor locales, such as Yosemite and Big Bear, became their favorite destinations. As time went on, Ivan and Annette bought a small motor home to replace the station wagon.

Judy had fond memories of growing up in Pico Rivera. "We lived in a house that my parents built," she said. "Both of them made the house over. Even Nancy and I helped. We were so poor in the beginning, Mom and Dad had to take out old nails from boards, straighten them out, and use them in the new construction. It took a long time to build that house and it was never truly finished.

"It was always family time at the dinner table. We would sit around and talk about the day's events. Especially when we went out to our cabin. Daddy liked to fish a lot."

Judy thought it was cute when her father began to wear a toupee when he began to bald. She said that he was laid-back and her mom was high-strung. "Mom ruled the roost. They were each half of a whole. Very in tune with each other. They loved each other very much."

Ivan Stineman was a supervisor in the credit card division of Chevron. There was a lot of pressure that went along with the job, and Judy said he often came home and drank Maalox for an upset stomach.

Ivan was transferred in time to the Chevron division in northern California. He and Annette and Nancy moved to the Concord area, while Judy stayed behind in southern California. She had a boyfriend there, who would later become her husband.

After moving to Concord, Ivan became a real estate agent for a while when he retired from Chevron, while Annette continued working there. They amassed a nice little nest egg by working hard. Once Annette retired, they went camping every chance they could get and also bought time-shares in such places as Lake Tahoe and Hawaii. They also invested their money with Morgan Stanley/Dean Witter, and Taylor Helzer became their financial adviser.

Nancy recalled, "On the rafting trip, Taylor took care of daddy. He made sure he was strapped in properly. It was a long trip on the river—about six hours, and mom was worried about the amount of time. But daddy did very well. He and Taylor seemed to get along very well."

On July 30, 2000, Ivan and Annette Stineman spent the afternoon at Coco's Restaurant in Concord with their friends Harry and Irma Dillon. They talked and laughed throughout the afternoon. Harry had been a fellow member of the Elks Lodge with Ivan for four years, and they were all good friends. In fact, Irma Dillon and Annette Stineman had been friends since they were nineteen years old and both worked for Chevron in southern California.

As they were talking, Ivan brought up the subject of an installation of HBO he had performed at his house recently. He mentioned that the young man who had done the job had taken a very long time to install the wiring. Only half-jokingly, Harry Dillon asked Ivan, "You sure he wasn't casing the house?"

There are some indications that Justin Helzer was the

young man that Ivan was talking about, and Justin was not doing this job as part of his AT&T work schedule.

The Stinemans and Dillons stayed at Coco's until 3:00 P.M., and then the Stinemans went home. It was just another warm lazy Sunday afternoon in late July as far as they were concerned. Afternoon turned into evening and around 8:00 P.M. the front doorbell rang at the Stineman residence.

Just before 8:00 P.M., on July 30, Justin and Taylor drove up in the Saturn to the Frayne Lane area in Concord. Dawn parked Justin's pickup at the corner of Frayne and San Miguel and waited. Justin and Taylor got out of the Saturn around the corner and started walking toward the Stineman home.

By an incredible coincidence, Alexandra Price, who had seen Dawn Godman at Debra McClanahan's that morning, was driving home to her place on Ryan Road. Her route took her by the corner of San Miguel and Frayne Lane. She did not see Dawn waiting in Justin's pickup there, but she noticed two strange young men walking down the sidewalk on Frayne. Price recalled later, "I saw two men walking on the left side of the street. They had dark suits on. They really looked out of place on a hot day. I thought maybe they were Mormon missionaries, though they didn't have name tags on. Then I thought maybe I was wrong about them being Mormons. One of them was smoking a cigarette. And they had their hair in ponytails. One had dark hair and the other light-colored hair. They were about ten feet apart and not talking to each other. I kind of kept my eye on them and watched them in the rearview mirror. They were so out of place. When I got home, I talked to a friend. I said, 'I think I just saw some hit men walking down the street.'"

Price was not the only observer of the two strange young men on Frayne Lane. David Carter lived with his wife and children across the street from the Stineman residence. David was sitting in a rocking chair near the front plate-glass window when he saw two young men in dark suits carrying briefcases. One man had dark hair and the other one lighter hair. Both of them had their hair pulled back in ponytails.

When the pair walked in front of the Stineman house, one of the young men stopped and seemed hesitant to go on. He looked at his feet and was apprehensive about something. David said of the men later, "My general impression was that they were trying to look more clean-cut than they really were."

As David watched, the light-haired man stepped in front of the dark-haired one and put his hand on the dark-haired man's shoulder. Then he made a gesture with his head toward the Stineman door as if to say, "Come on, let's go."

Strangely enough, it was Justin Helzer signaling to Taylor Helzer that they needed to put the plan into action.

Afraid that the young men really were religious missionaries, David Carter did not want to talk to them. He moved away from the window so they couldn't see him.

What exactly occurred inside the Stineman home can only be pieced together by evidence found later. What is known for certain is that Nancy Hall picked this exact moment to call her parents. Annette Stineman normally was very upbeat and chatty with her daughter. But not this time. She was sharp and abrupt, as if she'd just been interrupted in something important. She seemed stressed and rushed to Nancy, to the point of being rude. Nancy said later, "I thought something was going on at their house. But I didn't know what."

Annette abruptly said to Nancy, "We have company!" and hung up the phone.

Meanwhile, out in the pickup, Dawn Godman was sitting in the cab and smoking one cigarette after another. After a while, she thought that some people nearby were watching her. She was right. Rise Bradfield-Minder was looking for a friend to come to her house on Frayne Lane. She noticed a vehicle that was parked at the corner of San Miguel and thought it might be her friend. Rise went out to investigate and realized it wasn't her friend's vehicle. It was a pickup truck parked at an odd angle that nearly blocked traffic at the corner.

Bradfield-Minder went outside to smoke a cigarette and became aware of a silhouette of a woman inside the vehicle. The woman was smoking as well and flicking her cigarette butts out the window onto the street next to the pickup's door. The woman seemed to be agitated or angry. She smoked a lot and seemed jittery.

When Bradfield-Minder's friend arrived, they stood out on the front lawn and discussed the strange woman in the pickup. They wondered what she could be doing. Was she waiting for someone, or was she a lookout for some illegal activity going on? To Bradfield-Minder's eyes, the woman looked very agitated.

Bradfield-Minder and her friend discussed secretly photographing the pickup or even calling the police. Before they could reach a decision, a white van pulled out from a house on Frayne Lane and drove up to the pickup. [It was Stinemans' van stolen by Taylor and Justin. The Stinemans were being held captive in the back of the van.] Bradfield-Minder could see the silhouette of a man in the van. He had a ponytail. This person spoke to the woman in the pickup and she heard the woman say, "Did you get it?"

Bradfield-Minder couldn't hear the reply. As the van began to drive away, Bradfield-Minder heard the woman in the pickup say, "I'm right behind you."

But the strange woman in the pickup wasn't right behind them. Instead, she got out of her pickup and walked up to Bradfield-Minder and her friend. Without any preamble, the woman said, "I watched you watching me. A friend of mine was buying some weed from some shady people. I was the backup."

Momentarily stunned, all Bradfield-Minder could think to say was "Why are you hanging out with shady people?"

The strange woman answered, "It was a last resort."

Then she walked back to her pickup, got in and drove away.

Bradfield-Minder more than ever thought of calling the police, but in the end she didn't.

The Helzer brothers probably thought that they were unobserved as they took the Stinemans into their residence on Saddlewood Court. Little did they know that next-door neighbor Kaye Shaman was watching them from her window. She saw an elderly man and elderly woman being escorted by Taylor and Justin into their house. She noticed that the man had on a white rumpled shirt and wore gold-rimmed glasses. His eyes looked huge to her behind his glasses. She also noticed that he was taking exceptionally small steps as he walked toward the house. He seemed to be shuffling his feet, as if reluctant to enter.

The elderly woman even made eye contact with Shaman, or so she thought. Shaman couldn't read the woman's expression. She thought the elderly couple were the boy's grandparents.

When Ivan and Annette Stineman were brought

into the house on Saddlewood Court, they were hand-cuffed and forced to sit on the couch. Everything that happened next was related later by Dawn Godman. According to her, Justin sat in a chair with a loaded gun across from the Stinemans. Then he placed the gun on the floor as if daring the Stinemans to make a move.

According to Dawn, Justin was totally silent, but Taylor wouldn't shut up. He had been cranked up on meth for a week. Taylor told Dawn, "Things went really well. I know what I have to do next."

Taylor turned toward the Stinemans and asked if they were comfortable or needed anything. They didn't respond to being comfortable, but said they didn't need anything. Dawn noticed that the Stinemans were calm at this point.

Dawn and Taylor went into his bedroom and talked about how to access the Stinemans' accounts. They agreed that they had to ask the Stinemans about their normal habits so that their daughters would not become suspicious by their absence. They decided to do this by taking Ivan and Annette into separate rooms. Taylor also came up with questions about their financial affairs and statement accounts, and Dawn wrote them down. After all the questions were written down, Taylor took Ivan into one bedroom and Dawn took Annette into a room that was used as an office. Each was then asked questions outside of the presence of the other about their finances, so that they could not give each other code words or false numbers, or make up stories together. Then Taylor and Dawn compared their answers outside the presence of the Stinemans.

Since the answers seemed to be similar, they ascertained that the Stinemans weren't lying to them. Taylor and Dawn discussed the logistics of what needed to be done next.

Taylor went back to the living room, and according

to Dawn, he told the Stinemans, "I'm in trouble and I need a lot of money. People are after me and I need to get out of the country."

He told the Stinemans that they were going to have to sign over some checks to him and he would leave them handcuffed to a mattress once he and the others were gone. Once they were safe, he told them, he would call the police, three days later, and the police would come and rescue them.

Annette spoke up and told Taylor that with so much time going by, she was worried that she would soil herself. Dawn listened to Annette's tone of voice and concluded that she knew that Taylor was lying. It appeared to Dawn that Annette already knew that she and Ivan would be killed, no matter what happened.

Taylor said he was sorry if she soiled herself, but he couldn't help that. Then he brought a mattress into the living room and told the Stinemans to lay down on it and get some rest. He would talk to them again in the morning.

Justin stayed in the living room all night to guard the Stinemans. Taylor and Dawn went to her bedroom and began looking at the Stinemans' stock portfolio. They spent a long time analyzing it.

The next morning, Monday, July 31, Taylor had Dawn pretend on the phone she was Annette Stineman. Even though it was only 6:30 A.M., he had her call the Dean Witter office. George Calhoun was already there because he had to be in the office for the opening of Wall Street on Eastern Standard Time.

Calhoun remembered the conversation very well. He said later, "I received a call from a woman who claimed to be Annette Stineman. I was already in the office and the woman said that she wanted to have her accounts with us liquidated. It was because of a medical emergency. Her voice sounded like an elderly woman."

All of this seemed very abnormal to Calhoun, and he asked, "Are you sure you want to do this?"

Then he said, "Her tone of voice was nervous. There was an obvious level of tension. She responded to all of my questions very hastily. Supposedly there was a medical emergency on the East Coast. She was supposed to fly out there.

"What she was asking was to liquidate long-term investments. Mutual funds. It would be hit with penalties and taxes."

Calhoun looked up Annette Stineman's net worth. Her IRA before liquidation came to $167,000.

Calhoun brought in Greg Matthias, who was now Annette and Ivan's principal financial agent at Dean Witter. He and Matthias agreed there was something fishy about all of this. But Matthias thought that Taylor Helzer was working for some other company now, and Annette Stineman wanted to move her account there, and was too embarrassed to just come right out and say it, hence the made-up story about a medical emergency.

The woman caller by now was very nervous. She abruptly ended her call to Calhoun by saying, "I've got to catch a plane. It's an emergency. Take care of the trades. I have to go."

Having to take care of a client's wishes, and since the client on the phone knew privileged information, the trades started going through by 1:00 P.M. at Dean Witter. Once they were sold, they all went into a money market fund after three days. Personal checks could then be written against the full value of the money market funds.

Taylor and Dawn went back to wake up Ivan and Annette. Taylor took Ivan to make a call from a phone booth to cancel some appointments and leave a message for daughter Nancy so that she wouldn't worry.

Dawn went out to get coffee from a nearby Starbucks for Ivan and Taylor and herself. Polite as always, Ivan thanked her for it.

The lies to the Stinemans now took on a new form. To make Annette less worried about soiling herself, Dawn told the Stinemans she would stay with them for two days while Taylor and Justin made their escape. Once she knew that they were safely out of the country, she would take off. They would be on their own for one day before she called the police to rescue them.

For some reason at this point, Taylor decided to give Ivan and Annette six tablets each of Rohypnol. He thought it would make them compliant, but all it did was make them too drowsy to function well, and they still had some signatures to sign.

Ivan was taken to a bedroom, where he was forced to write a check. Annette was taken into the office, shackled to a chair, and watched over by Justin while this occurred. After Taylor was through with Ivan, he took Annette into his bedroom to sign a check. By this time, however, his use of Rohypnol was backfiring. Annette was falling asleep. To try and wake her up, he lit some meth in a pipe and put it up to Annette's mouth, but because she was too drowsy, he had to blow the smoke into her nostrils.

Even with the meth, Annette was still drowsy. After a long pause, he and Justin carried her to the mattress and laid her down, and laid Ivan down beside her. In total frustration, Taylor told Dawn she would have to practice writing a signature like Annette's signature. Dawn practiced for a while and then wrote out a check for $10,000 and signed the check with the name Annette Stineman. This was to be a test check to see if it would clear. If it did, they knew the rest of the money would be there as well.

Since Dawn was doing a reasonably good job of

signing Annette's signature, the Stinemans were no longer useful to Taylor. He dragged them into the bathroom. Annette was so groggy, she was practically asleep.

Justin Helzer was glad that the Stinemans were dropping off. He hoped that they would eventually be forced to ingest so much Rohypnol that they would just die in their sleep. He figured that would be the most peaceful way to die and he didn't want them to suffer.

But Taylor had other ideas—ones that made Justin extremely angry. Taylor woke up Ivan and Annette so that one of two things could happen. Either they could say good-bye to each other, or he could say good-bye to them. Justin would tell Dawn later, "That was totally unnecessary!" Justin was incensed by Taylor's action, but held his peace.

By now, both Ivan and Annette were restive on the bathroom floor and starting to struggle. So as not to get any blood on their clothes, Taylor stripped down to his underwear and had Justin and Dawn do the same. Taylor decided to kill the Stinemans by suffocating them. He placed his hands over Annette's nose and mouth, but that only seemed to make her struggle more. Justin did the same thing with Ivan. Tiring of the battle, Taylor ordered Dawn to bring in two large pieces of plastic and he draped one over Annette's face, while Justin did the same with Ivan. True to his nature, Justin did everything that Taylor did seconds after his brother took an action.

Even these large plastic sheets did not work. Ivan and Annette kicked and fought back. In total frustration, Taylor started banging Annette's head on the bathroom floor and against the edge of the toilet. Justin banged Ivan's head on the bathroom floor as well. But nothing they did seemed to kill the Stinemans.

Dawn, who was in the bathroom doorway, watched

as the elderly couple were being beaten. She said later, "I really couldn't believe this was happening. I just wanted them to die. I said to myself, 'Hurry up and die, so this will just be over.'"

By now, Justin was pounding Ivan's head on the bathroom floor very hard. There are indications from a later autopsy that Ivan may have died from a heart attack because of the beating.

Annette was even tougher. Tired of her struggles, Taylor dragged her to the bathtub, draped her body over the side and stabbed her in the lungs—once in the right lung and once in the left lung. Even that did not kill her immediately. As Dawn watched, Taylor slit Annette's throat. He pushed her face, down so that if nothing else, she would drown in her own blood. Finally, after incredible brutality, Annette Stineman died.

Within ten minutes of the Stinemans' deaths, Taylor told Dawn to get dressed and drive up to Petaluma, about fifty miles north of Concord, to deposit the $10,000 check. Dawn said, "I put on a cotton pantsuit that was lime green. Taylor, when he came out of the bathroom, was acting cool. Justin didn't look at me or talk to me."

With sheets of plastic on the floor and the tub area, Taylor and Justin got to work. No one was there to see them, and neither one spoke of what they did later, but certain things could be ascertained as to what happened. It became apparent to them very soon that human flesh cannot be readily chopped with a reciprocating saw. The brothers had to fall back first into slicing off flesh with knives. Only then could they use the reciprocating saw on the bones. Before long, the bathroom had to look like a slaughter-house. As the bodies were hacked into sections, they were placed in large plastic bags. Just what body part went into which bag would later become the province of a forensic medical examiner.

After her trip to Petaluma, Dawn was instructed by Taylor to stop at his parents' house in Pacheco and pick up some wood. Just what the wood was for, he didn't say, though it was probably intended for the fireplace at Saddlewood. Dawn did as instructed and brought a wheelchair back to Saddlewood along with the firewood. [Days before, Dawn had been instructed by Taylor to rent a wheelchair.] Once there, she noticed a big plastic tarp in the hallway with several black garbage bags placed on it. Dawn realized that chopped-up body parts of the Stinemans were in the garbage bags.

Justin was in the bathroom cleaning it and wiping down the surfaces. Dawn sat down with Taylor and discussed the trip to Petaluma. Then she said, "We talked about Selina and getting the money. About everything else that had to be done."

On Monday night, July 31, Debra McClanahan went to bed and awakened at 11:35 P.M. with a jolt. Someone was standing silently over her as she lay in bed. For one moment, she had no idea who it was and nearly freaked out. Then Taylor stepped from the shadows and spoke to her. He apologized for scaring her.

He gave Debra a hug and said he needed access to a key. He said that he couldn't stay long and that he needed to get into the safe. He asked where the key was and she told him it was beneath a tissue box.

Debra went into the living room to get a cigarette. When she walked back into the bedroom, Taylor was bent down on one knee, getting contents out of the safe. Inside the safe were packages filled with pills. Debra stepped forward and gave him a hug. Taylor asked for a large bag and she went and got him a gym bag. Taylor took a look at it and told her it was too small. Debra then got him a large garbage bag instead.

Even as Taylor fiddled around with the safe, he took enough time for Debra to lay down and he gave her a back rub. He said, "You're my best friend."

When he was done giving her a back rub, Taylor went out the door and said over his shoulder, "I put the key on the coffee table." But when Debra looked there later, there was no key.

Debra said, "I assumed he was going partying. He was all dressed up. It was yuppie casual. He was dressed to kill."

CHAPTER 7

**"Spirit says you get to know
this is not a dream."**

Dawn called various places on Tuesday, August 1, about renting a personal watercraft and was informed that the towing vehicle would need appropriate auto insurance. This glitch would throw off the timing for the Children of Thunder's plans.

While Dawn was doing this, Justin headed for an auto shop to have a trailer hitch put on his pickup. He arrived at Pep Boys at around 1:00 P.M. on August 1. The manager had him sign a form for work to be done, and after he talked to Justin, he had a work order put in for a trailer hitch to be put on a 1995 Nissan pickup. The work began at 1:17 P.M. and was finished by 2:50 P.M.

The manager recalled later that Justin had told him that he was in a hurry. "He wanted to get the [personal watercraft] fast. He said he was going to tow a boat or a [personal watercraft]. In fact, he even mentioned that he was going out on the Delta."

Justin did not stick around Pep Boys for the work to be finished. He called a cab company and they sent a taxi out to pick him up. In an incredible twist, stranger than fiction, the cabdriver turned out to be a buddy from Justin's old National Guard unit. They had served time together as MPs in Germany. The driver was Nicolai Nenad.

Nicolai and Justin talked about how things had been going for them since the service and about old times. Nicolai dropped Justin off at a house on Saddlewood Court.

Vicki Sexton had been a bank manager for nearly thirty years at various branches by the year 2000. On Tuesday, August 1, she was the bank manager of Cal Fed at the corner of California and Olympic Boulevards in Walnut Creek. At two-thirty that afternoon, she was sitting at her desk when a teller named Nicki brought a customer in a wheelchair to her desk. The young woman in the wheelchair was a heavyset young blonde who said her name was "Jackie."

Besides being in a wheelchair, this woman caught Vicki's attention because she was wearing a lime green pantsuit topped off by a large white cowboy hat. Jackie also wore driver's gloves on her hands. It was unusual attire for sedate and sophisticated Walnut Creek.

Dawn (as Jackie) started telling Vicki a convoluted story about Cal Fed customers, Ivan and Annette Stineman, about their supposed granddaughter Selina Bishop, who needed emergency medical care. Selina, according to Dawn, was in San Diego and needed open-heart surgery, but she didn't have medical insurance. (The place of the emergency had changed from the story given to George Calhoun.) The Stinemans were going to pay for the surgery, but they needed to put money into Selina's account. At that point, Dawn gave Vicki Sexton two checks with the Stinemans' signatures on them. One check was for $67,000 and the other was for $33,000. Both checks were made out to Selina Bishop.

All of this was so unusual, Vicki wanted to talk to the Stinemans, and she called a phone number that was printed on the checks. All Vicki got was an answering machine. The voice on the tape sounded like an elderly man's. The tape said, "Hello, this is the Stinemans' residence. We are not able to come to the phone right now."

Vicki left a message on the tape, stating, "Hi. This is Vicki at Cal Fed. Give me a call as soon as possible. I'll be here all day, until five-thirty P.M."

Dawn never anticipated Vicki calling the phone number printed on the checks. She told Vicki, "Oh, they just moved. Here's their new phone number." The new phone number was a pager number with a voice mail service that Dawn had purchased only a few days before.

Vicki called the new number and a male's voice came on the line, but it was not the voice on the answering machine. It sounded younger. (In fact, it was Taylor Helzer.)

Dawn repeated to Vicki that the checks needed to clear in a hurry. Vicki was certainly sympathetic, but she also knew that she needed to protect her bank and her customers. Vicki phoned Dean Witter about the checks, but couldn't get information from them about the transaction. The person there said he'd need the Stinemans' Social Security numbers. Vicki related this to Dawn, who said okay, she would find out what those numbers were. Then Dawn rolled her wheelchair out of the bank and through the front door. This was also unusual because wheelchair patrons came down an elevator from the parking lot on the second story. To go out the front door meant that Dawn had to negotiate sixteen steps with the wheelchair.

When Dawn left, Vicki Sexton felt there was something very odd about the whole situation. She went upstairs to the security department and had them put a "hard hold" on the checks that amounted to $100,000 and were destined for Selina Bishop's account. A hard hold meant that only Sexton could authorize clearance of the checks.

On August 1, 2000, at around 5:30 P.M., Richard Hundly, of Concord Insurance Service, received a call from Justin Helzer. Justin had been an automobile insurance client of his for about two years. Justin wanted to know how much extra it would cost to have coverage so that he could tow a rented personal watercraft behind his pickup.

Hundly said Justin's pickup would have to be photographed first to see if any damage was already there. He told Justin to bring the pickup down to the insurance office.

By the time Justin arrived, Taylor was already at the Concord Insurance Service, filling out paperwork. Hundly went outside and took a Polaroid shot of the pickup. While Hundly was doing paperwork, he overheard the two brothers talking about planning to take a trip with the personal watercraft in tow. Hundly was interested in personal watercrafts and he asked them where they planned to go. Justin answered, "Somewhere out in the Rio Vista area." This was out in the Delta of the Sacramento and San Joaquin Rivers.

Justin seemed relaxed to Hundly, though somewhat in a hurry because he still had to show the proof of insurance to the personal-watercraft rental place in Livermore, miles away, and it was getting near the end of the business day.

Once the policy was completed and signed, Justin phoned Dawn on his cell phone and told her that he now had insurance and would be over as soon as possible to pick up the rental.

Taylor, at this point, said he would get a cab ride home, but Hundly asked him where he lived. When Taylor said near Kirker Pass Road, Hundly said that was right on his way home. He offered Taylor a ride, and Taylor accepted.

On the way to Saddlewood Court, Hundly let Taylor use his cell phone. Taylor phoned Dawn and left a message. Hundly heard Taylor say, "I'm on my way home."

Dawn Godman arrived at Cool Rides in Livermore around 6:30 P.M. She asked co-owner Robin Miller how much weight the craft could handle. Miller told her a two-seater could handle 250 pounds and a three-seater about 350 pounds. Dawn noticed that there wasn't much room for cargo on the two-seater watercraft— there was only an area under the front seat that could hold a small amount of cargo. The three-seater, however, was almost like a small speedboat. It had runners alongside the craft, and Dawn realized these runners could hold duffel bags. In the end, she chose the three-seater.

Dawn made small talk with Robin Miller as time passed. Dawn told Miller what a hassle it had been to try and get a personal watercraft. She said that Cool Rides was the only outlet in the area that rented these. Then she added, "It took three of us working together to rent [one]."

Both Robin Miller and Dawn Godman were worried that Justin was not going to make it on time and Miller was getting antsy to close up the store for the day. It wasn't until nearly 8:00 P.M. that Justin finally arrived. As soon as he did, Miller turned on a mandatory safety video for them to watch as she filled out paperwork.

Miller had them give her their driver's licenses and a valid Visa card. The transaction cost $500, which Justin paid for, all in $20 bills.

Robin Miller heard Dawn call someone on her cell phone and say, "We got the [rental]."

Things still weren't going smoothly, however. While Robin filled out the paperwork, her husband, William Miller, realized that the personal watercraft they intended for Dawn and Justin to rent wasn't running properly. So he fueled up another one—#8.

Finally, after it was already dark outside, #8 was placed on Justin's trailer, and Dawn climbed back into the Saturn. As she drove away, Robin Miller noticed that there was a wheelchair in the backseat. She thought that was an odd item for someone renting a watercraft.

Later that night, Dawn left an outgoing greeting on voice mail supposedly from the Stinemans, but it was really her speaking, as well as Taylor. This voice message was in case Vicki Sexton called. It was supposed to fool her into thinking the Stinemans were in a hurry to get down to where Selina Bishop was having emergency medical surgery.

When Vicki Sexton got to Cal Fed on the morning of Wednesday, August 2, at eight o'clock, there was a note on her desk that someone had called and left the Stinemans' Social Security numbers for her.

A short time later, "Jackie" called and asked about the funds that were to go to Selina Bishop's account. Once again, Vicki had a gut feeling that something was not right. Jackie, in person, had a raspy voice. So Vicki asked the teller who had received the earlier call about the Stinemans' Social Security numbers if the person claiming to be Jackie on the phone had a raspy voice. The teller said that the caller indeed had a raspy voice. This was one more suspicious circumstance.

When Vicki talked to Dawn this time, she tried to trick her and said, "Thank you for calling last night."

Dawn responded, "I didn't call last night."

Vicki replied, "I need to speak with the Stinemans."

Dawn hemmed and hawed about the Stinemans not being available, which indeed they weren't—they were already dead.

Vicki Sexton phoned the number that Dawn had given her for the Stinemans and left another message on the answering machine. She said, "This call is very important. Please call back."

Then Vicki tried another number that Dawn had given her. A woman's voice came on the answering machine, claiming to be Annette Stineman. The message said, "I can't deal with this right now, Ivan." That was all.

Vicki said later, "I was weirded out by the message. I left one of my own on their machine. I said, 'Hi, this is Vicki Sexton from Cal Fed. We found your information. We'll call you next week.'"

Vicki Sexton's fears and the hard hold on the $100,000 checks was knocking everything off schedule for the Children of Thunder.

On the way home, Dawn picked up some food and she and Taylor and Justin all had dinner together. After dinner Taylor phoned Selina Bishop. Taylor was becoming very uptight about how things were progressing at this point. Dawn recalled, "Taylor was angry about Cal Fed. He thought something was wrong. Things should have been working better. He thought that I screwed up somehow."

Taylor didn't know that things weren't working according to plan because of Vicki Sexton's hard hold on the Stinemans' checks. More than anything else, it was disrupting the Children of Thunder's plans.

* * *

Taylor was also vaguely aware at the time that something that Jenny Villarin had done was going to come back to haunt him and everyone in the Villarin family. For what should have been such a small occurrence, it had terrible ramifications.

In late July, Jenny and her friend Rosanne Lusk Urban were aware that Selina was quite taken with a guy named Jordan. Urban said later, "Selina was quite enamored of this Jordan. She said she was really in love with him. But she was intimidated too. She said one of his former girlfriends had been a Playboy Bunny. This made her very self-conscious. She wanted to see a photo of a Playboy Bunny. So I bought her a copy. I thought the girl was cute, but not that big a deal. I think Selina was self-conscious because of her weight."

Selina had also told Lanelle Simon, Jenny's housemate in Novato, that Jordan came from a good family. Simon said later, "He was a nice guy and romantic. She seemed to have gotten what she dreamed of."

However, one time when Jordan phoned Selina, Simon answered the phone. As she recalled, "He said, 'Is Selina there?' He thought I was Jenny, her mother. He was very sickeningly sweet on the phone. He reminded me of Eddie Haskell on the *Leave It to Beaver* show."

Jenny was indeed curious about this mysterious Jordan, who was seeing her daughter, and she wanted to meet him in person. Rosanne Urban said later, "We assumed Jordan was a trust fund baby. He had a lot of spare time on his hands and money. Selina and Jordan were supposed to pick up some furniture from my house. Time after time, the dates were broken and he never did show up. Selina would make excuses for him."

Rosanne recalled, "On a Monday morning, Jenny didn't have to work. We went to breakfast early and drove to Woodacre. Selina had let it slip that Jordan was staying the night with her. I said, 'Let's go over there. But what do we say?'

"Jenny said, 'I'll say I need a fresh blouse for work.'

"I kind of egged her on and we went over there. Once I pulled up near her place, I said, 'Well, I can't go in. I'm not going to work and I don't have any excuse for being there.'

"So Jenny ran in and she was only there about five minutes. She sandbagged him. When she got back in the car, I asked, 'Well, how was he?'

"Jenny didn't seem overly impressed with Jordan. She said, 'He was cute, I guess.'

"She didn't say anything more, and I didn't press it."

In late July, Selina Bishop, her mother, Jenny, and Gloria LaFranchi all had lunch together at the Two Bird Café. Selina told the two women, "I like Jordan, but he won't open up our relationship. I'm really in love with him, but he wants to back off on the sex for six months to see where the relationship will go."

LaFranchi didn't say anything then, but recalled later, "I thought, what's up with that?"

Then Selina related to her that she and Jordan were talking of going camping in Yosemite. She wanted to go, but was worried by what Jordan had just said about their relationship.

Selina also talked to Rosanne Lusk Urban about the trip. Rosanne said something more prophetic than she realized at the time. She told Selina, "Everybody should see Yosemite once before they die."

Mulling over the situation about Jordan, Selina asked her boss at the Two Bird Café for some time off so she could go to Yosemite in the first week of August. Tony Micelli recalled, "She was going with her boyfriend, Jordan. She was very excited."

To Julia Bernbaum, Selina also seemed excited about

the upcoming trip. Bernbaum said that Selina and Jordan planned to go for only a couple of days up to Yosemite. And she thought this was odd, since it was a six- or seven-hour drive up from Marin County to Yosemite. They wouldn't have much time for sightseeing in the park because of the amount of time getting there and back.

"She was really gullible about a lot of things. I told her, 'I'm worried about you.' Selina said, 'I'm worried about me too. But I'm going.'

"Then we both dyed her hair pink and red. We were twenty-two years old. We did it as a lark."

Around this time, Selina wrote one of the most heartbreaking segments in her journal. It was written to Jordan, but he probably never read it.

She wrote that she wished she and Jordan could be together more often, and wondered why it was so difficult. She said that she'd found the person she'd been looking for and it filled her heart with joy. When they were together she was in a state of bliss.

When she was away from him, however, doubts crept into her mind. She wondered why he offered her only "crumbs of his time." She tried to imagine herself without him, and it was a painful thought to her. She realized that some women tricked the man they wanted into having a baby, by saying they had used birth control, when they had not. She said she understood this mentality, but she would not use it on Taylor, even though she wanted a part of him to be with her always.

Pulling back from her fantasies, Selina wrote that she really didn't know him any better than "a can of paint." She said that over time she would lose weight and her body would be more desirable for him. She still wondered, however, if that would be enough for Jordan.

Selina wondered if she was "too ghetto" for him, or he wasn't "ghetto enough" for her. She said that she didn't want to be a part of his "big plan." She didn't want a fancy house, expensive cars and clothing and a drug-filled lifestyle. All she wanted was a normal life with kids, a comfortable home and Jordan.

Rhetorically she asked, "Do I see a husband here?" She answered it by saying, that only time would tell. And she finished by writing that she loved Jordan, whoever he was.

One more person Selina spoke to about the up-coming trip was coworker Chris Caley. He had moved from New Jersey out to California and didn't have many friends in his new locale. Selina took him under her wing and was very nice to him. They often took cig-arette breaks together, and she told him a lot about her boyfriend, Jordan.

On Sunday, July 30, while the Helzer brothers were kidnapping the Stinemans, Selina and Chris Caley went to a rave in San Francisco. They arrived there at around 9:00 P.M. Caley said later, "They were playing techno music. There was a deejay spinning records. I danced some and then watched Selina dance. She seemed to be having a good time. She and I milled around and had a couple of drinks. I was there just as a friend."

While at the rave, Selina told Caley a little more about Jordan's supposed scheme that was in progress. He recalled, "She said he was involved in some kind of bank scam. I thought it sounded kind of shady. She talked about some financial things, and said that she still didn't know Jordan's real name. I thought that was odd.

"She said again that they were going camping. She

seemed to be concerned, but nothing outside the typical. Then she said about her boyfriend, 'We're working things out. It's a compatibility issue.'"

Selina and Caley left the rave about one o'clock on July 31, and she drove him home to Marin County.

On Monday afternoon, July 31, Selina sat in the kitchen of the Soladay home and chatted with Leora. Leora asked her about Jordan, and Selina sighed, then chuckled. She said, "Oh, he has a three-million-dollar plan."

Leora knew that Selina was planning a special dinner for Jordan, but he called thirty minutes before he was supposed to show up and said that he couldn't make it. Selina was very upset.

Selina was having a frustrating week, as far as Jordan was concerned. His plans for the trip to Yosemite kept changing, leaving her up in the air about when they would go. At one point, she even asked Lucia Villarin if she wanted to go along. But Lucia had a one-year-old baby and thought that it wouldn't work out.

Lucia also had her suspicions about Jordan. She wondered why he wouldn't tell Selina his real name.

Selina wrote about everything being in God's hands at that point. She said that Jordan was probably afraid to commit to her, that he might think of her as a burden. She said, however, that she was tired of trying to figure him out, and that she was particularly tired of his "secret agent bullshit."

Selina wrote that she desired to know if he really loved her. She said she was not looking for a soulmate or a husband, but just a boyfriend. If Jordan wasn't ready for that, then her search would have to continue.

Near the end of the journal entry she drew back from her ultimatum and wrote that all she wanted at the moment was to be held and loved. She said that her heart was always lonely when they weren't together and she told her mind to be quiet and take all the love he would give her, even if it was doled out a small amount at a time.

On Tuesday evening, August 1, Matthew King, of the Bison Brewery in Berkeley, looked up from the bar to see one of his regular customers come into the establishment. It was Selina Bishop. He knew her by sight because she and a young man had met there several times since June to have drinks and talk.

King said later of Selina, "She had a nice smile. I thought it was kind of romantic that she came from Marin County and he came from Concord, and they met halfway in Berkeley."

Of Selina's boyfriend, whom Selina introduced as Jordan, King would remember, "He was tall, well-dressed, with a professional-type ponytail. He had a swagger about him. Confidence. Cockiness. I thought of him as a ladies' man. Maybe even a porno star. They would walk in. Have a couple of drinks together. Hold hands. Maybe a hug. A girlfriend/boyfriend kind of thing."

Everything pointed to the couple enjoying each other's company for King, until August 1. On that day, Selina waited and waited for Jordan to show up. She exchanged some dollar bills for quarters and used them at a pay phone to call Jordan. When she returned from the phone, she told King, "I'm waiting for Jordan"; then she rolled her eyes. She added, "I don't know why I go out with him!"

Jordan finally did arrive at the Bison Brewery at about 6:30 P.M. King could see that Selina was perturbed at him. King recalled, "They talked and milled around for about half an hour. They never settled down. They finally left between seven and seven-thirty P.M."

Selina apparently went over to Lanelle Simon's place in Novato, where her mother was staying. She arrived about 9:10 P.M. All of them discussed going to a fair in Santa Rosa, but decided it was getting too late. Selina talked to Lanelle a bit more about her upcoming camping trip with Jordan. Lanelle said, "She seemed excited, but seemed hesitant too. She went back and forth with it."

Dawn said that Taylor's plans now went through various revisions. One plan was for Selina to pick up the money from Washington Mutual and bring it to Saddlewood. The next plan was that Taylor would actually take her to Yosemite until the money was transferred from Cal Fed to Selina's Washington Mutual bank account, and then would kill her.

Then Taylor became concerned that Selina might go to her ATM and discover that she suddenly had $100,000 in her bank account. That had to be prevented at all costs. On top of all of this was Taylor's long-standing plans to go sell drugs at "Reggae on the River" up in the redwoods on August 4 through 6. As he dwelled on all of these matters, he decided that things had to be wrapped up for him with Selina by at least August 4.

Even as he was planning to kill her, he admitted on a notepad that his thoughts about Selina had changed somewhat since targeting her as a victim in the spring. He wrote, "She is becoming a better person by being around me. I had a realization that people are changing for the better by just being around me. She is not evil, saintly or exceptional. But how can I take her life when she is becoming saintly?"

In the end, Taylor decided that his larger plans for

Transform America were more important than Selina Bishop's life.

About the same time that Taylor was writing his note, Selina made an entry into her journal. Selina wrote of a phone call between her and Jordan where he was making excuses once again about the delays for their Yosemite trip. She called it "his garbage." Then she wondered what she was going to do by herself for the next couple of days. She even told him she just wanted to forget the Yosemite trip and go to the theme park, Great America. Jordan told her he had something better planned.

The garbage that Selina alluded to was the killing of the Stinemans and their dismemberment, though she had no way of knowing this. The "something better" than Great America was Taylor's plans for her murder.

Taylor called Selina on Wednesday, August 2, and told her to meet him at the Marriott parking lot in Concord. The excuse he used was that his wife had just given him a treasure chest of gems and rings and he wanted them to be appraised at a local jewelry store. In fact, what he intended to have appraised were the Stinemans' wedding rings.

The last message Selina left on her phone message machine was "Hi, sweetie. I'm getting ready for the trip."

It's not clear if Taylor and Selina ever went to a jewelry store to have the wedding rings appraised. What is known is that Taylor and Selina drove to Saddlewood around dusk in their separate cars. Kaye Shaman noticed that a dark-haired young woman walked up to Taylor in the driveway and gave him a kiss. Then she and the man walked into the Saddlewood home. Selina sat down with Taylor, Justin and Dawn and they all played a game for a while. Dawn recalled, "Selina was happy. We all smoked some marijuana (except for Justin, who did not get stoned). She was at ease."

There was a plan in place to lure Selina into the bathroom. Dawn told her that they were remodeling the bathroom and wanted to show her what they'd done. It was remodeled, all right—the bathroom had been stripped of all the cabinets and shower curtain for the butchery of Ivan and Annette Stineman.

As Dawn went into the bathroom, Selina stood at the door, and Justin was behind her—with a hammer. As soon as Selina turned her back on Justin, he was to hit her in the head with the hammer until she was dead. But Selina never did fully turn her back on Justin. The plan was scrubbed and they all went back into the living room.

As they played the game once again, Taylor brought them all some wine. Unbeknownst to Selina, he had put some Rohypnol in her wineglass. He hoped she would just go to sleep and not wake up again.

Selina, however, noticed something floating in her wine and commented about it.

Taylor quickly said, "Oh, let me get you a clean glass," and exchanged glasses. Apparently, he didn't put any Rohypnol in the new glass of wine.

A short time later, Taylor talked with Dawn in private. He said that he would lure Selina into his bedroom. Dawn and Justin were to wait for a half hour; then when Selina was asleep, Dawn was to throw a towel over Selina's head, and Justin would hit her in the head with a hammer until she was dead.

Taylor did take Selina into his bedroom and the minutes ticked away, but after a while, he came out of his bedroom and told Dawn and Justin, "She's not falling asleep. I'm going to have her go into the family room and I'll give her a back rub."

As planned, Selina came out of the bedroom and Taylor spread a blanket on the family room's floor. He had Selina lie down on it and face the windows, away from the center of the room. Her head was turned away from Justin, who was standing nearby. She had no idea that Justin had a hammer in his hand.

Justin waited for fifteen minutes as Taylor began to massage Selina's shoulders and back. Then Justin moved forward, hammer in hand. Selina never saw it coming as Justin raised the hammer and slammed it down into her head with all his might. She cried out from the terrific blow. There is some evidence that Selina raised her hand before the second blow from Justin. Later, her body would have a broken finger and severe bruising up one arm. Justin slammed the hammer down into her head, again and again, at least four more times, for a total of six blows.

Dawn, who was nearby, said later, "I watched it all. They picked her up and took her into the kitchen area because she was bleeding a lot, and her blood was saturating the carpet. She didn't move anymore.

"Taylor told me to clean up all of the blood on the carpet. Then he and Justin went to the bathroom to get it ready."

At this moment, something very unexpected happened. Dawn was startled to hear Selina moan. She was still alive, after all. Dawn recalled, "I heard Selina moving around in the kitchen. But I just kept cleaning up the carpet. Taylor came out and saw her, and said, 'I'm sorry, Selina.' Then he hit her with the hammer. He did it at least three times. She stopped moving."

Justin and Taylor put a plastic garbage bag over the upper half of Selina to prevent more blood from getting on the carpet. Then they rolled Selina into a blanket and carried her and the blanket into the bathroom. Dawn kept cleaning the rug until Taylor called her into the bathroom. Dawn walked to the door and Taylor told her, "Spirit says you get to know this is not a dream."

He took out a large knife and slit Selina's throat. From the amount of blood that poured out, it was evident to experts later that Selina was not dead until that point, despite all the hammer blows to her head.

Dawn recalled, "Then I was scared of Taylor!"

Dawn quickly retreated to the family room and heard the reciprocating saw start up in the bathroom. She knew the sound of the saw from when she had used it working on the dog run in the yard. Taylor and Justin apparently moved Selina's body onto some sawhorses they had placed in the bathtub. They had laid plastic sheeting down in the tub. Dawn could hear body parts thump as they fell into the tub.

At one point, Taylor had Dawn come in with some chopsticks to pull body tissue out of the bathtub drain because it had fallen below the plastic. One thing they hadn't counted on was blood seeping up under the handles for the cold and hot water. As much as they tried, they couldn't get rid of all the blood.

In frustration, Taylor sent Dawn to a Yardbirds home improvement store to buy a couple of new handles, faucet and some disinfectant.

When Dawn came back, she replaced the handles and faucet, while Taylor and Justin started burning Selina's clothes in the fireplace. The firewood that Dawn had picked up at Gerry and Carma's house helped fuel the fire.

Taylor wanted to see if the dog, Jake, the Rottweiler, would eat human flesh, so he cut off the area around Selina's tattoo and held a small piece of flesh out on one of his fingers. The dog ate the flesh. Taylor held out a larger piece of flesh with the tattoo on it. Jake ate that as well.

There was a lot of cleaning and burning that night at the residence on Saddlewood Court. Since Selina's car was at Saddlewood, Justin drove it to a shopping center called Park 'n Shop, a few miles down the road.

Dawn and Taylor kept burning evidence in the fireplace. Dawn said, "Selina's blood on the kitchen area wouldn't come up. We put a lot of water on the carpet too. We put the handcuffs and hammer in the dishwasher and cleaned them."

Neighbor Joe Shaman was surprised around 10:00 P.M. when the doorbell rang and Justin was standing at his front door. Justin asked if he could use their hose because the water was shut off in his residence. Joe told him okay.

Joe mentioned this episode to his wife, and she recounted to him that she had seen a girl who was short, with long hair, going up the driveway with Taylor earlier in the evening. The girl had been wearing sunglasses and beach shoes. Taylor had put his arm around her neck and kissed her on the lips. Then they both went into the house. That had been around 8:00 P.M. and she hadn't seen the girl since then.

There had been a lot of racket coming from the strange neighbor's house on Saddlewood Court. There was hammering and sawing going on, and it got so bad at one point that Kaye held the phone up so that her mother on the other end of the line could hear the noise. Kaye even said to her mother, "It sounds like they're breaking bones."

Late that night, all the lights were turned off in the house with only the fire glowing. It was a scene straight out of hell, with shadows flickering on the walls and Selina's blood staining the family room's carpet. Taylor and Dawn talked about any loose ends that needed to be tied up. Taylor became worried about the fact that

Selina's mom, Jenny, had met him unexpectedly one day. This worry was intensified by a lie that Selina had told him. Perhaps because Jordan seemed so mysterious, she had told him that her mother was a private investigator. Nothing could have been further from the truth.

One thing Selina had told him was true, however. She had said that her mom would be house-sitting her apartment while she was away at Yosemite. This seemed like a good opportunity to Taylor to eliminate Jenny. He didn't want any person left around who could tie "Jordan" to him.

To this end, he packed two guns and clothing into a bag and left with Dawn on a mission. Dawn said later, "It didn't seem odd to kill Selina's mom. Taylor was always altering his plans."

Taylor went to Justin's bedroom before leaving, and Justin was lying down on his bed. Dawn heard Taylor give Justin instructions to go to Selina's car and look for an address book. This was in case Jenny Villarin wasn't staying at Selina's place. If that was the case, Justin was to inform him by phone where Jenny lived; then Taylor and Dawn would go there to kill her.

There were a couple of things Taylor didn't know as he and Dawn drove on their deadly mission across the San Rafael Bridge toward Marin County. One was that for once Justin would not obey his orders, and the other was that Jenny Villarin had a guest staying over that night with her at Selina's place. Her guest was Jim Gamble.

Jim wasn't even sure that he would go down to visit Jenny on August 2. He was visiting his mother in Yountville, up in the Napa Valley. She noticed he was vacillating a lot about going to Marin. Finally, around 2:00 P.M., he decided he would go.

As Jim drove into Nicassio in Marin County, Gloria

LaFranchi's daughter just happened to spot him. She told her mother that Jim was in town, and Gloria met Jim at Rancho Nicassio. Gloria said, "We had a couple of drinks and decided to have dinner.

"He talked about a trip that he and Jenny planned for Calistoga on the upcoming weekend. He had never been there and they thought it might be fun to visit the pretty Wine Country town."

Around 6:00 P.M., Jenny called from where she was working at the Paper Mill Creek Saloon. She talked to Gloria on her cell phone for a while and said that she'd like some dinner from the Rancho Market. Since James was already there, he volunteered to deliver the food to Jenny at Paper Mill Creek. He left Rancho Nicassio between 6:30 and 7:00 P.M.

Once James delivered the food to Jenny, he decided to spend some time at Paper Mill Creek and visit with his friends. He had a good time there and, because the hour was getting late and he'd had a few drinks, decided not to drive back to Yountville. Jenny offered him a bed at Selina's place, where she was staying, and James accepted.

Around 2:15 A.M., Leora Soladay heard Jenny and James drive up in separate vehicles and they were talking in the front yard. As they went through the garage, she could hear them speaking and laughing. After a while they quieted down, but soon one of them was snoring, and the noise kept her awake. Unable to sleep, she went to a spare bedroom next to Ty's, and there she drifted off to sleep. It was after three o'clock.

Her husband, Jay, also heard Jim and Jenny come to Selina's place. He said later, "I was in the master bedroom. I went to bed between nine and ten P.M. After a while, Leora left the bedroom."

* * *

Taylor and Dawn drove up on Redwood Drive in Woodacre and Taylor pointed out the Soladay home and Selina's apartment. Taylor backed the car into a little turnaround spot and Dawn scooted over to the driver's seat as Taylor got out of the car. In his hand, he carried the 9mm Beretta semiautomatic that Justin had purchased in Junc. Dawn had cleaned finger-prints off each bullet and reloaded the gun with them on the drive over from Concord. Taylor walked up the hill in darkness. Large trees cast shadows down on the yard. Within the house, all was still.

Dawn waited in the car and seconds seemed like an eternity to her. It was very quiet in this forested neigh-borhood. Suddenly, without warning, six gunshots ripped apart the silence.

Leora Soladay was startled awake by the noise that came from the lower portion of the house. She thought she heard five or six distinctive "bangs." She was shocked into inaction for several seconds, until she heard hurried footsteps in the yard outside. She did not see who was running from the house.

Jay Soladay had heard the gunshots as well. He raced into Leora's room and whispered, "What the hell was that!" Then he yelled downstairs, "*What's going on down there?*"

At first he thought kids had thrown firecrackers against the house. But the more he thought about it, the surer he was that they were gunshots. He said later, "I heard seven or eight of them." He claimed to have actually felt one of the shots reverberate on the floor below his room.

With remarkable nerve, Jay made his way down through the garage area, armed only with a flashlight and cell phone. Incredibly, Mike, a neighbor, phoned him right at that moment and said, "I think I heard gunshots at your home."

Jay was unsure and he said, "I think those were fire-crackers going off."

The neighbor phoned 911 and told the operator, "I'm in Woodacre and I thought I heard six gunshots. It illuminated our window. The shots came from outside of our house up the hill."

Meanwhile, Jay Soladay made his way through the garage area to Selina's door. He said, "What's going on in there?"

For an answer, all he heard was a faint moan. Jay started yelling, but there was no response except for the groans. Jay began to push the door open, but it was blocked by something heavy. He got the door open a crack and saw a man's arm and hand blocking the door. There was something dark on the man's chest. Jay was sure it was blood.

That was enough for him. He hurried back to the main part of the house. He told Leora, "There's two dead bodies down there."

In the next few minutes, a conversation between the Soladays and the 911 operator took place:

Soladay: There's two murders at my house. There are people on a bed with blood. We heard a vehicle drive away a few minutes ago.

Operator: Everyone stay inside the house. I understand you're scared.

Soladay: The person I went down to see. She came home with a guy.

The operator wanted to know if the woman was the Soladays' tenant.

Soladay: No, no. Her mother is house-sitting, and it's an older guy. The daughter is in Yosemite. I don't know the guy her mother brought home. I cannot believe this is happening at my house.

Operator: Was there an argument at your house?

Soladay: No.

Then Leora got on the phone, saying, "Please help us, right now. The people are dead."

The 911 operator contacted the county sheriff's office and Fire and Rescue. She said, "We have a possible shooting in Woodacre. We don't know if the suspects are still there."

A short time later, a sheriff's patrol car parked nearby. One of the officers was Blair Benzler. At around 5:02 A.M., in his patrol car, he got a call that stated, "Shots fired at residence in Woodacre."

Officer Benzler was on a prowler call in Fairfax when he got the call. It was about five miles down St. Francis Drake Boulevard from his position to Woodacre. As he sped toward the scene of the gunshots, he passed a dark-colored sedan going in the opposite direction. Benzler said later, "I noticed in my rearview mirror that the driver activated the brake lights. It looked like a dark-colored vehicle." There's a good chance it was Dawn and Taylor headed back to Contra Costa County. Benzler did not take notice of the license plate number of the car, however. He had more pressing business at the time getting to Redwood Drive in Woodacre.

Officer Benzler reported to the scene of the gunshots on Redwood Drive about ten minutes after the initial call from the dispatcher. He waited a very short time before another patrol car arrived at the scene. Then he and the other officer walked toward a house, where they met a man in the front yard. The man was Jay Soladay.

At first the officers didn't know who this person was, or if he was armed and dangerous. They made sure he didn't have a weapon, and then they questioned him. When it became obvious that he was the owner of the house, the officers began to make their way through the garage area. They both drew their service weapons as they approached a door.

Benzler said later, "The door swung halfway open and stopped. I could see a human hand blocking the door. There was blood on the carpet. There was a male victim, faceup, and a female victim, faceup, on the bed. The depression near her head was filling with blood. When I got in there, I tried to give aid to the victims. I checked their pulses. I heard gurgling sounds from the male victim. I checked, but the sound was blood filling the back of his throat. They were both lifeless."

The apartment did not appear to be ransacked as if a robbery had happened. Officer Blair Benzler began to look for shell casings. He found one on the bed near the female victim and noted it. Then he and his partner froze the crime scene and waited for detectives to arrive.

Meanwhile, Dawn and Taylor made their escape back to Concord, undetected. Taylor didn't talk to Dawn all the way back about what he had done, but she surmised that he had killed someone. Taylor was secretly stewing inside. He had given Justin a direct order, and Justin had disobeyed it. The plan had been for Justin to meet Dawn and him at the Two Bird Café. Justin was supposed to have checked Selina's car to try to find the address for Jennifer Villarin, just in case her mom wasn't at the Woodacre apartment. There was even a possibility that Taylor wanted to find an address of a coworker of Selina's at the Two Bird Café. He would express later that he wanted that person killed as well. But Justin had not shown up at the Two Bird Café or even called Taylor, and he was furious.

When they got back to Saddlewood, Taylor yelled at Justin, "Why didn't you go to the car like I told you!"

Justin answered lamely, "I was asleep."

Later that morning, Taylor called the Two Bird Café in an apparent attempt to create an alibi. Waitress Kabrina Feickert answered the phone. She recalled, "I picked up the phone. It was Selina's boyfriend. He asked for Selina. I said Selina wasn't there. I thought she was on vacation with him. He asked for Karen (another waitress). I said she wasn't there.

"He became very blustering. He started telling me he hadn't seen Selina all week. He was frustrated. He was supposed to meet her, but he hadn't. I thought this was strange, since I was covering her shift so that she could go camping with him.

"He was tripping over his words. He seemed nervous. I told him to calm down. It was very confusing. There was no relationship before between me and him, as to why he should be speaking to me now. He said Selina was playing games with him and he was sick of it.

"When he hung up, I told another waiter and Tony (the owner) about the call."

Even later that day, Taylor phoned a friend of Selina's named David Levi, who lived in Marin County at a place shared with Jordan Miller's boyfriend, Jesse Sullivan. Levi recalled, "Jordan was on the line. It took me a second to figure out who he was. He asked me if I knew where Selina was. Then he said he was worried about her. It wasn't like her to be that late. He said, 'Selina better not be playing games or fool with me, because I'm a lot older to be playing games!'"

Sergeant Don Wick had been with the Marin County Sheriff's Office (MCSO) for sixteen years by the year 2000. He was with the Crime Scene Investigation (CSI) unit when he and Detective Steve Nash went into the house on Redwood Drive. They went on a preliminary walk-through with the deputies and then settled down to business. Wick began processing and collecting evidence and had police barrier tape set up around the residence.

Detective Wick said, "We collected fragile things first—bodily fluids et cetera. Then we searched for shell casings. Some of these were clearly visible. One nine-millimeter shell casing lay on the bed next to Jenny's head, while another was against one of her arms. Another casing lay on the nightstand near the bed."

After collecting shell casings, Wick and Nash began to collect bullets from the crime scene. One bullet had gone through the door frame into a vent. Another bullet was recovered from the mattress next to Jenny's head. Other bullets were obviously lodged within the victims. Detective Wick noted that there were two bullet wounds on the woman's face. One was near the eyebrows, while the other was in the left cheek. The woman was found faceup and probably shot from the left side of the bed, judging from the angle of entry.

The man's wounds were more numerous. There was one through his right calf, one went into the left arm, shattered the bone in his arm, entered through his chest near the armpit, and came out his back. A third wound grazed his right forearm, went through the chest cavity and lodged there. And a fourth bullet struck his neck. Even if he had survived, he would have been a quadriplegic.

Items found in the bedroom included a purse with a wallet in it. The wallet contained $300 in $100 bills. There was also $1,000 worth of cash in a leather satchel under the nightstand. In the man's pants was a wallet that contained $168. It was fairly evident that robbery was not the motive for the murders.

One more interesting item was in the apartment. It was a journal that belonged to Selina Bishop. Detective Wick knew Selina personally, having met her in the past. Inside her journal were her expressions of love for someone named Jordan.

Another detective arrived on the scene a short time later. This was Detective Erin Inskip. She had to drive all the way from her home in Sonoma County to Woodacre and it took a while to get there. By the time she arrived, both Wick and Nash were there, along with Lieutenant Rick Russell and various members of the CSI squad. A question soon came up among them: where was Selina Bishop?

Jay Soladay told Detective Inskip that Selina Bishop worked at the Two Bird Café. Detective Inskip went there and spoke with waitress Kabrina Feickert. Feickert told Inskip about the phone call she had received from Jordan, Selina's boyfriend. Feickert said that Jordan was extremely agitated and angry at Selina. He made several disparaging remarks about her and then hung up the phone.

Feickert recalled, "She (Detective Inskip) and another detective sat down for a meal, and I was her waitress. They were very interested in where Selina was. They didn't know if she was okay. At the end, she (the detective) gave me a card."

Feickert did one more important thing—she informed Detective Inskip that Selina had a pager. Feickert thought that Jordan might have given Selina the pager.

Detective Steve Nash noted that day, "Because detectives of the Marin County Sheriff's Office have not been able to locate Selina Bishop, it is believed that the phone number from which her boyfriend called was the location Selina Bishop was to meet her boyfriend." (Taylor had phoned from a pay phone.)

"At this time, I believe it is important that Selina Bishop be located. She is the daughter of the deceased woman and is one of the persons most likely to have information relating to her mother's activities."

The detectives had another unpleasant task to perform that day. They had to inform the friends and families that Jennifer Villarin and James Gamble had been murdered. One of the first persons they informed was Gloria LaFranchi.

LaFranchi called David Villarin, Jenny's brother, and said, "Your sister is gone."

David was confused and asked, "Did she run away?"

"No," LaFranchi said. "She's gone for good."

David was stunned, speechless. This couldn't be happening.

Almost immediately he was worried about Selina. He knew how much she loved her mom and how this news would affect her.

David was always considered the rock of the family and the burden of telling others in the family about Jenny's death fell on him.

Olga was over at her mother-in-law's home when she got a message to call her brother, David. When David told her the news, Olga said, "I was shaking so badly, I couldn't even drive home. And nobody knew where Selina was."

Robert Asuncion's thoughts were also about Selina when he found out about Jenny. He didn't want Selina to get her first information about her mom's death in the newspapers.

Lydia Young was sitting down to dinner in Lake Tahoe, where she lived, when she got a call from David. He said, "Jenny's been shot."

In stunned disbelief, all Lydia could think to say was "Why?"

David answered, "I don't know."

Lydia was also concerned that Selina would hear about this from strangers.

When niece Jill got the news about her aunt being shot, she asked, "Is she going to be okay?"

David only had a one-word answer: "No."

Niece Jill said later, "I never expected that for someone who had been through so much. My first question was 'Where was Selina?' Nobody knew. I didn't want Selina to be alone and find out about Jenny."

Olga went to Marin County after being given a sedative. All the way there, she thought, *It can't be real. They have to be wrong.*

She recalled, "Lydia came over and we went to Gloria's house. We were all in a haze. For some reason, we went to a Target store to shop. To chill. We were all standing in the middle of Target, crying.

"We all stayed at Gloria's house. We couldn't go anywhere to get away from it. We went through everything to find Selina. I didn't want her to go back to her house, because her mom had been killed in her bed. We knew that Selina would want to curl up in her mommy's bed, but she never came home."

Lucia Villarin helped look for Selina that week. She looked all over Marin County, in places she knew that Selina visited. She looked in the towns, in the forest, everywhere. There was not a trace of Selina to be found.

Jenny Villarin's family wasn't the only one devastated by the news of the double murder. Jim Gamble's mom, Frances, recalled, "About midnight, August fourth, the light went on. I said, 'Jim?'

"It was Larry. He'd driven two hours to tell me. It was a terrible shock. From that point on, I didn't know what happened. I never got to say good-bye to my son."

CHAPTER 8

Murky Waters

Taylor wanted all the teeth removed from the heads of Ivan, Annette and Selina. This would make their remains harder to identify, if ever found. Dawn recalled, "Justin reached into the bag and got the three heads out and put them on a towel. I had to hold the people's heads while he tried to knock the teeth out of the upper and lower jaws with a chisel and hammer. I didn't think about anything while this was going on. It took at least thirty minutes for the whole process to take place."

They put the teeth and jawbones in plastic bags and the battered heads were packaged separately. In fact, Ivan's, Annette's and Selina's remains were intermixed to further confuse identification, or at least that was Taylor's thoughts on the matter.

On Thursday, August 3, the Children of Thunder drove toward the Delta with a personal watercraft in tow and nine duffel bags full of body parts. The bags also contained stepping-stones from the yard at Saddlewood to add weight to the contents. Dawn said they just hauled the duffel bags out of the garage in full daylight and placed them in back of Justin's pickup. To anyone on Saddlewood Court who saw them, it would look as if they were going camping. The craft they were towing added to that illusion.

The three of them rode in Justin's pickup truck, eastward to Highway 4, northeast on 160, and to the approaches of the Antioch Bridge over the wide San Joaquin River. They paid the toll taker $2 and proceeded across the bridge. Far below them the meandering waterways spread out like a three-dimensional map.

They drove up Highway 160 on the levee road paralleling the Sacramento River. Chinese workers had built the levees as far back as the 1870s. Before commercial fishing was outlawed in the 1950s, local residents known as "river rats" could make up to $1,000 a week netting catfish. Now it was the haunt of sports fishermen.

The Helzer brothers and Dawn turned east on Highway 12 and crossed the rich farmland of Andrus Island, to the North Fork of the Mokelumne River. They didn't know it at the time, but they were in the heartland of the great epidemic of the 1830s, where entire villages of Native Americans died. Then it had been a grisly scene of death and decay. It was about to become such a place once again.

The trio turned south on a small levee road that led to the marina of Korth's Pirate's Lair. Korth's Pirate's Lair was an oasis of tall trees and green water in the midst of the rich farmland. The Children of Thunder scouted a section of road nearby on a levee, where it came down to the water's edge. It seemed like a good spot to transfer the body bags to the personal watercraft, so they drove back to launch the rental.

Not many people were there at the boat ramp that time of day. Most had left early to go boating, and wouldn't be back until later. The trio drove the trailer down the ramp into the water, unhooked the watercraft and then drove the trailer back up to dry land. No bags were placed on the rental at this time.

Dawn drove Justin's pickup to the designated spot on the levee road as Justin and Taylor rode there on the watercraft. They pulled the rental up close to the bank and Taylor got off. He transferred two duffel bags with body parts onto it. The bags were placed on either side on the running boards. Then Taylor and Justin took off north, up the Mokelumne River as Dawn waited on the bank with the rest of the body parts.

She didn't see exactly where the Helzer brothers took the duffel bags to be deposited in the water. All she knew was that they were gone for about thirty minutes before they came back for the next load of bags. This routine went on through bag number eight, as Dawn sat in the pickup and read the book *The Four Agreements,* which Taylor had told her to read.

Before each trip, Justin plunged a knife several times into the bags. Dawn had come up with this idea. She said later, "There needed to be holes in the bags because gases would build up inside of them. If they weren't slashed, they might not sink."

It took almost all afternoon out on the Delta to get rid of the bags. While houseboats slowly glided by with vacationers, and water-skiers churned up wakes, Taylor and Justin went about their grisly business. Apparently no one was around when they deposited the bags into the murky waters of the Mokelumne River.

Taylor said he was tired and ordered Dawn to go with Justin to release the ninth bag. Taylor got off the personal watercraft and Dawn climbed on with Justin.

Since Justin was tired from running the craft all afternoon, he let Dawn drive it. As they went up the river, to a secluded spot, Justin dropped the last bag into the water. Dawn noticed that it took about a minute to sink. The water here was fairly opaque and nothing could be seen a few inches below its surface. The current, though not swift, was constantly moving, and undoubtedly moved the bag along as it sank.

After they had deposited all the bags, the Children of Thunder drove the watercraft and the pickup back to Korth's Pirate's Lair, and hooked it up to Justin's pickup. Taylor drove down the road and stopped at a bar because he had to use the rest room. After using the rest room, he and Dawn had a shot of tequila at the bar. They drove down the road a few more miles and stopped at a restaurant, where all three had dinner. Later, they all washed out the bed of the pickup truck.

Clear back in April 2000, Jessyka Chompff had invited Taylor to "Reggae on the River." It was a festival of reggae bands and alternative bands, up in the coastal redwoods along the Eel River. Taylor looked forward to going. He not only liked the music, he planned to sell a lot of ecstasy there. Since the Stinemans' checks had not yet been deposited into Selina Bishop's Cal Fed account, he felt that he could get away for a few days.

In the back of Chompff's mind, she was always worried that Taylor would "flake out." As she said later, "The tickets were pretty expensive and we had four of them—one for me, one for Alex, one for Taylor and one for a guy named Jamie. In late June, Taylor had called me and said he was involved in something that was taking all of his time. He said he saw circumstances that might make him unable to go. Then he said, 'I'm working on something big.'"

As Chompff said later, "I assumed it was something that had to do with drugs."

In late July, her concern that Taylor would just flake out became more prevalent. He was irritable and vacillating in conversations with her on the phone about whether he would make it or not. She knew that even under the best of circumstances Taylor was not someone you could count on. August arrived and Taylor was still telling her he wasn't sure if he could make it to "Reggae on the River." He didn't tell her the reason he wasn't sure that he could make it was because he was involved in murder and financial fraud.

Taylor and Chompff made tentative plans to leave on the morning of Thursday, August 3, but that fell through. The time was pushed ahead to noon on the August 3, but even that was too optimistic. Taylor, Justin and Dawn had barely left Saddlewood Court with the rental watercraft by that hour, heading for the Delta.

Jessyka borrowed a tent from Taylor's parents, because he said he was too busy to pick it up. What was even more frustrating for Chompff was the fact that Taylor said he didn't want her or anyone else to visit him at the Saddlewood residence. She assumed it was because of a big drug deal he was planning, but still it made the coordination for "Reggae on the River" difficult.

Noon of August 3 came and went, and there was still no Taylor. Finally, at one o'clock, he called her on a cell phone and said that he would not meet them until 3:30 P.M. That target time passed and there was no Taylor. Now Chompff was very worried that Taylor would not show up at all.

Late that afternoon, a very frazzled-sounding Taylor

phoned Chompff and said he would be at her house at 7:00 P.M. By now, Chompff was sure that Taylor would flake out. She and her husband had already spent $1,500 for tickets and camping preparations for the event, and she was not happy with Taylor.

More cell phone calls went back and forth between her and Taylor all evening long on August 3. She knew ahead of time if he was calling because she had caller ID on her phone that displayed his cell phone number.

Chompff recalled, "He said he was going to make it. He definitely wanted to go. It was nearly midnight when he finally showed up at our house."

While Alex and Jessyka sat around drinking coffee, Taylor was totally wound up and couldn't sit still or shut up. "He was agitated," she said. "Agitated and extremely tired."

Chompff admitted later that she didn't pay much attention to Taylor when he arrived after midnight. She said, "I was frustrated with him. He was wound up like he'd been to a nightclub. Like he'd been up, all day and night. Flighty and edgy, like he'd been to a rave. He looked hot and tired."

Finally, around 1:00 A.M., Friday, August 4, Taylor crashed and fell asleep in their home. It was about 7:30 A.M. when everyone was finally packed up and ready to go. It was about a two-hundred-mile drive up to "Reggae on the River." Alex and Jessyka drove in their truck, while Taylor and Jamie went in Taylor's Saturn. Even though the Chompffs were supposed to lead the way—because they had been to "Reggae on the River" before, and Taylor hadn't—Taylor would often zoom in front of them to take the lead. It only added to their frustrations.

Their trek took them up through Santa Rosa, Hopland, Ukiah and eventually through the small town of Laytonville. It was indeed ironic that Taylor was traveling through the same town of his victim James Gamble. Highway 101 was not all freeway, and in many places it curved and twisted over the hills and through the forests. Chompff said, "Taylor was driving badly and dangerously. There were lots of logging trucks on the road. At times it looked like he would run off the road. He was supposed to be following us, but he would pull ahead and then fall back. It was disturbing to watch him drive."

When they finally arrived at "Reggae on the River," near Piercy, everyone was frazzled. Since the Chompffs had been there before, Jessyka went with Alex to stake out a campsite. Despite the Chompffs' knowledge of the area, and camping in general, Taylor once again had to be in control. He found one excuse after another why the Chompffs' designated sites were not adequate. He kept wanting to move the tent to another location. To Jessyka's eyes, the areas he was trying to pick were worse. By now, she had had enough of Taylor. She snapped at him and he blew up.

"You're a manipulative bitch!" he yelled back, and continued to berate her in a loud voice.

"Taylor, we're all the same!" she countered.

And Alex said, "Hey, calm down, man."

Jessyka said later, "It was really embarrassing. There were all these other people around and he was making a scene."

Taylor stalked off, but came back later and apologized. For him, this gesture was a big deal. Normally, he thought of himself of incapable of doing wrong. Why apologize when he was already perfect?

Even though he apologized, it soon became apparent that Taylor was not part of the group. He listened to music with Alex and Jamie for only about ten minutes on Friday night, and then in Jessyka's words, he "went to do his own thing." She supposed his "own thing" was selling drugs.

Alex and Jessyka and Jamie saw Taylor in camp for a while on Saturday morning, but he slept all of Saturday afternoon while they hiked around the area. Even on Saturday night, Taylor kept to himself, and Jessyka once again assumed he was selling drugs at the event.

By Sunday morning, August 6, Taylor wanted to leave. Alex and Jessyka were determined to stay until Monday, having already invested so much money and time in preparation for the event. Even Jamie wanted to stay, but somehow Taylor convinced him to leave on Sunday. They packed up their belongings and were gone by 11:00 A.M. on Sunday, August 6.

While Taylor was at "Reggae on the River," Justin and Dawn had been busy in the Concord area. On Thursday, Dawn helped Taylor pack a suitcase with marijuana, ecstasy, meth and mushrooms for his trip to "Reggae on the River." Taylor gave instructions to her and Justin to get rid of all evidence connected to Selina and the Stinemans.

On Taylor's orders, Dawn and Justin were to dump the Stinemans' van in a run-down neighborhood of Oakland. His thoughts were that it would be stolen if they left it there. Dawn drove the van, and as she did, she threw the Stinemans' credit cards out the window, hoping that someone would find them and illegally use them. If this individual was later caught, it was assumed the incident would confuse the police.

The Stinemans' van was driven to Martin Luther King Way in Oakland and parked. To make it even more appetizing, they rolled the windows down, left the radio playing and a key in the ignition. Justin drove Dawn back to Concord in his pickup.

After their foray to Oakland, Dawn picked up Selina's vehicle at Park 'n Shop and drove it to Petaluma. Justin followed her in his pickup. Dawn parked Selina's car in a metered parking lot in that town and left the keys in the vehicle. On Taylor's instructions, she also left Ivan's wedding ring in the car on the front passenger seat. This was supposed to confuse the police into wondering why Ivan's wedding ring was in Selina's car. It was hoped they might even conjecture that he'd run away with Selina.

On the way back from Petaluma, Justin and Dawn dropped by Debra McClanahan's apartment to pick up a steam cleaner. To Debra's eyes, Justin did not look stressed, but she gave him a back rub anyway. Dawn was a little more agitated, and with good reason. She admitted later, "I couldn't get the smell of the Saddlewood house out of my nose. I didn't want to go back there." Even though she didn't say it at the time, the smell she was referring to was the smell of death.

Dawn read some newspapers in front of McClanahan for about a half hour and ate some spaghetti before she and Justin left to go back to Saddlewood Court. This was unusual. Debra had never seen Dawn read a newspaper before.

There was still plenty to take care of at Saddlewood Court. Selina's blood had stained the family room's carpet and kitchen area. The carpet in particular was troublesome. Dawn tried cleaning it with the steam cleaner, but it wasn't doing a very good job. Even though Dawn and Justin used household cleaners on the stains, they still wouldn't come out of the carpet, leaving it with a pink stain. Dawn and Justin finally decided they needed professional carpet cleaners to help.

Rebecca Clark worked for Bay Area Carpet Cleaning, and she received a phone call from someone named Justin in Concord. He said that he'd just moved into a house and had an accident. "I cut myself," he told her, "and got blood on the rug." He wanted to know if they could clean blood out of a carpet. Clark said that they could, but that she couldn't guarantee that it would be as good as new after the cleaning. Justin talked to her for about six minutes and she remembered him being friendly on the phone. He even cracked a joke. Justin made an appointment with her for Tuesday, August 8.

Apparently, later on, Justin became concerned about the length of time until August 8. He phoned Prestige Cleaning, on Sunday, August 6, and said that he needed an emergency carpet cleaning. Ed McCulloch was in church that Sunday morning and received a page about the request. The page indicated that someone needed carpet cleaning immediately because a roommate had a bloody nose and it made a mess on the carpet. Since McCulloch had to teach Sunday school that day, he passed the message on to his son-in-law, Tyler Douglass.

Douglass was also at church, but he contacted Justin and said that an emergency carpet cleaning would be very expensive on a Sunday and that he wasn't certain that he could find a technician to do the job.

Justin answered that the cost was no problem, and that Douglass should try and get a technician. Then Justin added that his roommate had left the carpet a mess.

Douglass couldn't find a tech for Sunday, but scheduled one for Monday afternoon. Justin seemed to be okay with this at first, but then Douglass received a message later that Justin had found someone else to do the job on Sunday, and to cancel the Monday appointment.

In fact, Justin contacted Chem Way Cleaning, of

Alameda, and spoke to Haji Balal. Justin said he wanted
a carpet cleaned on Sunday, and since Balal had a
tech in the area already, this was possible. Balal set it
up with his tech to get two blowers and antimicrobial
solution. The antimicrobial solution was to retard
mildew and make the odor go away.

While Justin was making all the appointments with
carpet cleaners, Dawn had been busy as well. She visited Debra McClanahan again and they went to Ap-
plebee's for lunch. Then on Saturday night, she called
McClanahan and lied, saying that some people had
found out about drugs being at Saddlewood Court. She
wanted to store them at Debra's place.

Concerned about illegal drugs being in her apartment, but still loyal because Taylor was involved, Debra
agreed that Dawn could bring them over for safe-
keeping. When Dawn arrived, she carried in a box
containing water pipes. She also had a suitcase that
rolled on wheels. Dawn didn't show Debra the contents
of the suitcase. Instead, she went into Debra's bedroom and locked the door behind her. From what
Debra recalled, "I heard the safe being moved off the
shelf."

The safe was indeed moved and being stuffed with
illegal items from Saddlewood. In the safe, Dawn had
placed various drugs, drug paraphernalia, victims'
identification, rings from the victims, knives and a
pistol. When she came out of the room, she told Mc-
Clanahan, "Now the safe is full. If the authorities ever
ask you any questions about us, get rid of the safe."

Debra later said, "At that moment, I thought, 'Oh,
shit!'"

Dawn also told Debra she had a wheelchair that
needed to be stored at the apartment. She didn't say
why she had a wheelchair, and McClanahan didn't
ask. They initially placed the wheelchair in the living

room, but then they stored it in Debra's daughter's room.

Dawn did not immediately go back to Saddlewood after the items were at McClanahan's. She said later, "I spent every moment I could away from the house. I just wanted to get away from it because three people had been killed there."

On Sunday, August 6, Dawn picked up a copy of the *Contra Costa Times* newspaper. Debra was with her and curious about this because Dawn had never shown any interest in newspapers, local or otherwise. A short while later, Dawn videotaped a segment of the news on television. The segment was about the murder of Jennifer Villarin and James Gamble. There was also news about the disappearance of Selina Bishop.

After this newscast, Dawn said she prayed. She later recalled, "I prayed to be guided by God. I thought maybe I didn't understand what Taylor was saying. That's why the plan wasn't working out."

On Sunday afternoon, Justin phoned Dawn at Debra's and told her to come home to Saddlewood. He said that the carpets were being cleaned. When Dawn arrived at Saddlewood, Balal and his wife had already spread an agent called Natural 2 on the carpets. The agent's bubbles pushed dirt out of the carpet, and when it dried, all of it could be vacuumed up later. The process went on for a while, and Dawn and Justin ate in the kitchen while the solution worked.

One stain in the hallway was particularly problematic. To Balal's eyes, it looked like a red Kool-Aid stain. "Did you spill Kool-Aid there?" he asked Justin.

"Yeah," Justin replied. "We spilled Kool-Aid."

A short time later, Dawn and Justin went to the movies. When they returned, Justin paid Balal $500 for the cleaning and gave him a $20 tip. Since the carpets were still wet, two industrial blowers were hooked up and kept running to dry out the carpets.

Dawn said later of Justin's demeanor that weekend while Taylor was gone, "Justin changed to be more outgoing. He spent more time with me. He was involved."

In the late afternoon, Taylor returned from "Reggae on the River." All that was needed now was for the two checks totaling $100,000 to clear. Then they could collect the money and make their escape from the area.

Around this time, next-door neighbor Kaye Shaman discovered something very odd in her yard. She was on the side of her house near the garden hose that Justin had used when she saw what looked like a bit of bloody flesh. "It looked like a bloody blob," she said later. She wondered how it had gotten there, but then surmised that a bird of prey may have dropped it. There were a lot of hawks and even eagles in the area.

Ivan and Annette Stineman's daughter Nancy Hall had tried calling her parents on August 1 and 2, to no avail. Normally they would tell her if they were planning to go out of town. Even worse, there was no tape in the answering machine to let her leave a message, and the phone rang continuously.

On August 3, she went to her parents' house on Frayne Lane because she wanted to have lunch with them, but also just to check up to see how they were doing. One of her main thoughts was to get their answering machine working properly again. Nancy arrived at their house at 11:15 A.M. as she went up the walk, she noticed that their Lumina van was gone, but a license plate was lying in the driveway. That seemed odd—so did the fact that there were several newspapers piled up around the front door. Nancy looked at the dates on the *Contra Costa Times* newspapers and they were dated from July 30 to August 3. There was also a Terminix receipt halfway under the doormat and it was dated August 1.

Once Nancy entered the house, she noticed a pan of moldy food on the counter. That was not like her mother at all, who always kept a spotless house. After seeing this, Nancy's thoughts turned to the two cats that her parents owned. Usually they stayed in the garage if her parents were gone for a few days. Food and water was left in there for them. Nancy searched the garage and couldn't find the cats anywhere. She went upstairs, opened the bathroom door and discovered a horrible surprise. One of the cats, Tooey, was frantic. It had no food or water, and had messed all over the bathroom.

"It was so pathetic!" she cried later. "I couldn't even tell it was Tooey at first."

Scared by what she discovered, because she knew her parents would never treat their cats this way, she went out and talked to one of the neighbors about where her parents might have gone. The neighbor had no idea.

This was so unlike her parents. Nancy recalled that "when my parents went on vacation, they would leave me a list of things. Mom would say, 'Now you remember this.'"

Very worried by now, Nancy phoned the Concord Police Department (CPD) and reported her elderly parents as missing.

Patrol Officer Mark Evans responded to a missing persons call on August 3 to Frayne Lane. He spoke with Nancy Hall outside of her parents' home and he also noticed several newspapers stacked at the front door and a license plate in the driveway.

As he went into the kitchen, she showed him the pan of moldy food and said her mother wouldn't allow something like that in the kitchen. As he and Nancy walked through the living room, she found a broken watchband in between the cushions of the recliner that her father often used. Nancy knew that the watchband belonged to her father. He always wore that watch.

Looking elsewhere, Patrol Officer Evans discounted robbery, since several expensive items in plain sight had not been disturbed. Evans went down the street a ways and talked with neighbor Clint Carter.

Nancy called her sister, Judy, in southern California and said, "I think we have missing parents." Then she spoke about the cats, the moldy food in the pan and a book with the quilted covers. The book with quilted covers was always taken along by her parents when they went on trips.

Judy recalled, "I tried to come up with answers. I couldn't think of any. I must have called my parents' house a hundred times that week. There was no answering machine. The phone just rang and rang."

Not far away on Saddlewood Court, a resident on the court named Steven Swantkoski had noticed something odd back on August 4. He had been awakened very early by his daughter who lived in Antioch. Her apartment complex had caught fire and she wanted him to come over there. He threw on his clothes, and as he pulled out into the roadway, he was surprised to see a man and woman in a white pickup truck talking. He looked at his watch and it was four-twenty in the morning. The people were most likely Justin and Dawn.

Swantkoski spent nearly two hours in Antioch before returning to Concord with his daughter and some of her belongings. He and his daughter arrived back at Saddlewood Court a little after 8:00 A.M. He didn't pay any more attention to the pickup truck, but his daughter spotted it. She noticed that on the back of it was a trailer that held a personal watercraft. The craft had bright colors and the words "Rent me" on the side.

Later that day, Detective Inskip interviewed Julia Bernbaum about Selina Bishop. Bernbaum told Inskip that Selina's boyfriend, Jordan, was from Concord. She also told Inskip that Selina had provided Jordan with a key to her apartment. Bernbaum said that Jordan was "secretive."

The lead investigator in the Marin County case was Detective Steve Nash. He had been with the Marin County Sheriff's Office since 1979 and investigated over two thousand violent crimes. He'd taken a post-identification technician course, blood spatter course and attended FBI-conducted fingerprint courses. He also received training from the Los Angeles Police Department Threat/Stalking Unit and was an instructor for the Marin County Sheriff's Office.

Detective Nash was trying to piece together not only clues from Selina's apartment, but information that other detectives were giving him as well. He learned from employees at the Two Bird Café that Selina's boyfriend was "concerned about revealing his true identity." Even they knew that Jordan was not his real name. One of them said that recently Selina had tried to take his photograph, and he had destroyed the film.

Detective Inskip told Nash that a pager was located at the Two Bird Café and reputedly it had been given to her by Jordan. When Detective Nash obtained the pager, he noted the area code was 925 (Contra Costa County) and the prefix was 597 (Concord). Jordan was supposed to live somewhere in Concord.

Nash had a theory at this point. He said later, "I personally viewed the photographs of Jennifer Villarin and

Selina Bishop. I also personally viewed the body of Jennifer Villarin. I believe that there is a very strong resemblance between Jennifer Villarin and Selina Bishop. I believe this would be especially true during the time of darkness when the murders occurred."

An all points bulletin (APB) was spread nationwide for Selina Bishop as a missing person. Detective Nash obtained Selina's journal and noted numerous references to Jordan and his drug dealing, his use of meth and his use of an alias.

On August 5, Detective Nash was able to obtain from Verizon Wireless information concerning a cell phone with a 925 area code that supposedly belonged to a Denise Anderson on Mayfair Avenue in Concord. The account had been activated in June 2000.

Detective Nash sent Detective Sergeant Barry Heying to Denise Anderson's address. He discovered that Denise Anderson had a different cell phone and knew nothing about Selina Bishop, Jordan or anything else concerning the case. One name was of particular interest, though. A name "Sky Anderson" was somehow linked to the cell phone. People in Marin County had heard that Jordan had a female roommate named Star. It was not too far a leap from "Star" to "Sky."

On August 6, Nash received an approved search warrant to obtain telephone records for a particular number. Nash compiled a list of numbers that were connected to that cell phone number. He noted that the same last name of Helzer popped up twice. It was Helzer who had a 925 area code. Further search showed that the Helzer in question was one Justin Helzer of Saddlewood Court, Concord. There was no direct link to Selina Bishop or Jennifer Villarin, but this was interesting.

Detective Nash requested a driver's license record from the DMV on Justin Helzer. He learned that Justin

Helzer owned a 1995 white Nissan pickup. The Soladays said that a white Nissan pickup had been used to help Selina Bishop move into her apartment.

An automated firearms system check showed that Justin Helzer had purchased a 9mm Beretta semiautomatic pistol in May 2000. This was a real eye-opener. Detective Nash knew that both Jennifer Villarin and James Gamble had been killed by 9mm bullets that probably came from a Beretta pistol or one of its knockoffs.

Detective Nash had Detective Lisa Lellis, of the Marin County Sheriff's Office, contact Lieutenant Norvell, of the CPD, to see what information could be found on Justin Helzer. What turned up, instead, was some data on a Glenn Taylor Helzer—a man who owned a 1998 Saturn sedan.

Odd bits and pieces of things kept surfacing now. Nothing to make a puzzle complete, but always intriguing. One of these incidents concerned Rodney Todd, who ran a computer business in Oakland, on Martin Luther King Way. He became aware of a Chevy Lumina van parked near his business on Friday, August 4. The windows of the van were down and the radio was playing. He said later, "It struck me as awkward. This was not a safe neighborhood to do something like that." Todd didn't phone it into the police, but he noted how long the van had been there.

It wasn't until a couple of days later that Officer Tim Shaffer, of the Oakland Police Department (OPD), noticed the same van on the 400 block of Martin Luther King Way at around 8:49 A.M. on August 6. There was just something about the van that looked wrong to him. It was nosed out from the curb a little too far and at an odd angle. He decided to investigate.

Once he approached the vehicle, he noticed a seat belt dangling out one of the doors. The windows were rolled down as well. The strangest facts of all were that there was a key in the ignition turned to ACC, the radio was playing and there was another set of keys lying on the dashboard in plain sight.

With all of these strange occurrences, Shaffer thought, *This is a stolen vehicle.*

He ran the plates and a missing persons report came up. The report concerned an elderly couple from Concord named the Stinemans. Officer Shaffer notified the CPD about what he had just discovered.

When the van was found in Oakland, Nancy Hall recalled, "I felt like the walls were coming down on me. My world was collapsing. It got worse each day. You didn't think it could get worse. But it did get worse."

That same day, Officer Nancy Vedder, of the Concord Police Department, went to the Stinemans' residence and found a notepad that mentioned the name Taylor Helzer on it. It also mentioned that Taylor had worked for Dean Witter. She found this on top of a desk in the master bedroom in plain sight. Written on the paper was "Check with Taylor." (Some have speculated that when Taylor and Justin invaded the Stinemans' home on July 30, Ivan was able to leave this one small note as a clue as to their whereabouts. Whether the note was meant to be discovered by the police or Nancy Hall is not known.)

This bit of information possibly connecting the missing Stinemans and the Marin County murders was enticing. Detective Nash had Detectives Inskip and Heying drive by Saddlewood Court in Concord on a surveillance run. They noticed a dark Saturn and a white Nissan pickup in the driveway. Nash then had Detective Fred Marziano get photographs from the DMV of Glenn Taylor Helzer and Justin Alan Helzer. Taylor's photograph was shown to Selina's friend and coworker at the Two Bird Café, Karen. Karen said that she was

75 percent sure the man in the photo was Jordan. She had a hard time telling, because Taylor (aka Jordan) had stuck out his tongue when the photo was taken.

Sergeant Birch, of the MCSO, contacted Rico LaFranchi and showed him a photograph. Rico positively identified the man in the photo as Selina's boyfriend, Jordan.

Detectives Nash and Lellis contacted Mike Small, of Red Hills Towing in San Rafael, about something that had occurred three weeks before. Selina had locked the keys inside her car at the Two Bird Café. When Mike Small showed up to help her, she was sitting in a dark-colored Saturn.

The surveillance team that kept passing Saddlewood Court noticed a young man get into a white Nissan pickup and drive away on the night of August 6. He returned after fifteen minutes.

Even later that night, the same man came out again and was gone for thirty minutes before returning. He must have been very distracted, however. He apparently did not put the pickup in park or set the parking brake. After he had gone back into the residence, the pickup rolled down the driveway and into the street.

In the early-morning hours of August 7, 2000, Detective Nash requested a search warrant for the Helzer residence on Saddlewood Court in Concord. Nash wrote that it was approximately 1:00 A.M. on August 7, 2000, and that Selina Bishop was still a missing person. She had failed to report to work at the Two Bird Café on August 4, and no one had seen her since August 2. On that date, a person who knew her had seen Selina at the Red Hill Shopping Center in San Anselmo.

Selina has been wearing a light-colored blouse and dark-colored pants.

Detective Nash went on to write that he believed Jennifer Villarin and James Gamble had been killed by a gun firing 9 mm copper-jacketed ammunition. Nash believed that Justin Helzer owned a 9 mm Beretta that was capable of firing 9 mm copper-jacketed bullets.

Nash noted that in Selina Bishop's journal, she had written of having difficulties with her boyfriend Jordan who happened to live in Concord. At 10:00 A.M. on August 3, Selina's fellow-employee at the Two Bird Café, Kabrina Feickert, had received a phone call from Jordan. He was extremely upset and agitated about Selina. Detective Nash wrote on the document that he believed Jordan was in fact Glenn Taylor Helzer. He also believed that Taylor Helzer would have access to his brother's 9 mm Beretta semi-automatic.

Nash drew out a request for the search and seizure of any clothing that might belong to Selina Bishop, any items that would account for her whereabouts, and the 9 mm Beretta and ammunition. His request stated that the search warrant was to help in finding the location and safety of Selina Bishop.

CHAPTER 9

Raid on Saddlewood

At 11:30 P.M., August 6, 2000, Detectives Inskip, Baker, Hart and Heying drove around the Saddlewood area, particularly keeping an eye on the home rented by the Helzer brothers. They kept their observations secret enough so as not to draw attention.

On August 7, at 3:30 A.M., Hynes attended a SWAT briefing at the Concord Police Department for an early-morning raid on the Saddlewood home. By 5:55 A.M., the SWAT team all got into position as the seconds ticked down toward zero hour.

Zero hour came at 6:00 A.M. as Detective Inskip knocked on the Helzers' door and announced the presence of the police. Sergeant Hynes and the others beat in the door of the Helzer home. Inskip said later, "After a knock and notice, I went to the back of the SWAT team and they used a battering ram and force. They eventually got in the door after a few hits with the ram."

As the SWAT team went in, Detective Erin Inskip

covered the front yard. Two people were detained inside the house. They turned out to be Justin Helzer and Dawn Godman. Taylor Helzer, however, was not so cooperative, and he made a dash for freedom. Taylor jumped out his bedroom window, leaped a fence and took off across a field toward Kirker Pass Road.

Detective Steve Nash saw Taylor take off running across the field and instructed other officers to track him down. Canine units were used in the chase. This was accomplished fairly rapidly, and Taylor was brought back to Saddlewood, wearing only a black T-shirt and nylon underwear.

Detective Lisa Lellis was there too, and detained Dawn Godman. Soon Taylor was brought back, handcuffed, up the driveway. One thing Lellis noticed almost immediately was a newspaper account of the disappearance of Selina Bishop. That section was folded and placed faceup on a counter.

While Lellis was dealing with Godman, Detective Inskip wanted to talk with Taylor Helzer and he agreed. At this point, Justin Helzer was the main suspect because it seemed that his gun might have been used in the murders of Jenny Villarin and James Gamble. So many officers were now in the Saddlewood home and in the yard that Inskip placed Taylor in her squad car. She wanted to talk with him, face-to-face, so she placed him in the front passenger seat of the vehicle. She decided to move the squad car a short distance from the house onto Saddlewood Drive because so much activity was taking place, and neighbors were starting to come into their yards to see what all the fuss was about.

Detective Inskip moved her vehicle a short distance down the block and parked. She and Taylor talked for a considerable length of time and he seemed to be cooperative. (One source would state later that Inskip and

Taylor talked for nearly forty-five minutes out in the patrol car.) The windows were initially all the way up on the vehicle, but Inskip pushed a button so the windows went down about eight inches to give them some air. Right after this occurred, Inskip received a call on her cell phone. It was a sergeant requesting more evidence bags from the trunk of Inskip's vehicle.

At this very moment, Taylor somersaulted through the window and took off running. Within moments, he was out of Detective Inskip's view. Inskip put out a call immediately to all the officers in the area that the person she was detaining had escaped.

Out of view of the officers, Taylor ran down Saddlewood Street. His main concern now was to get a vehicle and escape out of the area. Not far away, a middle-aged man named William Sharp lived alone with a Border collie, a malamute and a cockatoo. His morning that day began routinely with "bathroom, kitchen and coffee," as he stated later. He was just sitting down in his favorite recliner with a cup of coffee when a young man, clad only in a T-shirt and boxer shorts, literally ran into his house through the screen door.

As Sharp recalled, "He was a tall young fellow. He proceeded to scuttle from one sliding door to another. I thought, 'This guy's screwy.'

"He pointed his finger, as if he were pointing a gun at me, and said, 'I'll kill you if you don't give me your car keys.'"

Sharp could plainly see that the young man did not have a weapon on him. The whole scenario was somewhat ridiculous to Sharp.

"You can have all of the keys you want, but the cars don't work," he said.

"Just then the dogs started coming around the house

and [Taylor] saw them. So he ran out the back and jumped right over the back fence."

Taylor ran on down Laurel Drive and turned onto Helena Drive. At a house near the end of the block, Mary Mozzochi was calling Enterprise Rental Car because her husband had taken her car to work and the other vehicle was in the shop.

She recalled, "I was walking around the kitchen. My son was in the house sleeping because he stayed over the night. I started to go out the back door and spied my watch outside. There was a person there at the sliding door. He was wearing a black T-shirt and plaid shorts. I was surprised and asked, 'Who are you?'

"He grabbed me by the arm and came inside the house. He grabbed a knife off the countertop and he had a choke hold on me. 'I need to change my appearance, and get away,' he said. 'Don't call the police or I'll kill you!'

"He held the knife to about ten inches from my face. He asked for my car keys. He said a lot of profanity. He said, 'Give me the fucking car keys!'

"I said, 'See the phone book opened to Enterprise? My car doesn't work. I was about to call them.'

"He saw some replica Civil War rifles and a pistol my husband owned. 'Give me the handgun!' he said.

"'It's not a real gun,' I replied. 'It's a replica.'

"'I need clothes to get away,' he said. 'Gimme the fucking pants.'

"The pants were too big, but he took off his boxer shorts and put on the pants. Then he wanted a shirt. I didn't want to give him my husband's good golf shirts. So I gave him an old orange golf shirt.

"'Go sit in the corner!' he said. The pants wouldn't stay up, so he asked me for a belt.

"'Gimme something for my hair,' he said. 'Gimme scissors!'

"He grabbed his hair and cut off a large piece of hair, straight across. He asked who was home with me. 'Is there anybody else in the house?'

"I said, 'Yes, my son and his friend. But both of them were asleep.' I was glad my boy didn't appear.

"He said, 'Be quiet. You don't want any drama here. So you do what I say, or I'll kill you.'

"I answered, 'Look, I'm a nurse. I don't hurt people, I help them. So I'm not going to hurt you.'

"He wanted to make a call, but the cell phone had a dead battery.

"I asked him, 'Have you killed anybody?'

"He answered, 'Not yet.'

"I said, 'Okay, you have everything you need. So you leave!'

"'You come with me,' he said. He'd walked outside when he said it.

"'No!' I answered, and slammed the door shut and locked it. He took off running.

"Right then, I saw my son standing with a cell phone in the hall. He said, 'Mom, I've been on the phone the whole time, with nine-one-one.'

"They stayed on the line and guided him through it. An officer came soon."

In fact, there were several officers who saw Taylor Helzer trying to run away and detained him. Soon they had him back at Saddlewood Court, wearing baggy pants, an orange golf shirt and no shoes.

Mary Mozzochi was driven by an officer to Saddlewood Court. Standing outside the residence in handcuffs and wearing his bizarre attire was Taylor. Mozzochi looked out the squad car window and identified him as the intruder who had been in her house. Later, crime scene analysts and police dogs that could sniff out items spent the rest of the day at her house. Investigators found a large swatch of Taylor Helzer's hair right on top of the phone book.

After all the excitement of Taylor's escape, it was down to business for the officers on Saddlewood Court. Steve Nash soon realized that they were going to need a second search warrant with broader scope for all the items in the Saddlewood residence. The initial search warrant only allowed searches for clothing, weapons, shell casings and documents about the weapons. Initially their focus had been on the murders of Jenny Villarin, James Gamble and the clothing of a missing Selina Bishop. It was apparent now, however, that the people on Saddlewood were mixed up in a lot more than just those two murders. For one thing, there was an apparent bloody outline of a person on the family room's carpet, as if someone had bled there. And there were two professional carpet blowers running.

Once the officers obtained a second broader search warrant, the residence on Saddlewood Court became a beehive of police activity. Detective Nash noted and collected handcuffs and duct tape in the master bedroom. Items were collected all day long. The first day's search ran from just after 6:00 A.M. until 6:00 P.M., when the house was secured overnight. The next day, the searches began at 8:15 A.M.

Over the next few days, every officer and detective in the residence had specific tasks as far as evidence collection went. Detective Judy Elo, of CPD, collected a box of items that contained In To Me See business cards. She also collected various notebooks and papers with writing on them. One paper stated, "I choose the straight and narrow." On another was written, "There is no such thing as imagination. If I think it . . . it is."

There was a card in a Rolodex that contained

information on Dean Witter accounts. This was in Taylor's bedroom on a dressing table. Missing from the Rolodex were two items under the letter S. These two items were cards bearing the names Ivan and Annette Stineman. The cards were later found in an attaché case.

Detective Judy Elo also came across something called the Twelve Principles of Magic. Also found was a yellow legal pad with various questions. Some of the questions were numbered.

1. What are your top vacation spots?
2. Spell your daughters' names.
3. Ask about cell phone.
4. If going on vacation, would you call one, or both of your daughters?
5. Who would you call to let know other than your daughters?

These were topics that Taylor and Dawn questioned the Stinemans about on July 30.

Among other items was a script for Cal Fed for when someone was supposed to talk to them on the phone. In part, it read, "Okay, hon. I'll do it later. I'll be right there."

There was also a letter from Jordan to Sky. This was found on the floor of Taylor's room. Jotted notes stated that Dawn was going to Livermore. It also mentioned that she was having a hard time renting a personal watercraft, and noted that if he had to, he could rent one at Lake Berryessa.

Detective Elo also discovered that Taylor was in trouble with his credit rating. On an MBNA credit card, he was over the limit, and on a People's Bank card, he owed $2,640.

A receipt also stated that Taylor bought forty ounces

of red phosphorous. Elo knew that red phosphorous was used in the manufacturing of methamphetamine.

In a garbage can, she found a note that stated, "Escape plan." It told of creating resistance. In another part, it stated, "I'm not going to jail. I'm going to put a gun to my head. Justin is, too."

Things obviously hadn't turned out that way for Taylor or Justin Helzer.

Receipts for handcuffs were found from Not Too Naughty. There was also a Pacific Gas and Electric bill discovered for the Saddlewood residence, but the bill was in the names of Shirley and Emil Robinson. [Emil and Shirley Robinson were fictitious names used by Justin and Dawn for the purpose of obtaining water and electricity for the house on Saddlewood Court.]

Among the piles of papers was one written by Justin in Taylor's room. It described his life purpose and listed what he wanted for his future. Another document concerned something about a sex tour and prices for items that could be purchased for the tour. There was one catalog showing a bare-chested woman with a whip.

In Justin's room, Elo found an ad about better orgasms. Not far away was a nineteenth-century discourse about the LDS Church and their views on African Americans. In fact, Mormon documents were indiscriminately piled with sex articles and catalogs all over Taylor's room. One ad promised a bigger and better penis. There was also a 900 number to call, entitled 1-900-Cum-All.

Taylor had drawn up all sorts of schematics concerning women, sex and money. One described something with a woman with ten men for 50 percent. Another described five women with ten men for a total of $15,000. It was not clear what he meant, other than the possibility of sex for money.

There was an attached note to one document. On the note was written: "Afterwards, party-goers can meet girls one on one for prices significantly higher."

Even a quote from his mother, Carma, who was calling herself Teonae at the time, was mixed in with the other documents. She wrote, "There is one temple in the universe and that is the human body."

One of the most interesting folders that Detective Elo discovered went into detail about In To Me See. In it, Taylor spoke of dressing his girls nicely and training them how to take care of men, both sexually and otherwise. Then it went on to discuss 401K plans for the girls. The 401K plans would be set up by Taylor.

There appeared to be four levels in this particular program, even though there never seemed to be a consistent formula. In one document, Taylor mentioned things along these lines:

1st year—$388,000
2nd year—$649,000
3rd year—$987,000
4th year—$1,029,000

The amounts appeared to be what he hoped to make from the operation.

In another scheme he wrote: "$116,000 for the woman, $117,000 for me." Just what he based these numbers on was not clear.

In still another scheme he claimed that ecstasy = money. "What I need is the ability to manufacture. What I have is the process. What I need is someone who has the know-how and ability to buy."

Detective Elo also found papers referring to Taylor's stint in the National Guard, including the fact that he'd earned a sharpshooter status with an M16 rifle. Everything in his bedroom seemed to be a mixture of the worldly and the ethereal. There was a quote from Taylor that said, "Joyful relationships are created by only those who can see the truth." It was next to porno catalogs.

One schematic promised that for $800 to $1,000 per man, a male client could play strip poker with a beautiful woman, or dance with her, or play pool with her. Then they could have sex with the woman for a price she chose. All of this would take place in the Feline Club. The woman had to be free of drugs and alcohol. He promised to teach men how to take two women at the same time and "make them scream for you."

There were to be tutorials in the Feline Club about how to give and receive oral sex and how to stimulate a woman's clitoris so that she had a profound orgasm. A man could purchase a half-hour practice session with a live model for x amount of dollars.

Then there was something called "points." Points were to be given to the girls who worked in the Feline Club. A woman with the most points would get the first choice of clientele. A woman working for the club would get points by performing various sexual favors for the men.

Among the tracts on sex and religion, there were also documents pertaining to the mundane. Detective Elo learned that Taylor owed Carma $16,000 and he owed a Chase account $8,441. Chase was threatening him with a collection agency. Taylor owed MCI $1,230 and First Select $9,900.

Detective Elo discovered a Gothic-looking poster in Dawn's room. It depicted a misty landscape with demons and dragons. In Taylor's room, there was a demon ring and dagger. Nearby was a note about fear and love.

Another note nearby referred to magical stones. Each colored stone was reputed to have certain magical powers. He even claimed in the note to have a seer stone. In Mormon tradition, in 1827, Joseph Smith had obtained a seer stone that allowed him to read the golden tablets left on a hill in New York State. By this means, he was able to translate the wording into English. This version in time became the Book of Mormon.

Detective Lellis found a day planner while searching through the house on Saddlewood. It was in the kitchen, lying on a countertop in plain sight. There were also work order receipts and a receipt for leg irons.

Detective Lellis discovered three ski masks that skiers might use during chilly conditions, or could be used to cover up identities. There was also a receipt from the Home Depot for two spade bits, duct tape, a staple gun, a polyurethane sheet and a bottle of hair dye.

Sergeant Mike Crain of the Marin County Sheriff's Office was looking in the garage and found a business card from the Concord Cab Company. A scribbled note nearby read: "Alibi—Bob pulled a knife. He grabbed gun from me and shoot. Panic."

Then there was a flowchart on another piece of paper.

The chart read in part: with no mask/with mask; leaving; denial; use alibi; no shots fired; shots fired.

On another was: "Hair, shop, cut, clips for hair."

On a brown desk in the garage, Sergeant Crain found an owner's manual for a Craftsman variable-speed electric reciprocating saw.

He also found a tall wooden staff with a carved wooden skull on its top. Another staff contained a wooden eagle's claws grasping a large crystal.

Detective Nash was one of the leaders on the task force that was implementing the search at Saddlewood Court. While he was there, he found a briefcase

near the front door. Inside the briefcase were nar-
cotics, pills and mushrooms.

In Dawn's bedroom, Nash discovered a taser; in
Taylor's room, he found a wallet that contained money
and an ID card of Glenn Taylor Helzer. He also found
a note that referred to a PO box number.

Near the closet was an XL Hydrogen water-skier's
glove. A business card for In To Me See had the
name Jordan Andrew Taylor on it, along with an 800
number. There was also a cell phone on the floor
near the closet. On a dresser, Detective Nash found
a stack of yellow twist ties for garbage bags.

Moving to the family room, he discovered a pager.
Nearby was another pager and an answering machine,
along with two tapes that fit the answering machine.

Detective Nash made recordings of the answering
machine's tapes. One of the tapes stated, "Friday. Hi,
Dawn. This is (inaudible). Friday nine fifty-nine P.M."

Later on the tape: "Hello, this is Sophie. I've moved
back to Walnut Creek. Love to hear from you."

"Monday—three thirty-five. Hey, Justin. This is Mike
(probably Mike Henderson). Dude, call me
back."
"Eight-forty P.M. Hey, Justin. This is Mike. Give me a
buzz. Reporters are looking for you. It's about
that Bishop thing."
"Ten-ten P.M. Mike again."
Tuesday, 5:02 A.M. No message.
Tuesday, 9:07 A.M. "We have your dog." (This was
from the Animal Control Services.)
Tuesday, 10:03 A.M. "Carpet cleaning." (Requesting
to pick up dryers.)
Tuesday, 10:06 A.M. "Mike again. Call my cell phone
or the house."
Tuesday, 2:57 P.M. "Mike again. Some reporters are

looking for you." (These last three calls were probably placed on August 8.)

There were also phone numbers programmed into the phone for Sky and Selina.

Two handcuffs and keys were found in the Saturn's passenger side, and a button found in the fireplace, along with a lot of ashes. A bank statement for Cal Fed from May 3, 2000, to June 2, 2000, and a deposit from MBNA of $10,000 into a Cal Fed account was discovered as well.

Nash also saw that Justin Helzer owed people a lot of money. He discovered that Justin owed $6,409 to Household Finance, and a list of other debts totaled nearly $30,000.

Searching further, he found an owner's manual for a 9mm Beretta—the same type of pistol that might have been used to kill Jenny Villarin and James Gamble.

Even more intriguing was a note that simply said: "Two Bird Café."

On another note was "Ivan's check. Get him to fix it."

Items found in the bathroom of Saddlewood were a box of tools, screwdriver, valve from a sink, metric wrench, needle-nose pliers and a hammer.

Other rooms contained a military-style knife with serrated edges and a black knife with a seven-inch blade. There were more daggers, knives and even a sword in the garage.

Other things were more obscure as to their significance. There was a note about someone named Keri. It had a date of April 10, 2000, on it and the amount of $1,078.

Detective Nash also found a letter from Selina Bishop to Jordan. It read in part, "What's up buttercup." It was mostly a love letter. At the end, she signed it, "I miss you so much. Selina."

There were papers about addresses in Marin County, Vallejo, Richmond, Piedmont Avenue in Oakland, and Novato. When these were checked later, they all corresponded to Washington Mutual Savings branches. There was also a list of items to be performed:

Call Vicki
Mexico and taxi
Wake up at 5:30 A.M.
Date rape drug

And there was a last chilling item—"Head and teeth—two hours."

There seemed to be notes on an amazing array of things: plans to go to Mexico, guns and even crossbows. There was also a note stating wash cord, ashes, vacuum, toothbrush bathroom, wipe Taylor's stand and chair.

Detective Nash noted that an electrical cord was found in the bathtub and two ends of it tested presumptively positive for blood. There were also two vacuum cleaners in the house. Physical evidence specialists couldn't find anything of value in the fireplace, but on the kitchen counter, Detective Nash found a receipt from Not Too Naughty that concerned leg irons.

There were notes about computers, travel agents, cars and a safe—but a safe was not found at the Saddlewood residence. Detective Nash, just like Detective Elo, found a note about girls and points. But this one was different. It stated: $1 = 1 point. At 500 points, a girl could get full benefits. At 7,500 points, she could get a breast augmentation. And at 10,000 points, she would receive a vacation to the Bahamas.

Along with these notes on points were receipts that

added up to $60.98 from Yardbirds, dated August 5, for plumbing supplies. The supplies were paid for in cash. There were also receipts from Home Depot for sawhorses and concrete.

Receipts for supplies abounded at the Saddlewood residence. On July 12, 2000, the occupants had bought fence boards, window locks and reciprocating saw blades. The amount had come to $411.12. There were also receipts for duffel bags and attaché cases from Kmart.

Some receipts were dated July 30, 2000, and included such diverse items as hair coloring, Lysol, lighter fluid and acetone. There was also a receipt for barbell weights from Copeland's Sports.

Taylor, Justin and Dawn had left an incredible paper trail all over their Saddlewood home. In the mass of items were receipts for wine and cigars at the Cork and Bottle—July 30, 2000—to a receipt at Monument Car Parts. Every receipt led to some cashier with whom the detectives wanted to talk.

There were directions to Selina's house in Marin County and a phone number for Keri Furman down in southern California.

Detective Lellis found eleven Baggies of pills that contained cocaine or ecstasy. There were also Baggies of mushrooms and a bong.

Detective Barry Heying looked at videos on a VCR. All of them contained newscasts about either the murders of Jenny Villarin and James Gamble, or the fact that Ivan Stineman, Annette Stineman and Selina Bishop were missing.

Some of the more interesting bits of evidence were things that weren't there. These included several stepping-stones from the backyard that appeared to have been pulled up from the ground. They were not in the house or other parts of the yard.

Detective Ron Mingas videotaped the entire house and yard just as it was found. He also videotaped the apparent bloodstains in the family room.

Detective Nash noted that eleven swabs were collected in the family room in the supposedly blood-stained area. He also noted that the exterior of the entry door to the bathroom was swabbed and the side door to room number three. There were apparent blood-transfer stains in the bathroom as if someone's body had been dragged from there.

Around the fireplace, they found blood on the hearth and, of course, the apparent bloody outline of a body on the family room's rug.

Most intriguing of all the piles of documents and notes at Saddlewood were some that pointed toward the Delta. There was a receipt dated August 1, 2000, for a down payment on a personal watercraft that Dawn rented. Another receipt was of the actual rental. These receipts were from Cool Rides in Livermore, and signed by both Justin Helzer and Dawn Godman. According to the receipts, the watercraft was only to be used in the Delta and not taken out of the area. On a nearby scratch pad were handwritten directions to Cool Rides. The directions stated: "680 south to 5. 5 toward Stockton. Drive two miles to Enterprise car rental. Next door is Cool Rides."

Detective Mike Warnock went to Cool Rides and found that it was already closed, but he looked in the garbage cans, since garbage in the open doesn't need a search warrant to be searched or seized. Warnock found a torn-up rental agreement in the middle part of the trash. On the receipt were the names Justin Helzer and Dawn Godman.

On a later date, he got more details about the account from Robin Miller. She picked Justin out of a photo lineup. Detective Warnock also spoke to the manager at Pep Boys. The manager said that Justin Helzer had a hitch attached to his pickup truck. Justin had even told him, "I'm going out to a lake or the Delta."

The detectives also began to speak with people who were either mentioned in notes at the Saddlewood residence, or lived close to the Stinemans' residence. A detective talked to Rise Bradfield-Minder. She said she had known the Stineman since she was eighteen years old and knew of their habits. Shown a photo lineup of six men, she picked Taylor Helzer out of the group of six as the man she had seen walking up to the door of the Stinemans' residence on Sunday, July 30. She also picked out a photo of Dawn Godman from a six-photo lineup.

Minder and the detective reenacted the scene she had witnessed on the evening of July 30. She recalled very well seeing Dawn on the corner, sitting in a white pickup truck. She also was aware at the time that the van was driven by a man and there were no noises coming from the back of the van. In retrospect, however, she seemed to sense at the time that there were individuals in the back of the van.

Alexandra Price read some of the first news about the missing Stinemans, and had said to a friend, "I think I just saw a couple of hit men walking down the street."

She was watching television when she saw an arrest of the Helzer brothers and their photos. She thought, *Those look like the two guys I saw.*

In response, Price called the Concord Police Department and was asked to come in and look at a photo lineup. She picked Taylor Helzer out of a group of six mug shots.

With all of this going on, and her parents still missing, Judy Nemec and her husband flew up to the Bay

Area from southern California. They met Lieutenant Paul Crain, of the Support Services of the CPD. He was a liaison to the media, which was very interested in the case by now. It was still only understood dimly by the police on how the deaths of Jennifer Villarin, James Gamble and the disappearance of Selina Bishop and the Stinemans were interconnected.

Crain told reporters, "There's a connection based on what we found inside the [Saddlewood] house. We don't know if the Stinemans are still alive. The investigation is still classified as a missing persons case, but we are concerned about their welfare."

This was all big news in the Bay Area by now. Newspaper reporters swarmed the once quiet cul-de-sac at Saddlewood Court and the once equally quiet Frayne Lane. There were several television news vans parked on Frayne Lane near the Stinemans' residence. It was starting to take on a media circus aspect.

Judy Nemec said later, "I was in an emotional state of panic. It was like losing a child at the mall. We didn't know where my parents were."

The media was calling Nancy Hall at her home constantly, asking for updates. She said, "It was all very nerve-racking."

Nancy helped detectives at her parents' home as much as she could. She looked at a business card that had "G. Taylor Helzer" written on the front. On the back of the card, in her father's handwriting, was "Check with Taylor."

She didn't know exactly what the message was supposed to convey.

Nancy was shown a tin recovered from the Saddlewood residence. It was a tin which was owned by her parents, from Coco's Restaurant. Inside the tin were illegal drugs and a crack pipe. She knew very well that her parents never used any of those illegal substances.

After retirement, Ivan and Annette Stineman enjoyed vacationing
in their motor home and a time-share condo in Hawaii.
(Photo courtesy of Judy Nemec)

Selina Bishop, daughter of blues guitarist Elvin Bishop, was infatuated with Taylor Helzer. *(Driver's license photo)*

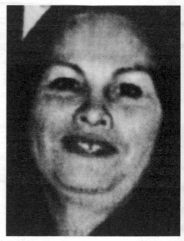

Selina's mother, Jenny Villarin, had suspicions about Taylor. *(Driver's license photo)*

James Gamble, known as "Gentleman Jim," was a good friend of Jenny Villarin. *(Driver's license photo)*

Taylor Helzer was an outgoing and popular student at Yganico Valley High School in the Bay Area of California. *(Yearbook photo)*

Justin Helzer was a shy and quiet student at the same high school. *(Yearbook photo)*

Future Playboy model Keri Furman (a.k.a. Kerrisa Fare) was beautiful even in high school. *(Yearbook photo)*

Taylor, Justin, and Dawn Godman began Children of Thunder at this suburban home on Saddlewood Court, Concord, California. Children of Thunder were supposed to initiate the Second Coming of Jesus Christ. *(Photo courtesy of Don Wilson)*

Taylor owned this bizarre wooden staff with a human skull depicted on top. *(Author's photo)*

By the year 2000, Taylor thought he was a prophet of God. He also convinced Justin and Dawn that he was a prophet.

Justin Helzer adored his older brother and followed his orders in Children of Thunder.

Dawn Godman was Taylor's third "core person" in Children of Thunder.

Mike Henderson visited his friend Justin at Saddlewood Court. Taylor told Mike he was a warlock, and Dawn told him she was a witch. *(Photo courtesy of Don Wilson)*

A wooden staff held a crystal that was a seer stone. Supposedly, it helped the Children of Thunder look into the future. *(Author's photo)*

Taylor took a pistol with him
to kidnap Ivan and Annette
Stineman at their home.
(Author's photo)

Taylor also took a Taser
to kidnap the Stinemans.
(Photo courtesy of Don Wilson)

Taylor and Justin were dressed as businessmen as they
approached the Stinemans' door. In their briefcases they carried
guns, Tasers, and a small blowtorch. *(Author's photo)*

Taylor and Justin used a Craftsman reciprocating saw to dismember the bodies of Ivan and Annette Stineman and Selina Bishop in the bathroom of the Saddlewood home. *(Author's photo)*

Selina Bishop took this photo of herself at a photo booth in a mall. She had less than two weeks to live after she took the photo.

07/24/00

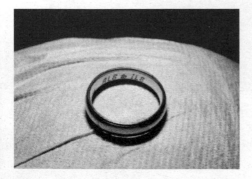

Taylor instructed Justin and Dawn to leave Ivan Stineman's wedding ring in Selina's car to further confuse policemen. *(Author's photo)*

Taylor, Justin, and Dawn took nine gym bags filled with body parts out to the California Delta for disposal. *(Author's photo)*

The area where the Children of Thunder deposited the body bags was a region of winding waterways and tules. *(Photo courtesy of Don Wilson)*

The body bags were deposited in the Mokelumne River from a personal water craft that the Helzers and Dawn rented. *(Photo courtesy of Don Wilson)*

In a bid for freedom from the police, Taylor Helzer forced Mary Mozzochi at knifepoint to cut his hair and give him her husband's clothes. *(Photo courtesy of Don Wilson)*

Sergeant Mike Crain was a key member of law enforcement who worked on the Stinemans' case. *(Author's photo)*

Detective Don Wick found a lot of important evidence connected to the murders of Jenny Villarin and James Gamble. *(Photo courtesy of Don Wilson)*

Detective Alicia Lellis found and catalogued numerous items connected to the Children of Thunder at the Saddlewood residence. *(Photo courtesy of Don Wilson)*

Detective Steve Nash linked the murders of Jenny Villarin and James Gamble to the disappearance of the Stinemans and Selina Bishop. *(Photo courtesy of Don Wilson)*

Ray and Mabel Carberry and Chris Darden were court observers
throughout Justin and Taylor Helzers' trials.
(Photo courtesy of Don Wilson)

Deputy DA Harold
Jewett sought the
death penalty for
both Taylor and Justin
Helzer. *(Photo courtesy
of Don Wilson)*

Judge Mary Ann O'Malley ruled on proceedings that dealt with hundreds of witnesses and items of evidence. *(Photo courtesy of Don Wilson)*

Attorney Suzanne Chapot presented a spirited defense for her client, Taylor Helzer. *(Photo courtesy of Don Wilson)*

In exchange for the removal of the death penalty against her, Dawn Goodman testified against Justin and Taylor Helzer in their trials. *(Photo courtesy of Don Wilson)*

When going to and from the courtroom, Taylor Helzer was always handcuffed and wore a waist chain. Bailiffs Howard Newman and Mike Harkelroad kept order in the courtroom during the proceedings. *(Photo courtesy of Don Wilson)*

Immediately after he was sentenced to death, Taylor smiled,
thanked the jury, and mouthed the words "It's okay" to his mom.
(Photo courtesy of Don Wilson)

Olga Land *(center)*, sister of Jenny Villarin, and Rosanne Lusk
Urban *(right)*, Jenny's best friend, had Detective Erin Enskip sit
with them at a press conference table after Taylor's death penalty
conviction. *(Photo courtesy of Don Wilson)*

Nancy Hall, the Stinemans' daughter, spoke to a room full of reporters after the jury ruled for a death sentence against Taylor Helzer. *(Photo courtesy of Don Wilson)*

The Stinemans' daughter Judy Nemec *(left)* and Detective Judy Elo held hands as Nancy Hall spoke to a room full of reporters after Taylor's conviction. *(Photo courtesy of Don Wilson)*

She also listened with a detective to audiotapes taken from her parents' phone message machine.

Message number one was of her father's voice telling to leave a message.

Message number two recorded, "Hello, this is Raymond from Terminix." It was about the pest control service.

Message number three was just an advertisement.

Message number four recorded, "This is Vicki Sexton at Cal Fed." It was the first call asking them to call her back.

Message number five recorded, "Hi, this is Vicki Sexton again. It's very important that you call me back."

Message number six stated, "Hi, this is Vicki from Cal Fed. We found your information and will call you next week."

Nancy didn't know what the information concerned. The financial and banking aspect of the Helzers' scheme was very shadowy to the detectives at this point.

Detectives also looked for Selina's car in Berkeley, but to no avail. Even more important than the car was the question: where was Selina Bishop? And for that matter, where were Ivan and Annette Stineman? More realistically at this point, the detectives were wondering where their bodies might be. The only link so far to the Helzer brothers and all the rest of this were some 9mm slugs found in Jenny Villarin and James Gamble and an array of cryptic notes and documents found at Saddlewood.

The first news coming out of Saddlewood Court was fragmented, illusory and stunning. The *San Francisco Chronicle* reported, "Tight-lipped Marin County Sheriff's detectives offered few details about the investigation, but said that a man is being held on drug

charges and is a possible suspect in the homicides."
(This referred to the deaths of Jennifer Villarin and
James Gamble.)

The *Chronicle* also said that detectives were interro-
gating him about the disappearance of Selina Bishop.
At present, all that the media knew was that Taylor and
Justin Helzer and an unnamed woman were arrested
for drug charges and seemed to have connections to
the other crimes.

Marin County Sheriff's captain Tom McMains told
reporters, "Taylor Helzer is a key individual because he
is the last person to see her (Selina Bishop). But I'm
not overly optimistic because I don't know where this
will lead us. This case has got a lot of twists and turns,
including some very surprising ones."

Little did he know at the time how right he was. The
twists and turns would meander like a delta slough of
murky water. Just below the surface, a vital piece of evidence was about to return to the light of day. It was
something that no one anticipated—but once it surfaced, it would blow the case wide open.

CHAPTER 10

The Delta of Death

When Steven Sibert discovered the first body bag floating in the North Fork of the Mokelumne River, it set off a chain reaction of searches and discoveries. Detective Steve Nash would later note, "The dismembered bodies of Ivan Stineman, Annette Stineman and Selina Bishop were discovered inside nine duffel bags, which were found floating separately in various locations in the Mokelumne River in the Sacramento River Delta.

"Some of the bags were discovered by civilians, some by law enforcement personnel looking for these bags and any evidence that might be related to them, and one was found by a biologist employed by the State Department of Fish and Game. All nine bags were in the water, some floating freely in the river and at least one was up against the riverbank. The people discovering two of the bags saw apparent body parts."

On August 8, in the *Contra Costa Times*, there was as yet no mention of body bags in the Delta. Lieutenant

Paul Crain told a reporter, "This is very unusual. We have very little information. There is nothing we can say that is a definite lead at this point."

Nancy Hall also made a statement to a reporter that she couldn't think of anyone who would want to hurt her parents. "They're just regular people," she said. "They had lots of friends and didn't get into confrontations."

By Wednesday, August 9, however, news of the discovery of the body bags was big news in all the local papers. The *San Francisco Chronicle* ran the story, "Marin County homicide investigators and Concord Police detectives are working closely with Sacramento authorities to identify the human remains discovered near Willow Berm Marina on Brannan Island."

The *Contra Costa Times* headline said: TWO CASES COULD BE LINKED. Within the text it stated, "In a sharp twist to a case mired in questions, police said the disappearance of guitarist Elvin Bishop's missing 22-year-old daughter may be linked to that of an elderly Concord couple."

Even then, Lieutenant Paul Crain admitted, "We're trying to find out who, if anyone from the Saddlewood house, has a connection to the Stinemans."

Captain Tom McMains told reporters, "At this point, we only know that bodies were found. We don't know if they have anything to do with our case."

Marin County Sheriff's Office sergeant Doug Pittman added, "There is nothing to tell me that Selina is deceased. It is our hope that Selina is alive. There is a chain of events surrounding her life which causes us to be concerned for her safety, but at this point I don't have any information about whether she has been harmed."

By Thursday, August 10, more information surfaced, and the *Contra Costa Times* reported that the Stinemans' van contained fingerprints that belonged to both Helzer brothers and Dawn Godman. Harold Jewett, a deputy district attorney for Contra Costa County, told a reporter, "I don't think I have words to describe what I'm beginning to see in this case. There is something truly horrible and perhaps evil in the commission of these crimes. It's obvious to us that the relationship between Taylor Helzer and the Stinemans was very suggestive of a motive."

With the news coming out, the media were heading in all directions—to the Delta, to Saddlewood Court, to Frayne Lane and to Woodacre. At the Paper Mill Creek Saloon, patrons were glued to the television set as more and more news hit the airwaves. A worker there told reporters, "Everybody loved Selina and Jenny and Jim around here."

A bulletin board was plastered with mementoes and recollections of the trio. One memo read, "Uncle James, I will forever miss your giant bear hug."

Another card stated, "Selina, your heart was bigger than this valley. Goodbye, sweet light."

The Helzer brothers' mother, Carma, was initially overwhelmed by the barrage of media questions. She spoke later of almost wilting under their persistent questioning. She did tell reporters at this point, "They (Taylor and Justin) haven't done anything criminal. This is a whole new experience for us." Then she answered a question by saying, "How am I getting through this? By trusting in God, man and the universe. In the end, everything is going to be okay."

An acquaintance of the Helzers, Paul Moses, of Martinez, was also stunned by the news. He told reporters, "They always seemed to be straight arrows. I never would have envisioned something like this in a million years. The brothers were very polite. Overtly kind. Their mannerisms were always like, 'Yes sir, yes ma'am.'"

Cousin Charney Hoffman said, "I felt sick. Literally. It was like someone kicked me in the stomach."

Aunt Dana Hoffman told reporters, "They were wonderful kids. They were an ideal family. Taylor loved people so much he was willing to go out of his way to help out the person who was not included. He was just an incredible young man."

A woman named Susan, who went to an LDS church in Martinez, said, "You couldn't find better kids. But you don't go from being a model Mormon missionary to drugs. Something had to happen in between."

Susan not only had taught Kelly Lord when she was young, but seemed to remember that Justin had been in her Sunday school at one time as well.

At a press conference in Concord, Gerry and Carma Helzer were besieged by reporters. Gerry said nothing, but Carma made a short statement, while crying. "They are innocent. I would like the victims' families to join me in prayer for the truth."

Flowers began to be placed at the end of the Stineman driveway by neighbors and friends. One card stated, "On your family's loss, may there be peace in knowing they are together. A neighbor who cares."

Dr. Gregory Reiber was a forensic pathologist with the UC Davis Medical Center. He'd been in forensic pathology since 1986 and had gone to Loyola University. By the year 2000, he'd done more than five thousand autopsies. In August 2000, he was about to do five more.

Initially he was on the Marin County murders of Jennifer Villarin and James Gamble. He noted that the body of Jennifer Villarin weighed 180 pounds, with dark brown hair and brown eyes. He also noted that she had two gunshot wounds that entered and exited her head. Gunshot wound number one entered near the upper corner of her left eye, near the bridge of her nose, and then descended through the rear of her head. Gunshot wound number two entered her left cheek, traversed her head in an upward path and exited from the left side of her head.

These were fairly round wounds, with abrasive rings around the edges. There was no soot deposit or gunshot residue (GSR) around the wounds, so he wrote, "These are distant-range wounds." The gun had to be more than two feet away from her head to have caused the wounds without leaving GSR.

Dr. Reiber also noted, "These would be fatal wounds. They went through the central areas of the brain."

One other thing that Reiber surmised was that the shooter at one point was at the foot of the bed. He believed that when bullet number one struck Jennifer, her head was propped up. As her head slumped down after being shot, he believed, bullet number two struck her at a different angle.

He also surmised that Jennifer Villarin probably did not live more than five minutes after being shot. He said later, "It's probable she never knew what happened."

James Gamble's wounds were much more diverse and complex. He was six feet two inches and weighed two hundred pounds. Bullet number one struck the right side of his neck. It was a through and through, which meant it struck no obstructions on its path through his neck that caused any deflection. Blood from this wound was, however, sprayed onto his chest.

Bullet number two went from the top of James's chest into his midchest. Dr. Reiber noted, "It was an atypical wound." This meant he didn't believe that it had hit square on, but might have wobbled after striking something else. It lodged in his neck near his spinal cord. This shot was probably fired from near his feet. The spinal cord was struck near the base of the brain and would have caused paralyzation from the neck downward.

Bullet number three hit James Gamble in his left shoulder, then his arm, and entered the left side of his chest, passed through muscle and then out his back. Bullet number four was a through and through on his right calf. Bullet number five was a graze wound on his right arm.

Looking at all the wounds, Reiber decided that the one to the chest would have finally been fatal. He inferred from evidence that Gamble had rolled off the bed after being shot and two more shots had been pumped into him while he was on the floor. In fact, Reiber decided that the fatal wound had occurred when he was on the floor and that Gamble had bled out.

Strangely enough, Dr. Reiber worked part-time for Sacramento County as well as Marin County, and he did autopsies for them. When the body bags from the Delta started showing up, he said, "It was a very complicated case."

The contents of the first bag came from a nylon Dunlop bag that contained cargo pockets. There was a stepping-stone in one pocket and three rocks in the other pockets. This first bag had been obtained near the Lighthouse Marina. Inside of the bag was the torso of an elderly woman with her organs removed.

The second bag was a black nylon Athletech bag with multiple cut marks. It contained the upper extremity of an elderly male, two lower extremities from an elderly male and the head of a young woman. The lower face of the young female had been mutilated, and the upper and lower jaws, and teeth removed. A red-beaded headband still clung to her hair.

The third bag contained several trash bags and their contents, which were the upper jaws and lower jaws of three individuals. Also within this bag were the lower extremities and the arm of an elderly woman. This bag was from the Willow Berm Marina area.

The fourth bag contained an elderly woman's head. There were overlapping cuts from several motions on the neck area. The soft tissue had probably been cut with a knife and the bony material with a saw blade.

In one of his notes, Dr. Reiber related, "It would take a great amount of work for disarticulation and some awareness of anatomy."

As far as the elderly man went, Reiber noted eleven stab wounds on the chest, some of them antemortem. But he concluded that these stab wounds were superficial and did not cause death. In fact, he would later say, "The cause of death was hard to determine on the elderly male. It was not from stab wounds. They were too shallow. And not from suffocation, because there would have been petechial hemorrhaging to the eyes. He might have suffered a heart attack from trauma. Or death could have come from his throat being slashed."

By the time Detective Alex Taflia arrived, Dr. Reiber had already gone through three bags and was looking at the fourth one. Even then, law enforcement was sending out more dive teams to see if they could find any more bags in the Delta.

Taflia noted in bag number four that there was a male left arm, skin from a hand and a male pelvis. In the same bag, wrapped in a plastic white bag, was most of a female head that was missing its upper and lower jaws. Gray hair on the head made it appear to be that of an elderly female.

The fifth bag was discovered on the South Fork of

the Mokelumne River and contained the pelvis of a younger female. It, too, had been altered by certain amounts of decomposition and the length of time it had been in the water.

The sixth bag was discovered on the North Fork of the Mokelumne River. It contained a male torso and paper-wrapped fecal material.

The seventh bag was found close to the sixth and included a female right arm, organs and sections of skin, liver, heart, lungs and intestines. It also contained the head of an elderly male.

The eighth was once again up the South Fork of the Mokelumne River and contained a young woman's torso and skin sliced away from the shoulder area. Eventually thirty-four separate stab wounds would be discovered in the torso. It was surmised that five of the stab wounds may have been inflicted while she was still alive.

The last bag, found near the eighth, contained a right arm and left arm, and a right leg and left leg. This bag was recovered by a dog team and Marin County law enforcement dive team.

Initially it was a job just to find out who these victims were. Pieces of bone from legs and rib bones were taken for DNA testing. And the discovery of the jaws with teeth were a big benefit. Even though they had been intermixed in a bag, all of the teeth were still there. These dental remains were turned over to Dr. Rawlins and Dr. Good.

One of the big questions early on was whether there was a fourth victim's body parts among the remains. With the help of dental records, and placing the body parts out on a table and reconstructing them to match a full body, there were only three victims.

Dr. Reiber said later, "It was pretty straightforward. We worked from the heads to the lower parts. There were three physically distinctive individuals. It was like putting together a jigsaw puzzle with some of the pieces missing."

After analysis, Dr. Reiber surmised that all of the victims had been cut initially with knives and not saw blades. He believed a saw blade was used second. He said, "There was mark action of blade upon bone."

It was noted that there were twenty-six stab wounds to the lower torso of Ivan Stineman. All were from a sharp, pointed instrument, probably a knife. A toxicology report showed caffeine in the brain tissue, but no other drugs. Ivan's heart and lungs were in place and attached to the diaphragm.

Annette Stineman's head and lower facial area were mutilated and the jaws missing. There was a discolored wound around the right eye and a fractured right eye socket. There were many injuries on the upper torso. He couldn't tell if some were antemortem or postmortem because of discoloration and the amount of time that she'd been in the water. Her abdominal organs were almost completely gone, and her right arm had been severed from the trunk. There were saw marks on the thighbones.

Dr. Reiber noted that her right lung had severe hemorrhages, so she was probably stabbed there before she died. A plastic bag with her organs was separate from the torso. Her chest organs and heart had to have been removed through the lower torso, not the chest wall, because of the incisions there. There were stab wounds on the head, but Dr. Reiber thought these were postmortem. There were trace amounts of meth in her brain. He determined the cause of death to be only as a hypothetical because of decomposition, and he determined that death was from multiple stab wounds.

The autopsy for the young female noted blunt-force injuries to the head. The left side of her head above the ear gaped open and showed brain tissue. There were skull fragmentations clear down to the middle ear. Dr. Reiber said, "The right and left side of the head showed trauma from a hard, heavy object. There had been at least half-a-dozen blows."

On the upper torso, there were multiple stab wounds that were postmortem. Five stab wounds in the central chest area had occurred possibly before death. These included stab wounds to the heart and each lung. This could be ascertained from the amount of blood that collected there.

A segment of skin had been cut away from the young woman's back. It was a section about 4½" by 3½" in diameter. This portion of skin was not found.

The young woman's arms were amputated far down from the shoulders. On the lower torso, there were twenty or more stab wounds, and stab wounds on the legs.

It was noted that she had two broken fingers on the left hand. These may have been defensive wounds—indicating that she may have thrown up her hand after being hit the first time.

Cause of death for the young woman was listed as multiple traumatic injuries. Blunt-force trauma to the head, or stab wounds to the lungs or heart, all of these could have been fatal.

Dr. Reiber told the *San Francisco Chronicle,* "I would say this is the most complicated case I've had to deal with in my career."

Besides just the body parts, law enforcement was also interested in the stones placed in the duffel bags. Detective Nash noted, "Eight of the duffel bags had been weighed down with rocks and/or man-made concrete stepping-stones. Most of the stepping-stones were concrete gray in color. All are about twelve inches in diameter and about one and a half to two inches in thickness. Officers from the Concord Police Department, the Marin County Sheriff's Office and criminalists from the Contra Costa sheriff's crime lab, who processed the Helzers' residence on Saddlewood, found similar concrete stepping-stones in the backyard of the property. Some stepping-stones had been placed in a pattern on the ground, while others had not. Obvious indentations where stepping-stones had previously been were noted within the pattern.

"A second type of rock was also present in some bags. It appeared to Concord Police Officer Vedder to be a type of broken/crushed rock, distinguished by rough and irregular surfaces and edges. Officer Vedder thought she had seen this type of rock used on river levees."

The news of the body bags being found in the Delta hit all the family and friends of the Stinemans and Selina Bishop like sledgehammer blows. Judy Nemec recalled, "Detective Crain said that a bag containing a young female's torso had been found in the Delta. Nancy immediately said, 'Selina!'"

Later, Crain called the daughters of the Stinemans again and said that a dismembered male torso had been found in a bag from the same area. Right after Nancy and Judy had gone to the police to give DNA samples, Crain told Judy, "You'd better prepare yourself."

Judy remembered, "We were in such a state of shock. I knew we wouldn't find them alive."

Nancy recalled, "They found a young woman's torso and arm. And then Daddy's arm. At first they didn't find any bags with Momma. I thought they might not find her. But they did."

Of Selina's family members, cousin Jill said, "We first heard about her from the media. It was a shock.

A microphone was shoved in my face and I was informed of the news. I was asked how I felt."

Jill was incensed by the callousness of the reporter. Any normal person would have known how she felt.

Another thing irritated her greatly. She said that after Elvin Bishop was informed about Selina, all law enforcement news went to him because he was the closest surviving family member. She and the others were now out of the loop and they felt shut out.

Lydia Young was also angry about the sudden clampdown on information. She said later, "We weren't next of kin. Elvin was. So we'd hear new stuff on TV. I was angry at the police."

Elvin Bishop, when contacted by the *San Francisco Chronicle* about the body bags, said, "I really don't want to talk about it right now."

Sacramento County sheriff's sergeant Dennis Arnal told a reporter in reference to the search for body bags, "When you find two eggs in a henhouse, you keep searching until you find more eggs, or you finish searching the henhouse." Then he added that the last two body bags were first identified as being similar by "weight, size and smell."

Two days after the first body bag was discovered, the Helzer brothers and Dawn Godman were arraigned at a court in Martinez. At the time, Taylor was only charged with burglary, use of a deadly weapon and making terrorist threats. This stemmed from his invasion of the Sharp and Mozzochi residences.

Justin and Dawn were only charged with auto theft at the time, concerning the taking of the Stinemans' van. The police let the media know, however, that further charges were pending. All three of the Children of Thunder were held in the Contra Costa County Jail without bail.

At the arraignment, Carma Helzer made only a

short statement to the press. She said, "We think that the truth is that our boys are innocent."

Deputy DA Harold Jewett, when asked about Selina Bishop, said, "It's a little bit more of a mystery as to how Selina Bishop met her end the way she did."

The mystery was only deepened when a friend of Selina's told police that Selina had suddenly started buying nice furniture for her apartment before she disappeared. She was also buying a lot of compact discs. Even though this money was probably coming from Taylor, no one knew how involved Selina had been in the plot against the Stinemans.

One friend of Selina's told the *San Francisco Chronicle*, "She was very naive." While another friend said, "She was so longing for this point in life. She would have done anything for him (Taylor)."

Family members who had known Selina all their lives were incensed by the implications that Selina might have been involved in the plot to kidnap and kill the Stinemans. A friend of Selina's told reporters, "She would have rather earned her money by working her fingers to the bone than by taking it from two elderly people."

Selina's cousin Tammy Young was sure that Selina and Jenny were marked for death because they knew too much about Taylor, or at least a person they knew as Jordan. Tammy said, "Selina told Jenny everything. Maybe he (Taylor) thought Selina had told her mother and was worried because he had been seen by her." Without knowing it at the time, Tammy Young was right on the mark.

Authorities were still looking at Selina as a possible suspect, however. They told reporters that they theorized Selina might have been in on the whole plot, but got cold feet at the last moment. They theorized that Selina had threatened to squeal on the others and had been killed by one or all of them.

In fact, Marin County sheriff's sergeant Doug Pittman told a reporter, "Right now, we're unclear about what Selina's involvement may have been."

Because Keri Furman's name and phone number were found on a bulletin board in Saddlewood, Detective Marziano contacted her by phone. Detective Marziano didn't know Keri's relationship with Taylor Helzer at this time, but he thought it might be important. Eventually he was able to contact Keri through her lawyer, Carmine Carlucci. A teleconference call was set up for the next day. At 3:00 P.M. on August 11, Detectives Fred Marziano, Steve Chiabotti and Dave Ishikawa were on a line in the Bay Area, while Keri and her lawyer were on a line in Las Vegas.

The detectives said hello, and Keri answered them in a friendly voice.

Detective Marziano introduced himself and related why he was calling. Keri was not surprised. She said, "I found out about it yesterday."

Keri was very frank about her and Taylor's use of ecstasy and his selling of the drugs at raves.

The detectives wanted to know about Impact America. She told them that Taylor claimed that God would show him the way about it. Then she said, "I didn't know what was going on. I didn't want to be dragged into his thing. I didn't support him in this idea."

She said Taylor finally didn't trust her with things about Impact America. He started talking to Justin and Dawn Godman about it in private.

Detective Marziano asked her, "Did Taylor think he was like Joseph Smith?"

"Yes," Keri responded. "He said he was now like a prophet of God."

One question zeroed in on why she had put money into Justin's account. She said she had borrowed $4,000 for her car and was paying it back. Taylor had told her to send the money to Justin.

On August 2, she had called Taylor and he was very upset to be receiving a phone call from her. He said he didn't want her phoning back. He said, "Don't call me unless you're dying or seriously injured." Of course, this was right in the middle of plans to kill Selina Bishop.

Keri told the detectives that at six o'clock on Thursday morning, August 10, one of her girlfriends, Alisha, had phoned her and said, "Taylor killed five people!"

Keri didn't believe her at first. Then she looked it up on the Internet. She saw that it was true and she said she got chills on her arms.

She told the detectives she remembered the knives and swords that Justin and Taylor used to keep in the garage at the Oak Grove residence. She was very cooperative with the detectives, but she did have one big worry. Her modeling career was just starting to take off. Her *Playboy* spread would be in September and she had a deal going with an alcoholic beverage company for a television commercial. She asked, "Is my name going to be released to the press?"

Detective Marziano answered, "Only if this goes to trial." Then he asked her, "Do you have a cell phone?"

She answered that she did.

She told them that she would soon be going to Dallas and Denver for part of a promotion tour. The detectives wanted to get in touch with her again.

The next day, Marziano decided they needed to talk to Keri in person. They agreed to meet her at her lawyer's office in Las Vegas. Then the detectives flew down to Vegas on Friday, August 11.

The interview was taped and all the detectives wore casual dress. They said later they didn't want to intimidate her. No guns or other weapons were displayed. Looking for more background on Taylor, Keri told them, "Most people will talk behind your back. Taylor would do it to your face. He would make you mad. I had given up what little self-esteem I had to be with him. He'd say something and you'd go, 'Ooohhh!'

"I never saw Taylor get angry. It was the other person who got angry. Actually, everything wasn't about Harmony. It was all about Taylor. He'd talk about walls and bringing them down. If you disagreed with him, he'd say, 'If you don't want to listen to me, I don't want to be in your space.' And then he'd leave."

Concerning Justin, she said, "He was very much a follower."

Detective Marziano asked Keri if she thought Taylor could have brainwashed Justin. He asked, "Do you think he could make Justin do whatever he wanted him to do?"

Keri answered, "Absolutely! If you were around him for a little bit of time, he could brainwash you. He would say, 'this is God's plan. You're my number one. I need you. He could also make a person feel like nothing, unless you were right on the same path with him. Otherwise, you were doomed."

Keri elaborated about Justin's life as well. She said, "He didn't have any friends, except Dawn and Taylor. He was very odd. He had things he didn't like about himself. About life. About people.

"Taylor told Justin to get that house (on Saddlewood Court) in his name. And Justin did. I felt bad for Justin. I knew that Taylor was never going to pay him back."

Keri told Justin about this and he replied, "You don't trust him and don't believe in him. He's going to make a lot of money."

Keri also talked about how Taylor began to dominate Dawn Godman. "He fed off people. I started getting jealous about his relationship with Dawn. I asked him, 'Why are you spending so much time with her?' He said, 'Because she believes in me. I have stuff to teach her.'"

The detectives asked Keri about In To Me See and Impact America. She admitted that she had helped with In To Me See. She said she was even the one who designed the colorful business cards.

She told of Taylor's ideas that changed so rapidly she could barely keep up with them. Underage girl prostitutes, Feline Club, yuppies and blackmail. It all started sounding too bizarre and unrealistic to her.

Keri said, "Impact America—I didn't want to be a part of it. I knew from the beginning it was just la-la land. I never thought he was a prophet of God. He'd say stuff likc, 'I'm feeling God's plan.' He said it would take a million dollars to make a million."

She told them that Taylor became upset with her after her professional *Playboy* shoot and her interest in a modeling career. He wanted her to be one of the three core people. He didn't want her going down to southern California. He wanted her to stay and soak in his wisdom of Impact America. As time went on, however, she felt that he was talking gibberish. He was moving toward the Days of Thunder, and she wanted no part of it.

Hundreds of miles away from Las Vegas, in Marin County, two hundred friends, family and the merely curious gathered at the Paper Mill Creek Saloon in

Woodacre. On a fence across the street were hundreds of messages for Selina Bishop, Jenny Villarin and Jim Gamble. Tom Pinkson, a next-door neighbor of Selina's, told reporters, "This is a valley of love, and that's been violated. We're going to have to heal that love. It's going to take a lot of work. If we stay with bitterness and anger, then we've lost twice."

Mark Land, who was married to Jenny's sister Olga, said, "With her patience and her insight, she gave my children the gift to read. She touched all our lives. I can see that here today."

Jenny Mehrtens spoke of Jenny Villarin always having a laugh and a smile: "The things in the paper and the news, we've got to forget about it. We've got to think about the things these people brought us."

Even a person who had not seen Jim Gamble in thirty-eight years was there. He was a classmate of Jim's from high school days. He said, "He was a real great guy."

Elvin Bishop's brother-in-law said of the guitarist and his family, "They're so overwhelmed by grief, they find it impossible to face anyone right now. But they're immensely touched by this gathering."

Robert Asuncion declared, "You can bet this family will be stronger. Every moment with your family is special. Don't let this happen to your family, where you lose touch, then get together to grieve."

CHAPTER 11

The Beehive

At the Concord Insurance Service, Detective Patrick Murray looked at Polaroid photos of Justin's pickup. He also talked to George Calhoun at Dean Witter and contacted AT&T, where Justin had worked. Detective Murray was put in contact with Don McNay, who was Justin's supervisor. He advised Murray that employees had their own vehicles and did not share their vehicles with other employees. Justin's vehicle was towed to the Concord Police Department, where it was eventually searched for evidence.

Edward Berry, of Double Header Pagers, talked to CPD and looked at a photo lineup. He identified Dawn Godman out of a group of six photos. Melissa Mahan at Not Too Naughty was asked about the purchase of handcuffs and leg irons. She also picked Dawn Godman out of a lineup.

Andre Lepage was shown a series of photos at Pep Boys. He picked Justin Helzer out of the lineup. Elizabeth Hand told police about Sky Anderson (Dawn Godman) buying Pro Grip ski gloves.

An interesting thing came to light from a Contra Costa County Jail inmate named Tammy Funderburk. A report on her from a jailer stated, "Funderburk was at the Martinez Detention Facility with several other women waiting for a court appearance. A television set was on showing news on the murders (of the five people connected to the Helzers and Godman). Dawn Godman was in the cell with her and said, 'Oh, they keep saying he's my boyfriend (referring to Taylor). He ain't my boyfriend. I've had sex with him and got him high, but he's not my boyfriend.'

"Godman then said that she had been in the Marin house and saw things there she didn't like. Godman was asked if she killed anyone, and she said, 'No.'

"Funderburk said that Godman laughed and smirked at the news about the murders. Her attitude upset the other inmates so much that Godman was removed from the cell for her own protection."

Dawn's pickup truck also became an item of interest to authorities. Jailers intercepted a letter from Godman's parents concerning the pickup, which had never been taken into custody, since no one knew its connection at the time. The parents said in part, "We're picking up your truck and bringing it home." Home was up at the small town of Ione in the Gold Rush country.

When officers went up there to search the pickup, they found a purse and small duffel bag in the pickup. Strangely enough, on the duffel bag the letters *MIA* were on a zipper tag. As an acronym, MIA can often stand for missing in action.

William Miller, of Cool Rides, was asked by detectives about the rental of the personal watercraft. He said that the rental in question had a fourteen-gallon tank, and when it was returned, it had four gallons of fuel left in the tank. He figured that the watercraft had been in operation for about two to three hours to use that much fuel. He also said he was surprised when Justin turned it in earlier than necessary. When asked by Miller why, Justin told him he was tired.

Detective Erin Inskip spoke with the Soladays about Selina's supposed trip to Yosemite. During this conversation, Jay Soladay mentioned a black Saturn. He identified the Saturn as belonging to Selina's boyfriend, Jordan.

Leora Soladay identified Justin's white pickup truck. She said it had been used to help Selina move into her apartment. Leora also picked out a photo of Taylor Helzer from a photo lineup and identified the man as Jordan.

Detective Wick spoke with Elvin Bishop. Elvin recognized a portion of an outgoing audio message on a phone tape that was Selina's voice. The message was directed to Jordan.

Justin's boss at AT&T was contacted. He showed the detective time card records that showed Justin called in sick for July 30, July 31 and August 1. Justin was scheduled off on August 2 and 3, but he never showed up for work again on August 4 or any days thereafter, although August 6 and 7 were scheduled vacation days.

CPD detective Steve Harn went to Sears and verified that a reciprocating saw had been purchased there. There was also a purchase of a six-inch and nine-inch blade. The name on a warranty registration was signed Sky Anderson.

Officer Vedder matched white plastic bags with red drawstrings, from the Saddlewood residence, to similar white plastic bags with red drawstrings that held the heads of Ivan Stineman, Annette Stineman and Selina Bishop.

The owner of the Concord Cab Company confirmed that a ride had been given to Saddlewood Court on Tuesday, August 1. Driver Nicolai Nenad was questioned, and it was learned he actually knew Justin Helzer. He related his story about serving as an MP with Justin in Germany.

In the week after the arrests, the media started to get a handle on elements of the case. In an edition of the *San Francisco Chronicle,* a story stated, "It would take nearly a week for investigators from the two jurisdictions to connect the seemingly unrelated events. When they did, they would uncover what authorities believe to be a bizarre and violent multicounty rampage by a pair of Contra Costa brothers who had had little prior contact with the law."

The article went on to speak of Selina acting like a lovesick teenager and being swept into Taylor's web of deceit.

In fact, at this point, no one knew for sure how much Selina was involved in the plot. Muddying the waters was a comment made by one of Selina's friends. This person told reporters that Selina was banking large sums of money and supposedly going to get 20 percent of some huge settlement that her boyfriend, Jordan, was going to get.

Even Contra Costa Deputy DA Harold Jewett admitted, "We have information that Selina Bishop did open a bank account in connection with this case."

The *San Francisco Chronicle* ran an article saying, "The financial entanglements . . . deepen the mystery over whether Bishop was a willful participant in the plot or an unwitting pawn."

Marin County Sheriff's Office sergeant Pittman shed no light on the subject when he said, "Right now, we're unclear about what her involvement may have been."

Then he added a new twist. Sergeant Pittman told reporters, "Although we seem to be focusing on these three suspects (Justin, Taylor and Dawn), we are not limiting ourselves to that. We're trying to contact people who might have seen or had contact with any of the victims before their deaths. Obviously the investigation still has a long way to go. There is a lot of follow-up to do."

On August 16, the newspapers added an intriguing new twist to what Pittman was implying. The *Contra Costa Times* headline stated: NEW LEAD IN BISHOP CASE. In smaller letters, it proclaimed: "Police seek a man videotaped at a Petaluma bank."

The investigators were indeed handing out copies of photos of the man videotaped at the Washington Mutual ATM machine on August 1, 2000. He was described as being white, between thirty-five and forty-five years of age, of average build, with short dark hair, wearing jeans and a light-colored T-shirt with sunglasses hanging from the collar. The time he was at the ATM was 5:28 P.M., and this corresponded to the time that a check for $10,000 was deposited into Selina Bishop's account. Even more intriguing was the fact that "the videotape also shows that this unknown suspect arrived and left the bank in a dark-colored sedan. He is not Taylor or Justin Helzer."

Lieutenant Paul Crain told reporters, "He's not a suspect, but he is someone we'd like to locate, identify and interview."

While the hunt for the elusive mystery man went on, in Concord, crime scene technicians were tearing up the Helzers' front yard with a backhoe. They were in the process of extracting the sewer line all the way out to the middle of the street.

Next-door neighbor Claude Reese told a reporter, "It looks like they took out the sewer line. I have a feeling they're looking for blood and body parts and whatever else someone might have put down the drain."

This supposition was given credence by a story told by neighbor Kaye Shaman. She told investigators that one day she went out to use the hose, the same one Justin had asked to use back in the first week of August, and found what looked like flesh and blood near the hose. She had no idea where it had come from at the time. She thought a hawk might have deposited it there. Now she had a whole new theory.

With new evidence being unearthed every day in the grisly crimes, Elvin Bishop told a *Contra Costa Times* reporter, "My immediate aim and ambition is not to go crazy. Blues was invented to get people through rough times. Since I'm lucky enough to have the blues, I might as well take advantage of it." He went on to say that he was seeing a counselor and seeking solace in music.

The story of the "mystery man" at the Petaluma bank kept mutating and growing. In fact, the *Contra Costa Times* reported that the Marin-based company Industrial Light and Magic was set to enhance digitally the videotape of that man at the ATM machine. This company was owned by George Lucas of *Star Wars* fame. It was ironic in the extreme that Selina had once played on a movie set left behind by George Lucas.

The possibility of a fourth suspect on the loose set nerves on edge in Forest Knolls and Woodacre. Some people feared for their safety. Sergeant Pittman tried to allay their fears by saying, "We have no reason to believe the public is in danger from the person in the photo." But after the brutality of the crimes and the discovery of body bags in the Delta, many residents weren't so sure.

On August 18, Taylor's attorney, Suzanne Chapot told reporters that Taylor was severely mentally disturbed. She said, "He doesn't know what happened. He hears things that people say in the jail and he is horrified."

Minutes before the court hearing that day, Gerry and Carma Helzer were served with subpoenas to testify before a grand jury. Carma testified before them for five hours; on leaving the building, according to reporters, she burst into tears.

On August 26, a lot more news was revealed about a conversation Taylor Helzer had with Detective Chiabotti back on August 7, after he'd been arrested. In an interview room, a very interesting exchange took place:

Chiabotti: Do you want to talk to me?

Taylor: I did . . . I do.

Chiabotti: You want to go someplace to sit down or do you want to talk here?

Taylor: Basically what I'm trying to say is . . . You know what? I'm getting freaked out here. I just wanna go back to my cell.

Chiabotti: That's fine. You can go back to your cell.

Taylor: Okay. What I'm trying to say is, I don't know. I just see things that I'm remembering now. Or am I having a vision because that happens?

Chiabotti: Okay. Do you want to talk about it now, or what?

Taylor: Yeah, I do. I'm telling you . . . right now that I'm remembering things regarding Selina and regarding Ivan and Annette. I told her (another detective) that I didn't remember. And I didn't at the time, but I'm starting to think these weren't dreams. 'Cause, see, there are two (Justin and Dawn) who shouldn't be in here. And I knew that already, but these two shouldn't be here. So as soon as—I'll just tell you this . . . as soon as I get to hug my brother and tell him I'm sorry in front of his lawyer, then I've got a lot to tell you regarding Selina and Ivan and Annette and myself.

Chiabotti: Okay.

Taylor: And I want to talk to them and tell them I'm sorry if I did anything for the betrayal of their trust because my actions have obviously made it look like they did something. Otherwise they wouldn't be here this long. I need to tell somebody this, but I don't need a lawyer to do that. I need to make sure they both have a lawyer before I say anything. I need to say my good-byes to both of them. Better get me in the same room at the same time. Whatever.

Chiabotti: Okay, well, let me run this by you. . . .

Taylor: Yeah.

Chiabotti: Probably when the woman detective talked to you, I guessed you asked for an attorney, so there's really nothing I can do about that. Now they've asked for their own attorneys, so they'll be provided with attorneys.

Taylor: So when I see that they happen to have an attorney, I've got some information to share with you guys.

Chiabotti: Okay, what?

Taylor: I'm not very good at things like this. I'm right now having a hard time.

Chiabotti: Okay, Glenn. Just so I understand this right, once they have an attorney and you're sure of that, then you're interested in talking with me?

Taylor: Right now, that's what Spirit says. Spirit says that I should not let them be here.

Taylor may have been feigning ignorance, but it may have also been a clever ploy to make sure that Justin and Dawn were "lawyered up" and not talking on their own. Taylor probably knew that a lawyer would tell the others not to talk. And by saying he was sorry that they were in jail, and shouldn't be there, he could indicate his loyalty to them, and they should do the same for him.

By August 28, the story of the mystery man was mutating once again. This time it placed him in Selina's car and had that car being driven by him out to the Delta. Television station KRON reported that divers in the Delta were searching for Selina's car there. This story got a certain amount of credence when it was learned that a large object, the shape and size of a car, was found to be in the Mokelumne River. The object was scanned by a side-scanning sonar system operated by the Tuolumne County Sheriff's Office (TCSO).

Marin County sheriff's sergeant Pittman told reporters, "We did locate one object in the water, and its shape and size is consistent with the shape of an automobile. Although it is consistent with a vehicle, it may be that we'll get out there and it won't be a vehicle or its not the vehicle we're looking for. The location is a known place where people often dispose of property."

The mystery man episodes continued, but the location of Selina Bishop's car was about to be solved far away from the Delta.

* * *

Greg McClish was a traffic control officer for the Petaluma Police Department (PPD). He had regular beats within the city and he would chalk tires on cars parked on certain streets. If a vehicle was left there longer than posted, he would fill out a ticket and place it on the vehicle's window.

On August 24, 2000, he was training a part-time officer as they moved through the downtown area of Petaluma. They came upon a blue Honda Accord with the license plate 4CQD822. The vehicles in that area hadn't been checked for two weeks since Petaluma had a budget crisis, and McClish had been doing all of the parking violation work by himself. He placed a parking ticket on the Honda when it hadn't been moved by his second trip around the area.

McClish came back to the same street on August 31, and the blue Honda was still parked at the same spot and collecting dust. McClish, by instinct, felt something was wrong about the car. Just to be on the safe side, he ran the plates and discovered that the vehicle was wanted in a Marin County homicide.

McClish called in his report to a dispatcher and waited. Fifteen minutes later, two MCSO officers arrived. Crime scene tape was placed around the vehicle and, at last, one mystery was solved. The mystery man at the bank was as elusive as ever, though.

Mysteries over vehicles did not end there, however. The next one concerned Keri Furman's little silver Eclipse sports car. In her September *Playboy* bio, she answered the question "When I feel the need for speed, I'm . . ."

Keri's answer was "Blasting tunes in my Silver Bullet (2000 Eclipse), flying to San Fran."

Two sources close to Selina called the police and said that they had seen a silver Eclipse in front of Selina Bishop's residence in Woodacre on July 16, 2000.

Since Jordan didn't own an Eclipse, only Keri did, it was wondered what she might have been doing there, especially since she said she wasn't anywhere near the area in July.

One of the sources told a reporter, "I noticed it. It stood out. You don't see them out here. Everybody has either a beater (beat-up car) or a truck."

In this case, the mystery of the silver Eclipse was never solved. It may have been just a case of mistaken identity.

Playboy magazine, which was already embarrassed by Keri Furman's (aka Kerrisa Fare) connections to Taylor Helzer, was not amused by this new revelation. *Playboy*'s spokesman Bill Farley told reporters, "It's been awkward having the magazine's name in connection with that grisly case."

Then he added that Kerrisa Fare was astounded by the fact that Taylor Helzer was connected to the murders. He said, "She felt he was a mild-mannered person that hasn't harmed anyone."

Then Farley went on to say that Taylor had approached *Playboy* to write his story. His asking price was $400,000. In fact, headlines in the *Contra Costa Times* declared, HELZER TRIED TO SELL STORY TO PLAYBOY FOR $400,000. This occurred from the county jail. The article went on to say that Taylor's lawyer said that he wanted the money to go to charity or a Selina Bishop fund. Carma Helzer chimed in and said, "The money could go to a charity, a fund for Bishop's memory or to fix up the county jail."

One of the biggest breaks in the case had nothing to do with vehicles, *Playboy* magazine or mystery men. CPD detective Darrell Graham conducted a routine interview with Debra McClanahan to determine what she knew about the Helzer brothers and Dawn Godman.

Detective Graham provided a later statement that McClanahan didn't provide any dramatic information initially. But later that same day, after he'd gone home, the Concord Police Department informed him that McClanahan had phoned back, wanting to talk with him. Graham phoned her about 8:20 P.M. and she told him that she'd just found a black metal cigarette case, with gold trim, inside her apartment and that it contained four movie tickets and a Denny's receipt, both dated July 30, 2000. She said that the cigarette case had originally been her ex-husband's, but then she had given it to Taylor Helzer.

Inside the cigarette case she found four theater tickets from the Brendan Theater in Pittsburg for the 8:10 P.M. showing of *X Men*. There was also a cash register receipt from Denny's on Sommersville Road in Antioch, from the same date, and stamped 11:37 P.M., for four people. The bill had totaled $33. According to McClanhan, she had gone to the Brendan Theater that same evening herself with her eleven-year-old daughter, but they had gone to the 8:10 P.M. showing of a movie. She denied knowing who the four movie tickets or the Denny's receipt belonged too.

Having all that information in mind, Detective Heidi Stephenson interviewed Debra McClanahan on August 22, and Debra began to open up a lot more. What she said was noted in a report:

Debra McClanahan said that she had known Dawn Godman for three years, and had met her at a Mormon dance. She was introduced to Taylor Helzer in November or December 1999. She had sex with him once, and it had been a one night stand. She said that she'd never known Taylor or Justin or Dawn to be violent. She did admit that any one of them might show up at her apartment at any time, day or night.

McClanahan denied that Dawn had a cell phone that had been rented in her name. She admitted that she had gone to raves with both Taylor and Dawn in Berkeley and had taken ecstasy. She also admitted that she knew Taylor was collecting disability money and that he had been a stockbroker.

She said that Taylor had phoned her on July 30 and that Dawn Godman had dropped by on the same day. McClanahan claimed to have asked Dawn if she could borrow a hundred dollars, and Dawn had left her a $100 bill. McClanahan did not reveal why she wanted the hundred dollars.

McClanahan told Detective Stephenson that on July 31, 2000, at about 11:30 P.M., Taylor had dropped by her apartment to say hi. He then said he wouldn't see her for a week, since he was going out of town. McClanahan said that she'd last seen Dawn Godman on August 6 at about 2:30 P.M.

Earlier that week, Justin and Dawn had called her on August 2 around 11:30 P.M., and actually came by her apartment on Thursday and stayed from around 2:30 A.M. until around 4:30 A.M. They played Canasta and no one seemed upset or agitated.

Debra claimed that Taylor, Justin and Dawn were supposed to meet her at the Brendan Theater to watch the movie *X Men* on July 30. She said she had arrived there with her daughter about 7:20 P.M. and couldn't find the others anywhere, so she and her daughter had watched the 8:10 P.M. showing. She said that she didn't know about any plans that Taylor had.

McClanahan did admit she had heard the phrase In To Me See which equaled Intimacy. As far as the cigarette case went, she said she had given it to Taylor and first discovered the receipts inside sometime after July 30. McClanahan denied ever having heard of the Stinemans or Selina Bishop. She did say she was with Dawn Godman when Dawn brought two pairs of handcuffs around mid-June, as well as a dildo. Asked what they were for, McClanahan said that she and Dawn enjoyed bondage in sexual encounters. She referred to the Not Too Naughty store as an adult toy store.

A lot of things didn't add up about many of Debra McClanahan's statements. Perhaps even she knew that she was now under suspicion by authorities. She called the Concord Police Department and asked if she could bring in a .357 revolver. She did so and Detective Graham took a look at it.

On August 24, Detectives Stephenson and Chiabotti reinterviewed McClanahan, and she began changing many of her previous statements. In this statement Debra said that Taylor had instructed her to take her daughter to the Brendan Theaters without him, but to buy four adult tickets to the movie. Then she was to go somewhere after the movie and purchase four dinners and keep the receipts. Someone was supposed to give her money for doing all of this.

Dawn Godman did show up at her apartment complex and met Debra at the pool area. Since McClanahan couldn't leave the pool area, because her young daughter was in the pool, she gave Godman a key, and Dawn left a hundred dollar bill in her apartment.

Debra told the detectives of her mission to the theater and Denny's. Then, however, she said that she put the receipts on a short wall in her apartment and, at some time uncertain to her, the tickets and receipt disappeared. "At various times between July thirtieth and August sixth, Taylor, Justin and Dawn all visited her apartment. At some time, Debra was aware that her ex-husband's metal cigarette case was on the short wall in the apartment. Debra knew she was doing a favor for the defendants and knew that they were asking her to cover something up for them, but she didn't know what specific behavior or crime that she was helping them conceal but thought it might be drug-related."

As to why she was starting to cooperate now, Debra said later, "I didn't know the extent of everything at the time. I only knew of two murders then (Jenny Villarin and James Gamble). I was thinking I could give this to the police department."

Detective David Chilimidos later got a tip about a safe stored at Debra McClanahan's apartment on Ryan Road in Concord. (Just who the informant was has never been revealed.)

With a consent to search, Detective Elo searched McClanahan's apartment on Ryan Road and looked in the bedroom closet. A safe was discovered in the bedroom closet and a wheelchair in her daughter's room.

In the safe were a number of important documents and items that were listed:

1. Checkbook of Ivan Stineman and Annette Stineman for a Morgan Stanley account
2. Washington Mutual account for Ivan and Annette Stineman
3. Checkbook for Annette Stineman on a liquid-assets fund
4. Numerous credit cards:
   a. Chevron card for I. L. Stineman
   b. Chevron card for I. L. Stineman
   c. Chevron Visa card for Annette Stineman
   d. Chevron card for Annette Stineman
   e. A Visa card for Ivan Stineman

Social Security cards belonging to Ivan and Annette Stineman were also found, along with a Social Security card and driver's license owned by Selina Bishop.

There was a paper with Selina's phone number on it, along with Cal Fed numbers, and a scrap of paper that read: "Sky and J meet me at 2 Bird Cafe at 5 AM. To go to Bolinas. But I sick. I stay home."

Along with these paper and plastic items was found a magazine for a 9mm Beretta pistol, razor blades, two diamond rings, two magazines for a .22-caliber pistol, a semiautomatic pistol with the serial numbers scratched off and a three-ring binder.

There were more esoteric items in the safe as well—crystals and green stones, a Digi Tech scale that weighed things in grams, hypodermic needles, a glass smoking pipe, handcuffs, a box of Rohypnol, a marijuana roach, Zig-Zag papers, a typed-out script and cigar box with Playboy Bunny logo.

The investigators also received a list of telephone calls from the Saddlewood residence to McClanahan's place. On August 3, 2000, there had been a one-minute call at 3:40 A.M., followed by a one-minute call at 4:30 A.M. There was a one-minute call at 5:21 A.M. and a two-minute call at 5:30 A.M.

The next day there was a search warrant executed for Gerry and Carma's residence in Pacheco.

On August 25, Detective Warnock brought Debra McClanahan into the district attorney's office in Martinez and then on to the grand jury. At last they had someone who knew some aspects of the crime spree and was willing to talk. Up to this point, there had been lots of evidence, but it was all mute evidence.

Detective Elo discovered in Justin's AT&T vehicle a bottle of Insta-Clean. This could be used to mask a drug test by putting a drop of it into the urine.

Detective Warnock talked to Olivia Embry, Richard

Hundly and Kelly Lord. He also talked to Jessyka Chompff about Taylor and interviewed the carpet cleaners who had been to Saddlewood. Detective Warnock spoke with Dawn Kirkland about the Helzer brothers' behavior at the Third Ward in Walnut Creek, and he analyzed the poster that held the Twelve Principles of Magic. This poster had been in the possession of Brandon Davids.

A gold ring from Selina's Honda was given by Detective Alex Taflia to Detective Mingas, and it was noted that an inscription on the ring stated, "ALS to ILS." The Stinemans' daughters confirmed that this wedding ring had been given by Annette to Ivan.

A roll of plastic film from the Saddlewood residence was also looked at. There was about fifty feet missing from the roll. It was later surmised that this amount of plastic had been used in the bathroom while the bodies were being dismembered. The plastic had obviously done a good job, as had Justin Helzer. It would be learned later that he'd gone over every square inch of the bathroom with a toothbrush. Not one drop of blood of any of the victims was ever found in the bathroom, despite all the bloodletting there.

Sergeant Andrew Gartner studied the voice mail greeting from Selina to Taylor. On one part, she declared, "Hi, sweetie. I'll call you in twenty or thirty minutes." In the background could be heard the voice of Jenny Villarin, sweet-talking to a cat.

Selina's diary was discovered and scrutinized for evidence. In late July, she had written that she didn't want to be part of Jordan's "big plans."

On August 1, 2000, she wrote, "I wish we could be together. Why is it so difficult?"

Then she wrote about wanting to go to Great America. Taylor cryptically answered, "I've got something better planned."

A pager message from Dawn to Taylor was found. The message said, "Hi, you've reached Taylor." Another voice message from Taylor stated, "You've reached Jordan Taylor for In To Me See."

Based on having heard Dawn Godman's voice in person, detectives thought the second message was from her to Taylor.

Clint Carter spoke with detectives at length about two male subjects he had seen walking toward the Stinemans' residence on Sunday, July 30. He said that the dark-haired male had stopped outside the door and looked hesitant. The blond-haired, or lighter-haired man, came up from behind, put his hand on the dark-haired male's shoulder and gave a gesture with his head toward the house, as if to say, "Come on." This surprised the investigators. Taylor had been seen as the decisive one, not Justin.

Detective Graham went to Washington Mutual in Petaluma to check out that angle of the case, and what he found at last put to rest the theory about a fourth suspect, the mystery man at the ATM machine. Graham spoke with the manager there to see what might be found on their video camera. She hoped to find out which teller had done any business concerning checks to Selina Bishop, and what day and time that might have occurred.

A time on the teller's record was processed for Monday, July 31, 2000, at 5:28 P.M., but when they looked at the videotape, the person at the ATM at 5:28 P.M. was no one that they knew who was connected with the Helzers and Godman. It was a photo of the mystery man. It had made them wonder if there were more people connected to the conspiracy than they knew about.

Finally it was discovered that the video camera's time was off by seven minutes. When they looked again, it was found that at 5:21 P.M. a large blonde in a wheelchair, wearing a cowboy hat and lime green pantsuit, was videotaped. It was, of course, Dawn Godman in disguise and the mystery man episode was finally laid to rest.

Joyce Sheehan, the branch manager, was asked to look at checks concerning Selina Bishop. She discovered that no transaction had been over $100 in all of July until a $10,000 check had been deposited. But the signature on the check was wrong. Instead of spelling Stineman correctly, the person wrote Stinman, without an *e* after the first *n*.

Detectives also had Nancy Hall look at various checks. She noted that a $33,000 check, dated August 1, 2000, to Selina Bishop had her father's handwriting. A check for $67,000 to Selina Bishop had her mother's signature. These were true and accurate signatures.

Christina Werk had a degree in forensic science and was a field evidence tech. She started doing fingerprint analysis of some items. She used powder method for lifting prints from vehicles and chemical method for paper items.

Micromatic powder was used on the Stinemans' Chevy Lumina and on Selina's Honda. It was dusted on with a fiberglass brush. She then used a fingerprint-lifting tape. One side of the tape was sticky, the other side not.

Eight "possibles" came from the Chevy van, she said later. These came from such diverse areas as the driver's side door, the rear driver's side, the passenger door and hood.

Fingerprint technician Sergio Solis became the custodian of record. He already had the fingerprints and palm prints of Taylor, Justin and Dawn.

Solis noted down:

80.1—Fingerprint driver's side door—Justin Helzer.

80.4—Fingerprint from Dawn Godman.

80.5—Palm of Taylor.

So all three members of the Children of Thunder had touched the Stinemans' van at one time or another.

Kenneth Fujii had been a criminalist for eighteen years by 2000. He was an expert in firearms and tool marks. He noted that the bullets recovered from the crime scene on Redwood Drive in Woodacre all came from the same gun, which he decided was probably a Beretta or Taurus semiautomatic. The Taurus in essence was a copy of a Beretta.

Fujii measured the trigger pull and the GSR when he received the Beretta from the safe to see if it had been modified. It apparently had not been modified. He noted that the Beretta ejected casings to the right. He also concluded that .762-caliber ammunition found at the Saddlewood residence was probably for an AK-47. This weapon was never found.

Another person who helped the detectives was Beverly Hodge, who worked for the California toll bridge agency in the Bay Area, which included the Antioch Bridge. Unbeknownst to the Helzers and Dawn Godman, when they drove the pickup with the personal watercraft over the bridge, they were photographed by a video camera. Officer Vedder asked Hodge to view all the videos from August 1, 2000, to August 4, 2000. She did this with Officer Vedder. They were looking for a white Nissan pickup truck.

These two viewed literally thousands of vehicles crossing the Antioch Bridge until they froze a frame from 1:28 P.M. on Thursday, August 3. They saw a white pickup truck pulling a trailer with a watercraft on it. There were three people in the truck, but the videotape did not give a good view of their faces, nor did it pick up the license plate number. But it did show a multicolored personal watercraft on the trailer. A logo read, "Rent me." This matched the crafts rented at Cool Rides.

One person who was a great help to the detectives was Cal Fed supervisor Vicki Sexton. She had been helping them ever since August 7. She related, "On Monday (August 7, 2000), I saw on Channel 2 that an elderly couple named the Stinemans were missing. I became very alarmed. I started processing information. Then I started hearing about Selina Bishop being missing. 'Oh, my God!' I thought. Those are my customers! I have to call the police."

She contacted the Concord Police Department and Marin County Sheriff's Office. She told them there was an account for Justin Helzer at Cal Fed. On July 11, he'd written a check to a store called Bags and Baggage. She also told them that $100,000 went into Selina Bishop's Cal Fed account on August 1, 2000. She'd placed a hard hold on these checks, however, and they had not cleared.

Detectives later noted about Vicki Sexton in their reports that she told Detective Norris that a white female in a wheelchair had shown up at the branch. The woman had been wearing a green top and pants, and a cowboy hat. This had occurred on Tuesday, August 1 at around 2:30 P.M. Sexton had spoken to this women who identified herself as Jackie, but was in fact Dawn Godman. "Jackie" was supposedly a good friend of the Stinemans and close to their supposed grand daughter Selina Bishop.

Godman said that Selina was in San Diego at a hospital and needed money for heart surgery, since she didn't have medical insurance. Godman claimed that

Selina Bishop presently lived in Petaluma. Godman said that she needed two checks to clear the next day. Then Godman said she had driven to the bank, which surprised Vicki Sexton because she was in a wheelchair.

Sexton told Godman that she had to verify the checks before completing the translation. Sexton dialed a phone number printed on one of the Stinemans' checks, and received a message from an answering machine with the voice of an elderly male. She left a message for the Stinemans to call her back, and Godman told her that the Stinemans had just moved and had a new phone number.

Sexton dialed this number, and received another message by a man purporting to be Ivan Stineman. This voice, however, sounded like that of a younger man. The voice was in a monotone and it sounded like he was reading from a script.

Sexton then phoned a Dean Witter office to verify that funds existed in the two accounts covered by the checks. A man there said he needed the Social Security numbers of Ivan and Annette Stineman. Godman said she would get these for Sexton. Sexton began the process of depositing the checks, but she put a hard hold on them until verification could be accomplished.

Financial Crimes Unit detective Patrick Murray, of the CPD, became involved in the money trail. On August 15, he contacted Morgan Stanley/Dean Witter and traced two checks—one for $10,000 and the other for $67,000. He wasn't able to track down a third check for $33,000 then, because it was still being processed.

Police work in all directions was spurred on by receipts and handwritten notes collected at Saddlewood. Edward Berry, of Double Header Pagers, was contacted. It was discovered that an account was made out to a Shirley K. Robinson. When Berry was shown a photo lineup, he picked out a photo of Dawn Godman as Shirley Robinson.

Detective Murray went back to Dean Witter and by then the third check had cleared. It was for the amount of $33,000 and the phone number on the check was the same pager number that Dawn Godman (Shirley Robinson) had.

Murray spoke with Greg Matthias at Dean Witter about Taylor Helzer. Then he spoke with George Calhoun. Murray began checking all the money that both Taylor Helzer and Justin Helzer owed various agencies. He learned that Taylor owed his mother $16,338. Justin owed large amounts to various places, such as $5,200 to Citibank, $5,000 to Metro 1, $7,600 to Household Finance and $2,400 to People's Bank. There seemed to be a financial incentive for murder, as well as some religious angle.

One interesting thing that popped up was a $185 charge to a place called Wet Pleasure in Napa. Murray surmised that Justin might have paid this amount to go "jet skiing" on Lake Berryessa as early as July 2, 2000. Later evidence indicated that Taylor, Dawn and Selina did, in fact, spend time there.

Strange names kept popping up on bills. There was Shirley and Emil Robinson for Pacific Gas and Electric and Concord Disposal Services. Dave and Sherry Birnauf showed up on Contra Costa Water District bills for the Saddlewood residence. Murray guessed that Justin and Dawn were using these false names to get services.

Robert Brady, of the CPD, analyzed the illegal drugs seized from the Saddlewood residence. From the twenty-six packages of pills (ecstasy) found, he concluded that each pill was worth from $15 to $20 dollars if sold at a rave.

* * *

Senior Inspector Ted Spyrow went for a more intensive and thoroughgoing interview with Keri Furman in September 2000. This interview took place in Carmine Carlucci's office in Las Vegas. Detectives Warnock and Oppit were also there. The detectives all wore plain clothes, and they brought along a series of photographs, documents and letters.

During the interview, Keri told them several new things about Taylor. She said, "He was going to find a married couple. [I] would have sex with the married man. Then Taylor would blackmail him."

They asked her about Taylor's fascination with numbers and their meaning in prophecy. She said, "His whole idea was having three core people. Justin was one. He wanted me to be another. He was testing my value of trust. Because I didn't handle it the way he wanted, he didn't trust me at all.

"He always wanted to see if I'd freak out. I was freaking out. He was afraid I'd turn on him. Like I've turned on him now."

Asked about the date rape drug Rohypnol, she said she was living in southern California at the time, away from Taylor. He came down for a visit and they both went to Tijuana and purchased the drug. Senior Inspector Spyrow brought up the plan about getting young women from Mexico to turn into prostitutes. She corrected him and said Taylor wanted them to come from Brazil.

About the Feline Club, she said, "Olivia and I were supposed to help with the operation of the club."

Asked about Taylor's dominance over other people, Keri said, "Taylor had an overpowering power of love. You felt the intensity in your bones. He said that God told him to go on disability. And to sell ecstasy. I was very confused about the teachings of Taylor. We were always butting heads. From day one, it was like that. He felt no guilt about anything he did. He could do no wrong."

When Senior Inspector Spyrow got back to the Bay Area, he looked at a map of the Delta region. At this point, the detectives had no idea where the Children of Thunder had launched their personal watercraft. Spyrow noticed that an area around Korth's Pirate's Lair was circled in ink on a map found at Saddlewood. He decided to go investigate and talked with owner Kip Korth.

Kip Korth owned a little bit of paradise on the Delta. Known as Korth's Pirate's Lair, it included a marina, tree-shaded mobile-home park, restaurant and launching facility. The place had been owned by the Korth family since the 1930s. Subsequent investigations proved that the Children of Thunder had indeed launched from the ramp there. There was a notation on a log-in sheet about a white Nissan pickup that launched a personal watercraft, along with the pickup's license plate number.

Like a giant circular puzzle, the leads, which had started with a duffel bag being found on the North Fork of the Mokelumne River in the Delta, were returning to close the gap on what had occurred during the Days of Thunder.

CHAPTER 12

Crossing the Bar

Taylor's schemes, plots and murders continued to drag more people down with him as the facts came out. In late August 2000, his mother, Carma, had to testify before a grand jury. At the time, it was still not clear to authorities if she had helped Taylor in any of his schemes. After all, he had written her name down on several notes.

Carma spent most of one day testifying before the grand jury, and even a part of a second day. The testimony was sealed, but at one point she did ask for a lawyer. For a short time, Gerry Helzer had to speak before the grand jury as well. He told a reporter later that they were being treated fairly, but he said about Carma's testimony, "She's being pounded in there."

Across town, Taylor Helzer sat in a jail cell along with Justin and Dawn. His lawyer, Suzanne Chapot, told reporters, "He's distraught. He doesn't know what happened." She indicated that he was suffering from mental illness and had done so for a number of years. She added that he was "remorseful and horrified" by what people in jail were telling him that he'd done.

The eighteen counts and thirty-nine overt acts against the Children of Thunder were incredibly long. The count list began with: "On or about March 2000 through August 2000, at Concord of Contra Costa County, the defendants, Glenn Taylor Helzer, Dawn Susan Godman and Justin Alan Helzer, did unlawfully conspire together to commit the crimes of murder, extortion, robbery, burglary, false imprisonment and obstruction of justice."

The overt acts ranged from "the defendants did kill Ivan and Annette Stineman" to "on August 4, 2000, in Oakland, the defendants abandoned Ivan and Annette Stineman's van."

Just where the trial would be held was a matter of conjecture. Jenny Villarin and James Gamble had been murdered in Marin County, while the Stinemans and Selina Bishop had been killed in Contra Costa County, and the body parts had been discovered in Sacramento County. Finally Marin County and Sacramento County agreed that Contra Costa was the appropriate site for the trial. Sergeant Doug Pittman said, "This decision is based on the fact that the circumstances leading to these killings had their genesis in Contra Costa County and that a majority of the overt acts attributed to the conspiracy to commit these murders occurred in Contra Costa County."

"Remorseful and horrified"—or not—by the crimes, Taylor Helzer had to face a hearing. During the proceedings, Deputy DA Harold Jewett alluded to the fact that Taylor had tried to sell his story for $400,000 to *Playboy* magazine. Suzanne Chapot made no comment about this matter, but Gerry Helzer did. He told a reporter that Taylor had thought of selling his story, then decided that if there was a buyer, he would donate the money to charity.

Justin's lawyer, William Veale, was trying already to distance his client from his older brother. Veale said, "I don't have any reason to believe that Justin Helzer killed anybody, hurt anybody or stole from anyone, and we will prove that in court."

Taylor and the others had plenty to worry about, however. Deputy DA Harold Jewett said that he would be seeking the death penalty against all of them. He told reporters, "The interests of justice would be served by the imposition of the death penalty for anybody who was directly involved in these brutal murders and really callous desecration of the bodies. It was methodical and almost clinical. There was almost sacrilegious mistreatment of the bodies."

In fact, some authorities wondered if there had been satanic rites performed because of the removal of Annette Stineman's internal organs. Her heart had been stabbed many times, apparently after it had been removed. There was no logical explanation for that.

Jewett went on to say, "I do not believe Selina Bishop was part of this extortion. There is some indication that she had prior knowledge of a grand get-rich-quick scheme by Taylor Helzer. I feel reasonably certain that not later than the time the Stinemans were killed, it became apparent for the Helzers that Selina knew more than was safe for them."

The proceedings for Taylor, Justin and Dawn came one month to the day after they were arrested. At one point during the proceedings, Taylor, who was supposedly suffering from mental illness, told Judge Michael Coleman, "Personally, I don't understand why we can't just say what happened to get it over with." His attorney, Suzanne Chapot, cut him off before he could say anything else.

Taylor, however, had a hard time being quiet. At another point, he told the judge, "Your Honor, I've wanted to tell about this for a long time."

When Deputy DA Jewett asked Taylor if he realized he was giving up his right to a speedy preliminary hearing, Taylor said, "I'm not sure what you're doing."

Irked by Taylor's behavior, Jewett responded, "Listen to me closely!"

After the hearing, Chapot told reporters, "He's disturbed and scared."

Justin's attorney, William Veale, said, "He's (Justin) got a gun in the house, but anybody who was in that house had access to it. Taylor Helzer had access to that house and to that gun. They (the prosecution) don't know who did what and they leapt to the worst possible conclusion."

At the proceedings, Jewett told Judge Coleman rather optimistically: "I hope that all of the forensic examinations will be completed by the end of November."

That Taylor, Justin and Dawn would not receive a speedy preliminary hearing was an understatement. It was eventually scheduled for January 5, 2001, and then moved to April. Even that was too optimistic. By the one-year anniversary of the abduction of the Stinemans, the preliminary hearing had still not taken place.

Even Taylor was frustrated by the delays. He told a judge during a brief hearing on July 28, 2001, "I wish it would happen a lot sooner. I don't understand why it takes so long for this process."

Part of the reason for the delays was the subpoenaing of 450 witnesses and the collection of thousands of pages of documents. Harold Jewett said, "There is a huge amount of information in this case. It is the largest and most complex case that I have ever seen."

In fact, the amount of documents and evidence filled two entire storage rooms.

On the one-year anniversary of the crimes, *San Francisco Chronicle* reporter Sam McMannis wrote, "If one thought the Helzer brothers' alleged crimes would drive longtime residents out of the neighborhood or make them cower inside their homes in fear, you are wrong. None of the seven home owners has moved or even considered leaving."

Alfred Rivera, who lived on Saddlewood Court, told him that the crimes could have happened anywhere. Rivera said that he felt sorry for the landlord. The house had not been rented since the murders in August 2000. Rivera also said he knew it would be difficult to find any renters for the place, considering its violent past.

Christine Rivera said that she'd lived in the neighborhood for twenty years and had raised two kids there. She added that the only way she was leaving the area was when they took her out in a pine box.

Neighbor Kaye Shaman, who'd found the bloody piece of flesh near her garden hose, said, "I'm not comfortable with the thing that happened. But I'm very comfortable with the court."

In fact, the neighbors often got together to discuss what had happened and to talk about the case as it moved along in the court. Alfred Rivera said he hoped the owner would just sell the place. Then he laughed nervously and added that if Mr. Cheng rented the place again, he hoped the landlord would be more careful about the renters.

Across the bay in Marin County at Forest Knolls, in a local park, an eight-foot-high grizzly bear had been carved from an old pine tree to commemorate Jenny and Selina's affection for bears. A potluck dinner was served at the Paper Mill Creek Saloon, followed by live music by Walt Dixon and the Sky Blue Band.

The summer of 2001 went by and still there was no preliminary hearing for Taylor, Justin or Dawn. There were arguments by the defense lawyers that Harold Jewett's murder and conspiracy charges were "vague" and should be thrown out. Jewett countered that his briefs were lengthy, cogent and detailed.

On top of this, a lawyer for Taylor, deputy public defender Simone Shaheen, asked that the upcoming hearing be closed to the media. The *San Francisco Chronicle, Contra Costa Times* and KGO-TV argued that very little media attention had been exhibited since the fall of 2000 and that there was a jury pool in Contra Costa County that numbered into the hundreds of thousands.

Jewett joined in the fray by saying media publicity was not only necessary, but therapeutic for the public. He added, "You could no more put a lid on the facts of this case than you could on the events of September eleventh. One of the reasons we have the Fourth Estate (the media) is so that we can know. So that we don't live in fear and ignorance."

In the end, Superior Court judge Douglas Cunningham came down on the side of the media. The hearing would be open to public scrutiny.

When the preliminary hearing did begin on December 3, 2001, more new evidence came to light. Detective Heidi Stephenson said that Taylor Helzer had not only killed the victims, but he had planned to fake his own death as well. By this means, he hoped to go underground after the crimes.

Stephenson also spoke about Debra McClanahan, who allegedly had taught Dawn Godman the pagan practices of Wicca.

When McClanahan took the stand, she confirmed

her allegiance to Wicca. She spoke of herself as a good witch. She also said that she had taught Dawn and Taylor some spells. She said that Taylor sometimes referred to himself as a warlock.

Debra even looked the part of a "good witch" on the stand. She wore a flowing black skirt with a white ruffled blouse.

Debra spoke of how Taylor had instructed her to buy four movie tickets and four meals on July 30, 2000. She said she knew she was creating an alibi, "But I didn't know what for."

Asked by Jewett why she had done such a thing, she answered, "Loyalty, fear, love, disbelief and denial."

Debra went on to say that Taylor had claimed that "he was legally crazy and that if he was ever caught, he would never be held responsible for his actions."

There were often contentious confrontations between Deputy DA Jewett and the various lawyers for the defense. At one point, Dawn's lawyer pointed out that there was a huge amount of paperwork and "the devil is in the details."

"Among other things!" Jewett sarcastically shot back, in reference to the attorney's client and Dawn's possible links to satanic rituals.

The preliminary hearing bumped along with objections and counterobjections by both sides. By February 2002, it was agreed that the actual trial would not take place before 2003, and the judge on the case would be the Honorable Mary Ann O'Malley.

Something happened on the way to trial, however. On August 4, 2002, Martinez jail guards were going to check Taylor Helzer's cell. Taylor barricaded the cell door with a chair. Deputies activated the SERT (Special Events Response Team), which was like a jail SWAT team. They broke into the cell and discovered a forty-foot rope that Taylor had constructed out of sheets and

T-shirts. On one end of the rope, he'd hooked a few feet of fishing line, which had somehow been smuggled into the jail. On another rope, he'd attached a screw and a pencil. Some in law enforcement believed this rope was to act as a garrote. Taylor could use it to strangle a guard if he needed to do so.

Taylor stated he planned to hang himself with the rope. That struck the SERT members as highly unlikely—it didn't take forty feet of rope to hang oneself.

In June 2003, Judge Mary Ann O'Malley ruled against a change-of-venue motion brought forth by Taylor's lawyer. The defense had cited a statistic that showed when four hundred Contra Costa residents were asked about the Helzers, 67.6 knew about the crimes. Judge O'Malley, however, said that press coverage of the crimes had been "factual and not inflammatory."

A new date of October 20 was set for the trial to begin, but all of this was thrown off track when Dawn Godman agreed to plead guilty if the death penalty was removed from her case.

Deputy DA Jewett told reporters, "Ms. Godman was specifically advised that because of the nature of the charges and her pleas, she would never be released. She understood that and she chose to plead guilty anyway."

In exchange for thirty-seven years to life, Dawn would have to testify in the trial against Taylor and Justin. This was a real coup for the prosecutor. Now he had someone within Children of Thunder to tell what had been going on all through May, June and July 2000.

Interestingly enough, Suzanne Chapot, Taylor's lawyer, had been angling for the very same kind of deal from Jewett for Taylor. She said, "We have three people blamed with murders and numerous offenses, and all of a sudden, three years into the case, the prosecution decides

one of them shall not be given death." Then she added
that Jewett had rebuffed her attempts for a plea bargain
that would have given Taylor life without parole. There
was a good reason for this, at least in Harold Jewett's eyes.
He never had a doubt, since the fall of 2000, who had
been the mastermind behind the Children of Thunder.

"The agreement came as a surprise to the attorneys defending thirty-three-year-old Taylor Helzer
and thirty-one-year-old Justin, who face the same
charges as well as the death penalty." Suzanne Chapot
told the court, "Ms. Godman's account of the events
that occurred during the week of July 30, 2000, radi-
cally alters my strategy for Taylor's defense," according to the *Contra Costa Times*.

She noted that Dawn's new confession to authorities lasted seven hours and was videotaped. Daniel
Cook, Justin's lawyer, said that he had not yet seen the
videotape.

Nineteen days later, Cook stated that Justin was
changing his plea to "not guilty by reason of insanity." Cook said, "This is something that has to be
done far enough in advance so that evaluations can
be done."

January 30, 2004, rolled around with another hearing for the Helzer brothers. As they sat with their
prospective lawyers at the long defense table, they
seemed fairly upbeat and chatty. By contrast, Harold
Jewett sat all alone on the prosecution side. He seemed
very focused on his paperwork.

Taylor's attorney Suzanne Chapot wanted a severance of her client's trial from that of Justin, and a
continuance as well because of all the evidence that had
to be read and absorbed. Judge O'Malley, however, said
that March 20 was late enough for jury selection to
begin, and denied the motion.

An argument soon erupted over whether a group of jurors should be present during voir dire, or if they should be brought in individually. Jewett testily said to Chapot, "We do not think that jurors are sheep."

Chapot shot back, "We are not saying jurors are sheep! I resent the implications of Mr. Jewett! We have conducted ourselves with the highest professionalism."

Judge O'Malley chuckled wistfully and said, "Oh, I see we're off to a good start."

Before jury selection began on March 20, Taylor Helzer threw everyone for a loop, including his own lawyer, over her objections. On March 5, Taylor dropped a bombshell on the court. "The announcement through his attorney that he (Taylor) wanted to plead guilty to eighteen felony counts stunned everyone in the courtroom and left the judge speechless," reported the *Contra Costa Times*.

This left Taylor without any deal in place from the prosecutor, and he still faced the death penalty. "He understands that this does nothing in terms of sentencing," Chapot said. "He is still facing a possible death sentence. But this is still what he wants to do."

Daniel Cook, Justin's lawyer, was just as surprised as everyone else. He told reporters, "This is a monumental change in the landscape. I have never been involved in or heard of a case like this."

Harold Jewett was very skeptical of Taylor's motives. He prodded Taylor with questions about his sudden plea of guilty.

Jewett: Are you doing this to assist your brother?

Helzer: No.

Jewett: Are you doing this to influence the order of trials?

Helzer: I have no expectation of that. It's just not okay for me to implicate someone else. I'm not necessarily trying to help my brother. I also have no intention of harming him.

Olga Land, Selina Bishop's aunt and Jennifer Villarin's sister, told a *Contra Costa Times* reporter, "It felt good to hear. We already knew it, but it was good to hear him say it (that he was guilty of the crimes)."

In light of these developments, Judge Mary Ann O'Malley agreed to a severance of Justin's trial from Taylor's sentencing trial. As reported in the *San Francisco Chronicle*, "Legal experts said the move was extremely rare but could help his brother (Justin) because separate trials generally favor defendants by allowing them to shift responsibility for the crime to their alleged accomplices."

Judge O'Malley ruled that Justin could not get a fair trial if his case was joined to that of an accomplice who had already pleaded guilty. Then the question arose— which trial should come first? Justin's lawyer Cook said, "Justin should be tried last so he could testify to his brother's childhood and close relationship."

Taylor weighed into the argument as well, saying he would waive his right to protect himself from self-incrimination and testify, but only if the matter of the death penalty had been resolved. In essence, he was trying to get in a "backdoor" agreement of a life sentence.

Daniel Cook was adamant about Taylor's knowledge of events. He told reporters, "No one, and I mean no one, can tell it (the story) the way he can."

Jewett responded, "This court has to examine, frankly, what is looking a lot like gamesmanship, whether or not Taylor Helzer would be a benefit to his brother if he testifies. I'd be happy to cross-examine Taylor Helzer right now."

That didn't happen, but Suzanne Chapot weighed in as well. She said, "Taylor wants to help his brother. He takes responsibility for this."

In the end, Judge O'Malley decided that Justin's trial would come first. It would consist of three phases. The first phase was to determine innocence or guilt. If Justin was found guilty, then there would be a sanity phase. If he was found to be sane at the time of the crimes, there would be a third phase determining punishment.

Jury selection began for Justin Helzer's trial in late March 2004. Even before this event, Deputy DA Jewett and Daniel Cook argued over the preamble to be read to jurors about Justin's alleged crimes. Jewett wanted a lengthy version, and Cook wanted a much shorter one. There were also huge differences about showing the jurors photographs of the nude, bloody bodies of Jennifer Villarin and James Gamble. Cook thought these were too inflammatory, while Jewett said they showed the brutality of the crimes. Judge O'Malley ruled that the photos would stay in.

Judge O'Malley did side with Cook on the matter of Taylor Helzer's supposedly feigned mental illness and what he had told Keri Furman about it. O'Malley said this was too remote from Justin's trial to be admitted and that it should be a part of Taylor's trial and not Justin's.

More legal wrangling followed on March 25. One area of contention was Taylor's ties to Wicca and witchcraft. Cook wanted all of this excluded, saying that Justin was no part of it, but Jewett alluded to both brothers' relationship with Debra McClanahan and Taylor's statement to Justin's friend Mike Henderson that he was a warlock at the Saddlewood home. Then he added,

"Justin followed Taylor's prophecies into departures from reality. Intentions and motivations are a part of this case. They (Justin and Taylor) were with a self-proclaimed witch."

Cook responded, "We already know the scenario with witchcraft. Justin never said he was a warlock."

Judge O'Malley finally ruled, "I can see that there might be a possibility on this issue. We'll have to wait and see." She left the door open on the issue of witchcraft admissibility. Then she cautioned, "This will be a fine line. Everyone is on notice about this."

There was even contention between the prosecution and defense on when jurors would fill out the questionnaire. Cook wanted jurors to air their feelings about the burden of proof before filling out the questionnaire. Jewett responded that if that happened, "they might answer the questionnaire with all the frivolity of answering questions at a cocktail party. It is vital that they be mindful of their civic duties."

Cook declared, "I cannot imagine that anyone coming into this room will mistake this for a cocktail party! What I want to see is if someone has a difference of experience [about the court system], and if they cannot put that aside, there is a danger that people will conceal their true feelings on a questionnaire."

Judge O'Malley responded to Cook by saying, "I see your point. But I have to say, even after having questioned hundreds of potential jurors, I'm surprised how naive people can be about a courtroom. I've had people say it was a good experience after eight weeks of trial, and they certainly didn't feel that way when they came in. I think the questionnaire is so specific, we'll get a lot of honest opinions. They will be forced to write down what they feel."

On April 5, 2004, the jury selection began in Justin Helzer's trial with a jury pool of 350 people. The possibility of a change of venue still hung in the air, even while this was going on. Daniel Cook told reporters, "If we are confronted with what we think is prejudice created by experience of the media, then we might seek to renew our request for a change of venue."

In the matter of publicity, one unforeseen situation was helping deflect a lot of media attention that might have been there otherwise. Across the bay in San Mateo County, the Scott Peterson trial was under way. It drew news agencies from around the country. Judge Mary Ann O'Malley, by contrast, would not allow any cameras, video or still to be in her courtroom during witness testimony, and only very limited use of a still camera during recesses.

The *Contra Costa Times* noted that "maybe we're in the shadow of [the Peterson trial] right now."

Shadows or not, the process of culling potential jurors from the pool was lengthy and arduous. After dismissing many for hardship reasons, the ones who made it past that still had to answer a questionnaire that had 130 questions. As the potential jurors were whittled down from 350 to the final twelve (two men and ten women), with four alternates, Cook told them, "All I want of you is to go back into that room when you deliberate, with an open mind. I'll tell you right now, if there is a guilty verdict in this case, you will be asked if he is sane or insane."

One potential juror replied when questioned, "I think anyone who commits a murder must be insane."

Cook replied, "I agree with that."

Cook also asked jurors if they thought an insanity plea was just a gimmick to escape the death penalty. Some of them did, and others didn't. One woman said, "You have to take it one step at a time. You can't be looking at the end result."

This was the kind of juror that both Cook and Jewett were looking for.

At one point, Justin looked straight at a pretty young blond woman who was being questioned. A short time later, she looked straight back at him and said, "It's a personal thing now. But I honestly believe I can keep an open mind."

The topic of gruesome photos as evidence came up, and Jewett said, "I have to know if viewing them will be a problem. You have to look at them, but they're horrible."

Cook also addressed this issue. He said, "I need to know if your experience would be—they'd be so troubling, you couldn't focus after that."

Other issues came up as well. One woman's grandparents were Mormon. Cook told all the potential jurors, "There are some people who think the Latter-Day Saints are terrible. Others think it is the greatest thing on earth. I have to ask how you feel about the Church."

Cook also touched on the death penalty issue. He said, "In California, only people who commit first-degree murder under special circumstances are eligible for the death penalty. But not all of them get the death penalty. As jurors, you must decide which ones should, and which ones don't."

Cook's lengthy questioning of potential jurors began to reach the point of repetition. Frustrated by the lengthy process, Judge O'Malley told him, "We have to get through twenty-four people today, not twelve people today."

Five days later, the process was still going on, and Jewett said, "The decision whether a person lives or dies is a personal one. If we reach that phase, by that time you would have been here three months. Then it won't be an abstraction. I am compelled to ask you, could you really impose the penalty on Justin Helzer? Could you?"

Most of the jurors looked directly at Justin sitting at the defense table. He did not move a muscle as the jurors wrestled with that question.

Jewett's question was more than just rhetorical. One by one, he asked the potential jurors if they could impose the death penalty on Justin Helzer. One person answered emphatically that she could not. She was eventually let go.

Even Charles Hoehn, Justin's other defense attorney, asked the potential jurors, "Are you right for this trial? If not, now is the time to say so."

On April 29, 2004, two men and ten women, and four alternates, had come to grips about whether or not they could impose death on Justin. They were no longer potential jurors—they were actual jurors in the case of *The People of California* v. *Justin Alan Helzer.*

Daniel Cook told reporters, "This case is so unusual, it's going to be difficult for everyone involved in it. This is an enormous undertaking."

Deputy DA Harold Jewett agreed. He said, "It has more evidence than other trials and some unique qualities. We've got a long road ahead."

Just as everyone predicted, the following months of spring and summer 2004 would be focused within four walls of Department 4 of the Bray Courthouse in Martinez. By the time they were done, their lives, those of the victims' family members, and that of Justin Helzer, would be changed forever.

CHAPTER 13

The Forum

A trial is an odd combination of high drama, tedium, hard work and incredible theater. Unlike theater, however, the ending is never predictable, nor is the script. The law keeps everything within certain boundaries, but human emotions on both sides of the table, within the jury and within the gallery come into play. In the four-month ordeal that would be the Justin Helzer trial, the gallery became almost a second home for several residents of Contra Costa County. Coming from different backgrounds, age groups and viewpoints, they would form a bond not only among themselves, but with the victims' families, and even to a degree with Justin's mother and sister, and the attorneys and Judge O'Malley.

One of these court observers was Martinez resident Roger Riddle. Riddle was not a stranger to violence—he had been an infantryman in Vietnam during the worst years of the conflict. He'd not only seen his share of horror there, he'd been the victim of a violent crime when he lived in Vallejo, California. An intruder came into his house, knocked him unconscious, robbed the house and left him for dead. Luckily, a friend stopped by the next day and found him still alive. He was rushed to the hospital and recovered.

When asked why he was attending the Helzer trials, Riddle answered, "The crimes were so horrendous, I wanted to see these guys in person. I'd seen the crimes in the newspaper and on television and I'd been to other trials before. But I'd never seen anything like this."

Retirement community residents Ray and Mabel Carberry also became faithful court observers. Ray was an ex-navy man, who had been in ports around the world, and Mabel's son-in-law was a deputy district attorney in a different county. They were drawn to a trial that was sure to be very dramatic. Some of the events had happened not far from where they lived. Even more strangely, they were married on the very same weekend, July 29, 2000, when the Helzer brothers kidnapped the Stinemans.

Thirty-one-year-old Chris Darden, a helicopter pilot, got hooked on the case when he volunteered to search by helicopter for Ivan and Annette Stineman. He later said, "I lost some faith in humanity when I listened to the details of the Helzer brothers' grisly crime spree. Now I don't put anything past anyone. This wasn't a Hollywood story. It happened and it happened in Concord!"

Forty-four-year-old Juley Salkeld also became a court observer. She was a law student who planned to be a prosecutor one day. She said, "All the phases of this case and trial are fascinating."

In time, these court observers would even be written about in the *Contra Costa Times*. The headlines stated: COURT WATCHERS PLAY UP THE PART.

Reporter Matt Krupnick wrote, "Like a Broadway musical, the Justin Helzer murder trial has bit players who are unheard but know their cues intimately. Chris

Darden sits in the middle of the back row and always leans forward to keep his injured back from hurting. Mabel and Ray Carberry usually sit somewhere in the third row, with Mabel scribbling notes and sketches on a bound notebook. Juley Salkeld sometimes arrives late, but almost never misses a day."

If ancient Greek drama had a chorus, the court observers in the Justin Helzer trial were a modern equivalent. Victims' family members, bailiffs and even Judge O'Malley noted when they skipped a day, and said that they missed their presence.

On the last day of April 2004, the trial of *California* v. *Justin Alan Helzer* began. Judge Mary Ann O'Malley presided in a black robe. Yet not even the austere robe could hide her charming grace and good looks. At one point, Chris Darden whispered to Ray, "She looks like Princess Diana."

Ray, who is Irish, scoffed at the "English Rose" allusion, but admitted that "Judge Mary is very sweet and friendly." Then he noted that her last name was O'-Malley, after all.

Judge O'Malley was more than just a figurehead or a pretty face, however. She had a keen intellect and incisive understanding of the law. She also had a firm grasp of courtroom dynamics. On several occasions, she thanked the jury for being so attentive and focused. She won them over by her frank appraisal of different situations and her good humor during breaks. She even led them in stretching exercises during breaks, knowing how tedious it can be to sit hour after hour, listening to sometimes boring testimony.

Mabel Carberry said, "The time it took to get qualified jurors, and all the work, I credit Judge Mary Ann O'Malley for staying the course. She called the shots, gave the jurors exercise time on the spur of the moment and allowed beverages in the courtroom. She was outstanding, personable and lovely."

The formal counts against Justin were so numerous, it took nearly a half hour for the court clerk, Tom Moyer to read them. They ranged from Count 1 to Count 18, with thirty-nine overt acts tacked on.

Deputy DA Harold Jewett got things rolling by laying out the entire case in chronological order, starting with the lives of Ivan and Annette Stineman. He delved into their marriage, the birth of daughters Nancy and Judy, and Ivan's taking on Taylor Helzer as his financial adviser. He spoke of Taylor befriending the Stinemans, and even taking them on a white-water raft trip. He spoke of Taylor's betrayal of their trust. He also spoke of Justin's overwhelming admiration of Taylor.

Jewett spoke of Taylor's feigned mental illness at Dean Witter, his life with Keri Furman, raves, drugs and his growing ambitions. Impact America was detailed, the Children of Thunder, and Dawn and Selina as well. Jewett spoke at length about the murderous week of July 30 to August 7, 2000, and the depositing of body bags in the Delta. He talked about how Justin followed almost all of Taylor's orders, no matter how murderous, or how bizarre. By the time Jewett was through, his voice had reached a crescendo and three hours had elapsed. Still, he'd only scratched the surface of the incredible events perpetrated by Taylor, Justin and Dawn.

By contrast, Justin's main defense attorney, Daniel Cook, was soft-spoken. In looks and style, there was a touch of Bobby Kennedy in him. He told the jurors, "Please keep your minds open. Mr. Jewett laid out a good road map. But we need more than road maps. To understand the truth, we have to look at why the case is about a test of faith. It's about a test of faith [for

Justin] in his brother. That brother spoke as if he was a prophet of God."

Cook spoke of Taylor's overwhelming influence on Justin. "Justin wanted to do good. But Justin was a nerd. He was slow and he had no self-confidence. He would do what his mother wanted, but it was never enough.

"Taylor, on the other hand, could light up a room. He could charm your socks off. He felt he was always right. He tolerated no dissension. Taylor preyed on people. He was powerful and skillful. He could quote scripture. He always made sure his circle of people were under his control.

"The evidence will show that Justin was not a schemer, a planner or a criminal. Justin was a follower who worshiped Taylor. And Taylor knew that Justin would do anything he asked.

"When Justin grew up, he was straight as an arrow. He never drank a beer, smoked a cigarette or masturbated. He couldn't get a date, couldn't hold a job, and he was not good at school. He eventually got a two-year degree. He also went on a two-year mission for the LDS Church. This was considered good by his community. He achieved something. He became a man.

"But Taylor said the Church had it all wrong."

Cook told of Taylor and everyone in his orbit going to Impact and Harmony. Cook said, "Harmony stripped away Justin's last layer of defense. From then on, Justin jumped when Taylor said to jump."

Then Cook put a hand over his heart and said, "We have to find the truth. A man will be here every day in this court. He is not here today, but he is powerful. A skillful manipulator who consumed everyone around him. Justin is not that man. The man is Taylor."

Opening arguments lasted until 2:24 P.M. on the first day of court. At that point, Jewett told Judge O'Malley that there was a matter he needed to address.

The jury was led out of the courtroom into the hallway by bailiff Mike Harkelroad.

When they were gone, Jewett said, "I got a voice mail message during the lunch hour."

At that point, Judge O'Malley said, "I want this in camera (in private)."

As she, Jewett and Cook started for the judge's chambers, an AP reporter suddenly stood up and declared, "I object in the name of freedom of the press!"

Everyone was momentarily stunned, including Judge O'Malley. She frowned at the female reporter but did not respond. Judge O'Malley and the others went into chambers.

On their return into court, O'Malley said, "Now on the record, I will not have any outbursts in my court! If you do, you will be removed."

Confrontations with this reporter were far from over, however. During a break, she was out in the hallway, talking to her editor on a cell phone. Unfortunately for her, she was speaking in the presence of two jurors about the trial. The jurors were so upset about this, they both complained to the bailiff about it. When the bailiff brought this to Judge O'Malley's attention, O'Malley became incensed, after having already given a warning.

When court reconvened, Judge O'Malley said to the reporter, "Explain yourself."

Reporter: I called my manager.

O'Malley: Why in front of my jurors?

Reporter: This is not my experience. I said, "The judge has gone into closed court. What should I do?"

O'Malley: I don't want my jurors to hear comments.

Reporter: You don't want any of us phoning out in the hall?

O'Malley (stern voice): You will not phone in front of the jurors! Maybe a mistrial will happen and, I assure you, not even your manager would want that!

The next trial day, Monday, May 3, 2004, was all business by comparison. Harold Jewett began the long parade of witnesses with people who had known Ivan and Annette Stineman, including their daughter Nancy Hall.

The next set of witnesses were neighbors and people who had seen two strange young men in suits approaching the Stinemans' door on Sunday, July 30, 2000.

Jewett then questioned Jeanette Carter about Taylor, Justin and Dawn's life in the Mormon Church and her meeting him on "Murder Mystery Night" at the Singles Third Ward in Walnut Creek.

Jewett's questioning of Bishop Brett Halversen, of the LDS, delved into the matter of Mormon doctrine and the Helzer brothers' deviation from them. Halversen had been a Mormon since the age of eight, and he was now sixty-seven years old. He spoke of the foundations of the faith, which according to Mormon doctrine went back to 2200 B.C. centered in the Holy Land of Palestine. Key to the faith was the period from 600 B.C. to 400 A.D that chronicled the history of the Nephites. According to Mormon doctrine, Nephi lived with his family near Jerusalem around 600 B.C. and an epochal event happened when Nephi encountered Laban, who was keeper of the holy records of his people and their covenant with God. Nephi knew that Laban was not the right man to be keeper of the golden tablets that recorded the history.

Laban refused to give over the sacred tablets to Nephi by right of ownership, nor would he sell them to him. Realizing that Laban was drunk and unworthy of the sacred tablets, Nephi used Laban's own sword to kill him. Then putting on Laban's clothing, to fool the guards, Nephi secreted the tablets out of their hiding place.

According to Halversen, "Nephi received inspiration from God to do the act. He got an okay from God to kill Laban."

This was an important concept, not only for Nephi in 600 B.C., but for Taylor Helzer and the Children of Thunder in 2000 A.D. All of these individuals believed they received divine sanction to kill to further a greater good. To have turned their backs on God's command in their estimation would have been sacrilegious. But whereas Nephi received a divine message from God, according to Halversen, Taylor Helzer did not.

Halversen also spoke of how Nephi and his family traveled from Palestine to the New World of the Americas. Daniel Cook objected to the long narrative of Mormon history and scripture, saying it was irrelevant. He was overruled by Judge O'Malley.

Bishop Halversen then spoke of Nephi and his family in the Americas, and the split between himself and Laman, his brother. Two separate and antagonistic cultures evolved from this split—the Nephites and the Lamanites. The epic of their struggle was eventually written down on golden tablets and became the Book of Mormon. Around 400 A.D., according to Mormon doctrine, the golden tablets were buried beneath a hill in what would later become New York State. It was the hill of Cumorah, near present-day Manchester, New York.

There the golden tablets would rest until discovered by Joseph Smith in the 1820s.

Halversen spoke of the "Latter-Day" portion of Latter-Day Saints as a reference to their belief that they were living in the latter days of the world before Christ's Second Coming. Halversen said, "Perhaps the Last Days are now. It would be a time of the decline of moral values and moral issues. They would be days of darkness."

Halversen also delved into the importance of certain numbers in the Mormon faith. The number 3 was important and would lead to Taylor's insistence on "three core people" in his group. Twelve was also important, because of Jesus' Twelve Apostles. And 15 was as well, adding the 3 and 12 together. Halversen spoke of the three top leaders in the Mormon Church and their twelve apostles. He said, "An individual can receive a revelation from God for themselves. But only the fifteen can have a revelation from God for the Church as a whole in the world."

He added, "Spirit is the essence of the Heavenly Father's will. The Holy Spirit prompts people to do God's will. All individuals have a spirit. They were spirits before they were born, and become spirits after death."

The Mormon faith went along with the Book of Revelation in the Bible about the "war in heaven." The War in Heaven contained such passages as:

He is clad in a robe dripped in blood, and the name of which he is called is the Word of God. And the armies of heaven, arrayed in fine linen, white and pure, followed him on white horses. From his mouth issues a sharp sword with which to smite the nations, and he will rule them with a rod of iron; he will tread the wine press of the fury of the wrath of God the Almighty.

And when the thousand years are ended, Satan will be loosed from his prison and will come out to deceive the nations which are at the four corners of the earth, that is, Gog and Magog, to gather them for battle; their number is like the

*sands of the sea. And they marched up over the broad earth
and surrounded the camp of the saints and the beloved city;
but fire came down from heaven and consumed them and the
devil who had deceived them was thrown into a lake of fire
and brimstone where the beast and the false prophet were, and
they will be tormented day and night for ever and ever.*

In an interesting comment that could have easily
been about Taylor, Halversen said, "Lucifer had
charisma to draw his brothers toward evil."

Bishop Halversen also brought up anecdotes about
the importance of seer stones in the Mormon faith. In
the Introduction of the Book of Mormon, it is stated:

*In due course, the plates were delivered to Joseph Smith who
translated them by the gift and power of God.*

Smith, according to the Book of Mormon, was able
to do so by the use of seer stones:

*He (Moroni) said there was a book deposited, written upon
gold plates, giving an account of the former inhabitants of
this continent. . . . Also, that there were two stones in silver
bows and these stones fastened to a breastplate, constituted
what is called Urim and Thummim—deposited with the
plates; and the possession and use of these stones were what
constituted seers in ancient or former times; and that God
had prepared them for the purpose of translating the book.*

Taylor also laid great stock in seer stones. Several
gem-type stones were found in his bedroom, and one
of the staffs in the house held a large crystal in carved
eagle's claws, although this particular one apparently
was owned by Dawn Godman.

Halversen's questioning from Jewett wasn't all about
Mormon doctrine—he was questioned about his per-

sonal relationships with Taylor, Justin and Dawn as well. Halversen had been bishop for the Singles Third Ward in the 1990s and knew Dawn very well. He said, "She was a person coming off the street. She had great needs. She had a child part of the time. A boy of five or six. She sought financial assistance and we gave her money for food and shelter. She made progress while a member of the Latter-Day Saints. Her ability to be in society. As a whole person, she was better."

Then he said, "In the summer of 1999, she wanted money to attend Harmony. It was that one of the twelve apostles of the LDS said to avoid self-awareness programs. So my response was no, for Harmony."

Around this time, Halversen became aware that Taylor Helzer was starting to attend meetings at the Singles Third Ward along with his brother, Justin. Halversen recalled, "He (Taylor) was unusual. His clothing was atypical. He had a long beard and his appearance was unkempt. He looked like a nineteenth-century preacher."

Taylor's parking-lot meetings were disturbing to Halversen, because he seemed to be deviating from Mormon doctrine. Many of the things he had to say made no sense in the prescribed teachings of Mormonism.

Halversen said, "The Latter-Day Saints never recognized Taylor Helzer to receive divine revelations for the Church."

Halversen had conversations with Justin around this time and discovered that Justin had many ideas that were contradictory to the Mormon faith. By now, Justin had started to believe many precepts encapsulated in Buddhism and Zen philosophy.

Besides all the witnesses on the stand, there were also several court battles about the admissibility of evidence. One such confrontation concerned Taylor's flight from detectives at the time of his arrest at Saddlewood. Jewett wanted this to be heard by the jury, and Daniel Cook did not.

"I want to contest the events of the flight as inflammatory and had nothing to do with Justin. It is prejudicial and the jury may think that egregious conduct is linked to Justin," Cook argued.

Judge O'Malley sided with Cook on this matter, and the events about the flight of Taylor was not heard by the jury. On other matters, Cook was not so lucky. He wanted to get in evidence that Justin was nonaggressive at Harmony meetings and stories from all the people who maintained what a "nice guy" he was.

Cook: Justin went to Harmony in 1999. It is not a remote issue.

O'Malley: You are getting in inadmissible evidence.

Cook: He was nonaggressive there.

O'Malley: I don't want to go there. You're trying to go back to family occurrences. He's a nice guy, et cetera. I don't want any more incidents like that.

There were times that the prosecution and defense also had problems with witnesses testimony. Jeanette Carter seemed to have made statements to Detective Chiabotti in 2000 different from the ones she was making on the stand now. Jewett asked her, "Were you trying to deceive Detective Chiabotti?"

Carter answered, "No."

Jewett asked, "And are you trying to deceive the people in the jury box today?"

Carter once again replied, "No."

Other witnesses were very helpful on the witness stand for Jewett, however. Michael Henderson was one of the few people to have been allowed at the house on Saddlewood. He told of Justin showing him the 9mm Beretta semiautomatic that Taylor would use to kill Jenny Villarin and James Gamble. He also told of being invited to dinner at Saddlewood and Dawn proclaiming to be a witch, while Taylor said he was a warlock.

Mabel Carberry said of Deputy DA Jewett, "He was dynamic. He kept the jurors and gallery captivated with clear and positive evidence. He was honest with the victims' family members and let them know what was coming. When you consider the crimes happened four years in the past, he made everything seem like yesterday."

Other witnesses were helpful for the defense, even though they had been called by the prosecution. Kelly Lord told Cook, "I always thought Taylor did the killing. I believe he did all of the killing. I find it very hard to believe that Justin murdered any of them. I look back on all of this and think, 'There but for the grace of God, I could have been Dawn Godman.' As for Godman, Lord said, "Dawn was Selina. Either one of them could have been killed."

Some of the court observers admitted that Cook had a very hard task to perform. Ray Carberry said, "Cook worked very hard on a difficult case." And Juley Salkeld agreed, by saying, "He paid attention to what was happening. He showed passion when he needed to. At one point, he said, 'Your Honor, I'm fighting for my client's life.'"

Other witnesses were very reluctant on the stand, such as Jessyka Chompff during portions of her testimony. She was embarrassed that her affair with Taylor was coming to light in a most public way. Discussed in front of the jury and the gallery, was the fact that she had sex with Taylor and her husband. She admitted that Taylor was a gift from her husband on their wedding night. All three of them were in bed together, and then Alex left and it was only her and Taylor there. Compff said, "Taylor couldn't get an erection, so we did other things."

Christina Kelly was also a reluctant witness at times, especially talking about her involvement with Taylor and Keri about the Feline Club. She was being very careful in her testimony, trying to imply that the Feline Club was an escort service, not a prostitution service. Finally in frustration, Jewett said, "Tell the whole truth!"

If Kelly was being very guarded in her testimony to Jewett, it was nothing compared to the intransigence of Keri Furman. There were problems with her right from the beginning, starting with her no-show at 9:00 A.M. on May 12, 2004, as she was supposed to do.

Keri had been subpoenaed to show up at that hour in court, but she informed Jewett she had written down the wrong flight times from southern California to the Oakland airport. She claimed to have written down 7:51 A.M., rather than 7:15 A.M. There was no way she could be in Martinez for the morning session.

Jewett was not pleased. He asked for a bench warrant and said that if Keri did not arrive in court by 1:30 P.M., she should be arrested and brought into court in handcuffs.

When Keri (now Keri Mendoza) finally did take the stand, she and Jewett were both in a contentious mood. She often answered his question with "I don't remember," or "I don't recall."

At one point *Chronicle* reporter Demian Bulwa counted Mendoza saying, "I don't remember—I don't recall" sixteen times in five minutes.

A constant refrain from Jewett was "Didn't you say . . . ," referring to her comments to detectives in Las Vegas, and her different answers now.

At another point, he was frustrated by how she was now portraying the interview with detectives in Las Vegas. He had proof via audiotapes that her demeanor there had been cooperative, friendly and forthcoming. Now she was saying the detectives had badgered her and intimidated her.

Jewett said, "I'm asking about your conduct in Las Vegas."

Keri answered, "Your messengers (the detectives) were very unprofessional." She accused them of slamming a pile of documents down in front of her, being threatening and even trying to have her sign autographed copies of her nude *Playboy* photos.

Keri's refrain of "I don't recall" became even more pronounced when Jewett asked her about placing $4,000 in Justin's Cal Fed account in June 2000. Jewett asked her, "Do you recall talking to Taylor about depositing money into Justin's Cal Fed account?"

"I don't remember," Keri responded.

"Did you call Taylor on August second?" he asked.

At that point, she said, "I called and he was angry. I just wanted to know how he was doing. I didn't talk about a payment of money."

She did admit a short time later that she supposedly owed Taylor for a loan he had given her to buy her sports car. Then she added one more thing. Keri said that Taylor told her over the phone, "The deal is working out."

Asked by Jewett what the "deal" was, she responded testily, "I didn't want to know, Hal! I didn't want to associate with it."

Jewett said, "Remember, you are under oath."

He asked later, "Did you give any thought [in Las Vegas] of what they were arrested for?"

Keri responded, "You had detectives come see me the same day this happened." (Actually, the detectives met her five days after the arrest.) "You sent your dogs down there!"

"I sent my dogs down there?" Jewett asked incredulously.

"Yes. I didn't want to think about it. I had my career to think about. I don't like you, Hal. You're not my friend. Taylor lied to me, Hal!"

Then she complained that when she received a subpoena recently to appear in court, the deputy serving it in her southern California county had supposedly blocked her in her driveway and threw the subpoena in her face. "You threatened me with arrest!" she cried.

The "dogs" remark particularly piqued Jewett's interest. He asked her, "Ever see any dogs at Saddlewood?"

"No," she said.

Jewett asked Keri about In To Me See and her role in it, especially about helping on the questionnaire.

With barely concealed scorn, she answered, "I don't remember any questionnaire, Hal."

And concerning the Feline Club fronting for a prostitution ring, she said, "I was not a part of that!"

"Weren't you supposed to train the girls?" Jewett asked.

"No!" Keri replied.

Asked if she had told Detective Marziano the truth during his visit in Las Vegas, she was evasive at best. "I was under a lot of stress then," she answered. "I'm not having a very good day now. I don't deserve to be treated like this. I did my part, Hal! I think this is unfair."

Perhaps frustrated by Keri's lack of cooperation,

Judge O'Malley told her that no one was having a good day, and that it would all be over quicker, and less of a torture for her, if she just answered the questions.

Keri was crying almost nonstop by the time Jewett asked her about the Twelve Principles of Magic. She said that Taylor had placed the poster on a refrigerator so that she would have to look at it every time she passed by. Jewett asked about Taylor's contention that there was no right or wrong, and what did she think about that. Keri answered, "I'm not like him. But he didn't like the terms 'right' and 'wrong.' It was the best thing of my life to leave him."

Jewett asked, "It was the best thing of your life to leave him?"

She practically spat back in his face, "What do you think, Hal!"

Asked about a safe, she denied any knowledge of one. Asked about the manufacturing of drugs at Oak Grove, Keri said that she never wanted any manufacturing to take place there and was incensed when she found out about Taylor trying to do that in the garage.

Keri's testimony would have been through in one day, but because of her late arrival and constant verbal battles with Jewett, she was held over for another day to testify. Arriving in court the next morning, she wore the same outfit as the previous day, not realizing earlier that she needed to pack a bag for a two-day endurance test.

At least in the questioning by Daniel Cook, Keri began to feel that she was on safer terrain and regained much of her composure. She talked about a rough childhood and lack of confidence while growing up. She spoke of how Taylor had overwhelmed her when she was still young and naive. She said he had taken advantage of her vulnerability.

Asked if Taylor had ever threatened her, she said,

"Not physically, but near the end, I was scared. I really didn't know this person. I didn't want to know some things about him. Justin never talked to me about what he was up to. They both shut me out."

Keri was finally through on the stand, but her previous statements were not. Jewett wanted to impeach a total of thirteen of her statements that she had made under oath, with variant answers she had given to the investigators over the phone and in her Las Vegas interview. He also wanted to show that the Las Vegas questioning had not been done in an intimidating manner, as she now suggested. In fact, it had not been confrontational at all, and on the audiotapes her willing cooperation and often friendly manner could be heard.

Cook, on the other hand, had a problem with only portions of the transcripts being admitted now. He said that to let the prosecution pick and choose sections from the entire transcript could be unfair to his client, Justin. Cook added, "There are errors in those transcripts. The heart of the matter is, my client has the right to a fair trial. To allow parts of a transcript to be read is not consistent with due process."

Then Cook said that Keri's statements mainly dealt with her days when she shared a house with Taylor and Justin on Oak Grove Road. "Those [thoughts] were focused on certain subject matters there. Ms. Furman's knowledge of Taylor and Justin came from that shared residence." Cook pointed out that Keri had never been in Saddlewood or known anything about the development of Children òf Thunder.

Cook wanted the whole transcript brought in if any portion of it was read. He said, "Keri even told officers that Taylor was a parasite to both her and Justin. In those transcripts, it details [Taylor's] blackmails, crazy ideas, raves, Harmony and questionnaires. Taylor talked about all this stuff as if God were talking to him. I consider Taylor a brainwasher. He could brainwash someone to do anything he wanted."

Cook pointed to a statement Keri made: "Justin would follow anything Taylor asked him to do. So would Dawn."

Cook stated, "All of this is relevant. The rule of law and spirit of the law is such that we must approach this broadly."

The crux of the matter for Judge O'Malley was that if the entire transcript was presented, it would take at least an hour and a half to go through it. She was mindful that the jurors might be lulled into complacency by the droning speech of something being read for that long a time. Cook, however, cited the California Constitution, Article 1—Section 28. It referred to the fact that the time element should not be a factor in deciding how much material was presented before a jury. He said, "We've been here a couple of months, and will be here for a month more. Mr. Jewett has presented exhaustive details and I should have the same right. In the big picture, it won't take that much time."

To Judge O'Malley, it seemed that the rules of law applied to Section 356 of the California evidence code. She said, "My understanding of three fifty-six is that by its nature it doesn't allow the entirety (of a document). The whole is only allowed if it makes understandable the main area of evidence. I didn't find that the entire transcript needed to be played to make it understandable. As for certain statements you (Cook) feel are not impeachable, in number thirteen, she says, 'You (the detectives) can call me anytime. I want to be helpful. You can even call me at three A.M.' This impeaches her statement about Mr. Jewett sending his dogs (the investigators) to Las Vegas.

"Number ten deals with the signature on a center-fold. This is not impeachable."

When the jury was brought back in, Judge O'Malley explained to them why there had been a lengthy delay. Then, polite and conscientious as always, she said, "You have witnessed in this trial three of the best attorneys you will ever see."

Dawn Godman took the jurors through every aspect of her life before and after her conversion to Mormonism. She told of first meeting Taylor at the murder mystery night at the Third Ward. Like many other young women close to him, she said, "He was charismatic and powerful."

Even with a sentence of thirty-seven years to life, she still admitted, when asked by Jewett, that she still wasn't sure if Taylor was a prophet of God or not. Dawn said, "Breaking away from Taylor has been a back-and-forth struggle. It's been a continuous process over the last four years."

She even admitted that after her incarceration, "I believed no matter what happened, Taylor would work with the angels to set us free."

Then she said something that startled the victims' families. Dawn declared, "I've always tried to live life without regrets. If I had to go back and do my life over again, I wouldn't change a thing."

She quickly added that she did regret having ever met Taylor Helzer.

Dawn covered everything about the Children of Thunder without flinching. Her plea bargain depended on it, and unlike Keri Furman, she rarely said, "I don't recall." She spoke of every aspect in the scheme from July 30 through the killing of Jenny Villarin and James Gamble in the early-morning hours of August 3. She told of cutting up and packaging the body of Selina, and depositing all the body bags in the Delta. She even said that later she couldn't get the smell of the residence at Saddlewood out of her nose for two weeks afterward. Jewett would later refer to this as the "smell of death."

Dr. Reiber's testimony was extensive and graphic in the extreme. Every word he said about the autopsied body parts was backed up by extremely graphic photos on an overhead screen. Jewett had warned the victims' family members they could leave if they did not want to sit through the showing. They all stayed. Carma Helzer and Justin's sister, Heather, however, left the court. Only Justin was left from the Helzer side, with his lawyers sitting next to him. During the showing of the photographs, he would not look at them. He stared down at the desk in front of him with determined concentration as Jewett referred to the photos as "Justin's handiwork."

Court observer Juley Salkeld said, "Dr. Reiber's statements were very damaging to Justin. Especially when he talked about putting the body parts back together. In some ways, that was the worst part."

Chris Darden added, "It was Dr. Reiber and Detective Nash who blew this case wide open. Their testimony really hurt Justin."

Various bumps along the road in the trial came as one side or the other objected to certain evidence being introduced. Cook objected that Jewett was trying to introduce the safe at Debra McClanahan's residence, and this had to do with Taylor and Dawn, not his client, Justin. Judge O'Malley ruled that the safe and its contents would be allowed. One of the pieces of evidence in the safe was the pistol that Justin had purchased.

Then Cook objected to Jewett actually turning on the reciprocal saw so that the jury could hear the sound it made. He said, "There is no evidentiary value in the operation of the saw. It would influence the passions of the jury."

Jewett argued that Dawn Godman knew the sound of the saw because she had used it to construct the dog run. She could listen to the saw in court and say that it sounded the same as the one she had used. Jewett said, "It goes to state of mind and their deliberate commitment to kill."

"It's nothing more than a grandstanding move to influence their (the jury's) passions," Cook countered.

Jewett: The saw brings home loud and clear the nature of this crime.

Cook: The shock and theatrical effect does not assist the jury in the facts. It's merely for dramatic effect.

O'Malley: In considering to allow the saw to be turned on—I look back to other homicide cases that have been before this court. In other homicides, I allowed how weapons were used. For instance, in the case of a shooting, it showed how you load a gun and how it would become fully operable and the sound of the process. It goes to intent and state of mind. I think it is relevant if it was to show how you get this instrument (the saw) to work. If it is an item that makes a loud sound, so be it. This just happens to be a saw rather than a gun.

Cook was luckier with his contention that no mention should be made of Taylor's flight to evade officers on the morning of August 7, 2000, at the time of his arrest on Saddlewood. Cook said that Justin had been no part of that process and had willingly allowed himself to be arrested by officers. Jewett wanted the evidence in, saying that Justin was a co-conspirator and there were notes about what he and Taylor would do if ever arrested.

Judge O'Malley allowed the nature of Taylor's detention by Detective Inskip to be mentioned, but not the matter of his flight or terrorist threats to William Sharp and Mary Mozzochi.

If Cook was worried about the impact the sound of the reciprocal saw made in front of the jury, it was nothing compared to one of Jewett's most dramatic moments in court. Jewett was talking about the hammer blow from Justin on the back of Selina Bishop's head as she lay on the floor receiving a back rub from Taylor. Suddenly, without warning, Jewett brought a hammer down on a stack of papers in the courtroom. Almost everyone jumped by the loud impact, even Judge Mary Ann O'Malley.

Closing arguments can be very dramatic by their very nature. They are a summation of testimony and a counselor's right to delve into oratory beyond the scope of mere evidence. Harold Jewett began for the prosecution in the guilt phase by saying, "This is one hell of a case. We had five people brutally killed. Each person was a unique and special person."

He spoke of Annette Stineman enjoying mystery novels, gardening and her spinning wheel. Ivan enjoyed romance novels, working in the yard and his friends. Jewett pointed to Justin and said, "This defendant took the lives from the Stinemans. The brutality of the crime reflects about his heart and soul."

Jewett spoke of mens rea, the criminal's state of

mind, and the anguish of the Stinemans—the horror of "what they saw in the last moments in the bathroom at Saddlewood."

Jewett then turned to Jenny Villarin. "She was a child of the '70s. A free spirit. She was about the same age as Selina when she met Elvin Bishop. He truly did 'fool around and fall in love.' He fell in love with Jenny.

"Selina was a little on the wild side, but she had lots of friends and was sweet. James Gamble was a classic gentleman. He helped his friends. He helped Jenny. He was a generous man.

"You have all the evidence, but how do you apply it? This case is all about power! It's the usurpation of power and the controlling of lives. You cannot consider punishment at this time. You must consider guilt."

Jewett spoke of Justin's malice aforethought and his express intent to kill. He said that premeditation of thought preceded Justin's acts. That made his killings, murder in the first degree. Jewett added that Justin, Taylor and Dawn intended to kill up to five people at Bob White's house. He spoke of them carrying guns, knives and a blowtorch. They didn't care whom they killed once they were inside the house.

Jewett also said that Justin was part of the plot to kill Jenny Villarin, even though he wasn't at Woodacre. Justin was supposed to find Jenny's address in an address book in Selina's car. Even though he didn't follow through on that, he was still a co-conspirator.

"It was a natural and probable consequence to the murders of Jennifer Villarin and James Gamble. A consequence of the original crime. Jennifer had to die because she could be tied to the extortion plot. The Children of Thunder was all about a conspiracy. All the acts preceding the crimes—the buying of guns, ammo, [personal watercraft]—were all overt acts because there was an intent to commit a crime. If you join a conspiracy, if you have knowledge of criminal events, you are liable for the crimes. The criminal acts of one are the criminal acts of all."

Jewett added, "I shudder to think what would have happened if Steve Nash hadn't been involved. Would anybody at the Two Bird (restaurant) have been safe? Would Leora Soladay?"

Jewett next spoke of Justin killing Ivan Stineman. Justin tried to smother him with his hands. When that didn't work, he tried smothering him with a sheet of plastic. When that failed, he banged Ivan's head on the floor until he was dead. Jewett said that even if Ivan died of a heart attack, it was Justin's actions that caused him to die.

"All of these acts were concurrent with kidnapping and robbery. You have the image of Justin in a chair with a gun on the floor, and the Stinemans on the couch. We'll never know if that was a dare.

"Children of Thunder was still in effect after the deaths. Extortion proceeded and Justin aided and abetted these proceedings. Both Taylor and Justin inflicted blows to Selina Bishop's head. It remains a mystery who inflicted the antemortem wounds to her body. Even if it is never known, Justin aided and abetted in these acts. I can't point to this knife (Justin's knife) and say this was it. But the wounds to the body are consistent with it."

Referring to the photographs of Ivan, Annette and Selina's dismembered bodies, Jewett said, "You didn't see blood in those photographs. But those guys (Justin and Taylor) were covered in blood. One had to hold a body down while the other one cut. It took a minimum of two people. What happened there shows the heart and soul of Justin Helzer."

Jewett recounted that Justin was not a total robot to Taylor's instructions. His journals spoke of religious ideas and concepts that were different from Taylor. He dabbled in mysticism, sorcery and Buddhism.

"Besides murder, there was extortion, robbery, kidnapping and possession of illegal drugs. As to the drug use during the week of July thirtieth to August seventh, Justin was the one keeping his mind clear. He was straight and sober."

Jewett pointed directly at Justin and said, "He was the anchor for Children of Thunder! He provided the haven for the crimes. He put up the money for Saddlewood. We have Justin's writing on a flowchart. Justin contemplated what would happen if they got caught. He made up an alibi for himself before the crimes were ever committed."

As to reasonable doubt, Jewett said, "The burden of proof never slides down to the other end of the table [in the guilt phase]. We didn't even need Dawn Godman for this case. There is a mountain of evidence, both direct and circumstantial, as to Justin's involvement. I don't have to go farther than Clint Carter and Detective Solis. Justin's fingerprints are on the Stinemans' van. There are dozens of pieces of evidence. All of them corroborate Dawn Godman.

"We have evidence that Justin walked first to the Stinemans' door. He gave his brother a nod of the head. 'Okay, we're ready. Let's get this puppy done!' That was Justin's state of mind."

Jewett reiterated the witnesses' testimony, one by one. To Dawn Kirkland, Justin had mentioned religious ideas that did not correspond to Taylor's ideas. It showed that he was capable of making up his own mind on issues. Johnette Gray, Justin's fellow AT&T worker and housemate, told of him meditating and even telling her that he sometimes leaned toward her own belief of atheism.

Jewett also spoke of Justin having a mean streak.

When Sarah Brents said she only wanted to be friends with him, he told her, "I've only been friends with you to see if I could fuck you!"

Jewett recalled, "Justin had two sides, sweet and hostile. He would shout obscenities in the bathroom."

As far as Taylor and Justin planning together, Keri Furman had said, "I had to leave the room when Taylor talked to Justin."

Jewett noted, "Taylor needed Justin and Dawn for Children of Thunder. Dawn was the secretary." Then he pointed his finger at Justin and said, "Here's the enforcer!"

Jewett spoke of Brazil and Justin's role in it. "Taylor planned to put it under Justin's control. The board of twelve in Brazil would include Debra McClanahan and Carma Helzer."

Jewett pronounced that on July 30, 2000, the Children of Thunder declared war on Satan to the Universe. "There was no turning back. They all understood the impact of Children of Thunder. You heard that Mr. Nicolai [*sic*] called Justin a kind of Opie. I don't see Ron Howard anywhere in the defendant!"

Of his lengthy presentation, Jewett said, "I'm a builder. I spend a lot of time laying a foundation, even if it's boring listening to it. I build the structure, piece by piece.

"I'll say it [again], Children of Thunder was all about kidnapping, robbery and murder. The whole idea was to get huge amounts of money. They used sex and drugs. They preyed upon human weaknesses. There was a key word on a scratch pad with monetary figures."

It was hard to read, but Jewett said, "The word looks like 'wow.' The wow is about a lot of money, not peace and joy and the war on Satan.

"It was Justin's handwriting about the Cal Fed branches in Piedmont, Novato and El Cerrito. Eventually they went to Cal Fed in Walnut Creek. Justin did the research in this.

"Justin made a list when they moved into Saddlewood. He made a list of all his debts. All while Justin did his work at AT&T, his thought processes were on Children of Thunder."

Jewett recounted that when the body parts were placed into plastic bags, Justin was part of the process. Jewett said they didn't need Dawn Godman to testify about this. The evidence itself spoke of Justin's involvement. Justin was right-handed and Taylor was left-handed. Fifty percent of the twist ties on the plastic bags containing the remains of Ivan and Annette Stineman had been tied by a right-handed person. This happened while Godman was away and heading for the bank in Petaluma.

Jewett noted that Justin once thought of himself as a troll from medieval fantasy. Then he rhetorically asked about the dismembered bodies of Ivan and Annette, "What kind of troll does that? It certainly doesn't come from the Book of Mormon. It sounds kind of vampire-like.

"Those people were mercilessly killed for Children of Thunder directly by the hands of Justin Helzer. Through Children of Thunder, he is responsible for the deaths of Jennifer Villarin and James Gamble."

Jewett walked to a copy of the Bill of Rights hanging on the courtroom wall. He pointed at it and said, "Rights come from a thing called law. One instruction I want to remind you of is that a jury may not adopt a fixed opinion. We want you to deliberate. That is your responsibility."

Then as sort of a parting shot at Justin, Taylor and Dawn, he said, "They're not the only ones who have some thunder!"

* * *

If Harold Jewett's voice reached a crescendo of anger near the end of his presentation, Daniel Cook's voice was soft and restrained. He took a jab at Jewett for recalling testimony of 116 witnesses by saying, "Don't worry, I won't do that."

Cook said, "I saw that you were watching carefully during this trial. We have a ways to go, and the most important thing right now is to maintain our focus. You cannot be ruled by passion and emotion. I'm depending on every one of you to stay on track.

"Remember your very first instructions. You are not to be influenced by sympathy or passion. This is not a contest to see who can exhibit the most outrage or shock. All of our consciences have been shocked. But we have a job to do. Approach this path dispassionately and fairly.

"I feel that it is very important to point out an instruction that statements of lawyers are not evidence. The last thing I need to do is talk down to you. The shaking of his finger (by Jewett at Justin) is not evidence. You now have enormous power and authority. The system relies upon you. Rage and anger, maybe they are deserved, but they are not evidence. Don't let theatrical demonstrations replace your good sense, for some blind pursuit of vengeance.

"I don't know that you needed a hammer pounded on the table. I don't know if it was important to turn on a saw in this courtroom. Stay focused on the process.

"I want to get right to the point. Counts five, six and eighteen have not been proven. The murders of Jennifer Villarin and James Gamble are not Justin's responsibility. The question is: are these [crimes] proven beyond a reasonable doubt? I say, no.

"Dawn was the classic aider and abetter. She shared the intentions and purpose in these murders (of Jennifer Villarin and James Gamble). She was the driver in that crime. Justin went to bed when the plot to kill Selina's mother began between Taylor and Dawn.

"You need your greatest powers to review evidence. The evidence doesn't show that Justin was one of the planners. You're smart people. You have common sense. I don't have to stand here a day and a half (like Jewett) and tell you what to do. I have every faith in you. You will throw out the charges that haven't been proven."

Harold Jewett had a few words of rebuttal. "We don't care what Mr. Cook concedes and contests. Mr. Cook, why did I pound the hammer on the table? I would be negligent if I didn't display the weapons of the crime. It showed the kind of force needed to cave in Selina's head. At least one hundred thirty pounds of pressure, according to Dr. Reiber.

"The same thing with the saw. It made a lot of noise. Dawn Godman could hear it in the other parts of the house."

As for the length of time it took to make his closing arguments, Jewett said, "We start from scratch and build a case. The case is reality. It is in the dimension of time. I won't say that Mr. Cook told falsehoods, but he certainly ignored a lot of things. If Justin had knowledge of the plan to kill Jennifer, then he is guilty. The nine-millimeter gun was his. It was Justin's gun that killed Jennifer and James.

"I do get fired up. I defy anyone not to feel emotions in this case. You have been working hard and attentive, but you've got a lot of work ahead of you. I hope you'll look at all the evidence."

CHAPTER 14

The Fatal Phases

It was not an unexpected event when the jury came back in on Tuesday, August 3, 2004, with a verdict of guilty for Justin Alan Helzer in the murders of Ivan Stineman, Annette Stineman and Selina Bishop. They did not find him guilty in the murders of Jennifer Villarin and James Gamble. According to Chris Darden, not one juror would look at Justin while the verdicts were being read. Darden also noted that it was exactly four years to the day since the murders had reached their culmination in the killing of Jennifer Villarin and James Gamble.

After the verdicts had been read, Chris asked Carma Helzer, "How are you doing?" She answered, "Okay. I've been dealing with this for four years."

In fact, many of the court observers, and perhaps even Carma herself, agreed that Daniel Cook was saving his "legal ammunition" for the sanity phase. They basically believed that it was here where the real test of whether Justin Helzer would live or die would occur. The lack of witnesses called by Cook in the guilt phase seemed to confirm their suspicions. They also noted that to be ruled guilty by reason of insanity, in California, a defendant first had to be found guilty of the crime.

As the sanity phase began, Justin wore his usual green sweater and slacks, but he seemed more talkative and animated with his lawyers. His mother, Carma, sat in the second row behind him, looking tired but alert. Gerry, his father, came in later and sat down by her side. Farther down the row, to the left, sat the Stineman daughters and relatives of Selina and Jenny.

Unlike the guilt phase, the defense started opening remarks in the sanity phase. Speaking originally for the defense was Charles Hoehn. He said, "Our hearts go out to the victims' families. This case is not like any other that I have seen. Mental illness underlies this case.

"I'm here to put the evidence into context. Was Justin Helzer legally insane during the week of July 30, 2000? I believe he was. You're going to learn about his life and his parents. Twenty-eight years of trying to be a good boy."

Hoehn spoke of how Taylor was diagnosed with mental illness in 1999, and how his mental state played a factor in Justin's own mental illness. Hoehn told the jury that they could consider someone's mental condition before and during the crime. He said, "Justin was always in the shadow of Taylor. Justin was never really loved by Carma. Not the way she loved Taylor."

Hoehn brought up the Hinckley case, where John Hinckley Jr. so desired Jodie Foster's affection that he attempted an assassination of President Ronald Reagan. Hoehn compared that to Justin yearning for affection from Taylor. To lose Taylor's love would be devastating for Justin. He would rather follow Taylor into murder than lose the affection of his older brother.

Hoehn said, "Mental illness is not a choice. Mental illness is a tragedy. Because of Taylor's beliefs, Justin truly believed he was acting as a warrior for God."

Hoehn brought up the fact that Justin was pushed by Taylor toward Mark 3:17 of the Bible:

James, the son of Zeb'edee, and John, the brother of James, whom he surnamed Boanerges, that is "Sons of Thunder."

"Taylor overwhelmed his brother," Hoehn said. "Justin was only a pair of hands to complement Taylor's evil plans. According to experts, Justin could not tell right from wrong because of his mental illness. Justin was diagnosed with a shared delusional disorder called folie à deux. This was a shared mental disorder."

Hoehn explained how Taylor was put on antipsychotic medication in 1999. "He was taking a smorgasbord of drugs. He suffered from grandiose delusions. The shared psychosis between Taylor and Justin was that Taylor was a prophet of God.

"The Church may have left Justin (his excommunication), but Justin never left the LDS Church."

Hoehn spoke of the Book of Mormon passage that declared that the faithful servant will get his just reward and admittance to the celestial kingdom. Hoehn said that by doing Taylor's work, Justin believed he would be admitted into the celestial kingdom.

Hoehn also spoke of the great differences between the brothers' personalities. "Taylor was a Jim Jones–type person. The only male disciple he had, however, was his own brother, who he dominated all his life."

At this point, Jewett objected to Hoehn's presentation, stating that Hoehn was doing a closing argument instead of an opening statement. Judge O'Malley tended to agree and said, "You are doing a closing now. You need to tell what your witnesses will say."

Hoehn had a long conversation with Cook and then continued. Hoehn said, "Brandon Davids said Justin was weak-minded. Another cousin said Justin was mentally ill and that his family treated him as if he was retarded. 'He was weird, but he didn't make me nervous like Taylor.'"

Hoehn stated, "This family were extremely devout Mormons until Impact. Justin went to Impact. He had a mental breakdown and began to sleep under the stairs. This is an American tragedy of untreated mental illness.

"Did Justin know what he was doing was illegally wrong? Yes. But [to him], it was to save millions of lives. A divine waiver existed that superseded human lives.

"Justin seemed to be composed, but he was encapsulated with delusions. Attention disorder. Socially antisocial disorder. The mania from Taylor was communicated to Justin."

In a very real sense, the battle for Justin's life now would be played out by contending psychiatrists and psychologists. It was their testimony that could sway the jury into believing Justin was either sane or insane. It boiled down to whether Justin had understood the nature of his acts at the time of the crime. Both Jewett and Cook understood the important nature of this phase, and Jewett made several motions to restrict certain admissibility. In one motion, Jewett wanted to question each doctor about how much he had been paid by the defense to interview Justin. Cook argued that the jury wouldn't understand that being such a long and complicated case meant that the doctors had needed a lot of time to write up their reports after having spent hours with Justin. This led to high costs because of the time spent on those reports.

Judge O'Malley decided that Jewett could ask about the itemized expenses because those went to credibility.

Another motion by Jewett concerned the fact that he had never received any notes from Dr. Dolgoff. Jewett said, "According to Code ten fifty-four, I am entitled to any and all writings of any type, i.e., notes, reports, anything that has to do with the Helzer case. Therefore I cannot effectively nor actively cross-examine someone when I have no idea of their position."

Cook responded, "Mr. Jewett is full of nonsense, and he knows it. The defense had turned over more than is required by law. I have never received a report from Dr. Dolgoff, therefore I cannot submit something I do not have."

Dr. Stephen Raffle took the stand for the defense. He had a B.S. in physiology from UC Berkeley, and attended the Chicago School of Medicine and also taught for eleven years at the Hastings School of Law. In his career, he had studied somewhere between three thousand and five thousand cases. In the 1990s, he was an expert witness in ten murder trials.

Jewett asked him during voir dire, "How many times have you testified to the diagnosis of shared delusional disorder?"

Raffle admitted, "Never."

Hoehn noted that Dr. Raffle had interviewed Justin Helzer five times in jail in 2003, and one time in 2004. After these interviews, Dr. Raffle came to several conclusions about Justin. One was that Justin had a delusional disorder with Axis 1—a current or recent onset of the disorder—and Axis 4—psychosocial stressors, i.e., fired from a job, which brought on depression. He also concluded that Justin was afflicted with the rare but severe shared delusional disorder. Dr. Raffle explained this as being when two people are in an extremely close relationship, and there is one active dominant person. The active person already has a delusional disorder, and the passive person develops the shared delusional disorder so as not to lose the active dominant person from their life.

Dr. Raffle said that Justin lost his own grip on reality when Taylor had a mental breakdown. To prove that Justin was insane, Raffle administered the MMPI test on him, which is the standard psychiatric test worldwide. He also checked to make sure that Justin was not malingering or faking his insanity. To do this, Dr. Raffle compared his notes with four other doctors. All of the reports stated that Justin was telling the truth during interviews.

To further check into the possibility of shared delusional disorder, Dr. Raffle had two meetings with Taylor Helzer in the Martinez County Jail. He noted that Taylor talked very fast, as if he were on meth, even though he hadn't had any in a while. Taylor couldn't seem to concentrate on any one subject for any prolonged period of time. Raffle said, "He was restless, nervous and jittery."

Taylor explained to Dr. Raffle at one point that the way he dealt with voices in his head was by shouting at them. Dr. Raffle concluded that Taylor was a borderline neurotic and psychotic. He also surmised that Taylor's afflictions had been visited upon Justin's fragile ego.

Hoehn asked, "How could a person (Justin) with no criminal record, after twenty-eight years, just lose their moral compass?"

Dr. Raffle answered, "Justin became delusional, believing that Taylor was a prophet of God, and that Satan embodied the United States government."

Hoehn asked why Dr. Raffle's diagnosis was at odds with portions of those submitted by Dr. Good and Dr. Carol Walzer. Raffle said that those doctors had only seen Justin for two hours, while he had spent thirteen hours with him. Therefore, he had a much clearer idea

of the severity of Justin's mental problems. He also said
that neither one of those doctors had obtained a history of Justin's state of mind directly after the crimes
had been committed. Nor had they looked into Justin's
family background. Had they done so, they would
have noted that there were mental problems in Justin's
extended family.

One comment by Dr. Raffle was a two-edged sword.
He claimed that Justin did understand that what he had
done was legally wrong, but he did not understand
that it was morally wrong. According to Dr. Raffle's
reading of the California code on insanity, a perpetrator
had to understand that what he was doing was both
legally and morally wrong.

As for Children of Thunder, Dr. Raffle said the hierarchy of that organization was already familiar to
Justin. Justin recognized its similarities to the hierarchy of the Latter-Day Saints Church. It was a hierarchy
he could be comfortable with.

On cross-examination, Jewett zeroed in on what he
saw as Dr. Raffle's shortcomings in the process:

Jewett: No tests, no written reports, were viewed by
you before Justin's NGI (not guilty by reason of insanity plea) in October 2003. Is that correct?

Raffle: Yes.

Jewett: So only after Justin entered a NGI plea, is
when you began to review reports on Justin's insanity?

Raffle: True.

Jewett: At any time during the interview, did Justin
tell you Taylor was hearing voices?

Raffle: No.

Jewett: In fact, Justin specifically told you that Taylor did not actually hear any voices, but instead they were more like thoughts?

Raffle: Yes.

Jewett made Dr. Raffle confirm many things that Justin had said about Taylor and about his own views as well. Dr. Raffle had noted that Justin said:

"Taylor didn't really know if the Spirit revelations were true or not. Taylor was weighing it all and using me as a sounding board. There's no right way, just differences. As an example, a drunk driver who hits a pedestrian is not entirely at fault. The pedestrian put themselves in the way too and was partly to blame. It was a karmic reaction.

"I first thought that Taylor was a little nuts. But then I decided the ends justify the means. Selling dope was okay because it really wasn't hurting anyone and we needed the money to save America from destruction.

"Killing for greed, laziness or self-indulgence is not right, but killing for God's work, to better the People, is good. God didn't command us to kill, but he gave us the green light."

After Justin was arrested, he admitted, "Being in jail caused me to rethink my beliefs in Taylor. I started to believe my brother wasn't a prophet of God, but a devil in disguise. Otherwise, things would have turned out okay and we wouldn't be here in jail."

The trial on Tuesday, June 29, was delayed on Cook's request, and for a very good reason. During the late-night hours, around midnight, Justin's cell was searched and it was discovered that he had been hoarding some medication. When the jailer asked him if he was contemplating suicide, he refused to answer.

According to Cook, deputies removed Justin from his cell and placed him in a padded room. They used leg irons to shackle him to the floor and took away his pillow and blanket. With those items gone, Justin hadn't slept all night long.

Cook related that Justin kept asking to speak with his lawyer, but he was never granted that privilege. He did speak with his mother sometime around 1:00 A.M., and she called Cook's office and left a message there.

Cook said, "I find it odd that these interrogators, whatever their motivation, would find the need to hurry to court, and alert the court about this, but at the same time would not call Justin's lawyer."

Judge O'Malley interrupted Cook and said, "I don't know all the facts yet because they are still coming out."

She paused for a moment and then said, "Mr. Cook, I was just given the incident report by my bailiff. In reading the information in here, it looks like your client was asked a question whether he was suicidal, and your client refused to answer. Martinez County Jail has a policy, when they suspect prisoners may be suicidal, that they take them to a padded room and take away instruments and objects from them, such as a pillow or blanket, so as not to harm themselves in any way.

"All Justin had to do was answer the question. He would have either been in a padded room or remained in his jail cell. Because your client refused to answer the question, the sheriff's deputies had no choice but to follow protocol and place him in a suicide watch. They checked on him every fifteen minutes, and wrote a brief report every fifteen minutes.

"Even as recent as seven-twenty A.M., the sheriff's deputies asked if your client was suicidal. He refused to answer the question and stated that he wanted to talk to his lawyer before he answered the question.

"I even gave your client an additional thirty minutes

this morning before court, between nine and nine-thirty A.M., to shower and get cleaned up while we were waiting. It turns out that your client refused to shower as well."

Cook replied, "I am puzzled just as well as the court why someone would refuse to take a shower. But I do know that because Justin was forced to sleep on the floor with shackles around his ankles, without a pillow or blanket, Mr. Helzer (Justin) is very upset and extremely tired, due to not getting any sleep all last night. Because my client is very tired and also very upset, Mr. Helzer is unable to focus on the trial today and cannot listen to the testimony that would be given. Mr. Helzer is also unable to assist his counsel with his defense, due to his tiredness and lack of sleep. I ask the court to delay this trial while I get the rest of the facts and my client's status changes."

Judge O'Malley countered, "It is nine-thirty A.M. now. As long as your client refuses to answer the question, then your client's status is not going to change! This is not something we're going to be dealing with every day. So I suggest you talk with your client after we recess. I will excuse the jury for today and order them to come back tomorrow at nine A.M."

Court did resume the next day without the jurors ever knowing what had happened on the previous day. Dr. Raffle admitted that Justin had scored in the top 75 percent of the population on the Wexler IQ test. Raffle also admitted that he had no opinion on what negative effect Impact and Harmony might have had on Justin. He did say, "Justin was a loner and okay by himself. But (Taylor) declared war on Satan. Justin said after that, 'Soldiers kill, they don't murder.' Justin knew it was legally wrong, but not morally wrong to do what they planned. In Justin's mind, there was a difference between 'kill' and 'murder.'"

Dr. Raffle added one more interesting thing. Before the guilt phase, Justin had declared that if he was acquitted, he wanted to go to Tibet and spend the rest of his life in a monastery.

Dr. Raffle also had the task of reviewing other doctors' reports on Justin. He told of Dr. Larry Wornian stating that Justin had been a model Mormon boy and had been ordained as a deacon at twelve years of age. He had become a priest at sixteen, and was an elder at nineteen. He left on a mission that year, but he had a hard time with it. When he came home, he felt disillusioned about the LDS Church and himself. He felt "wimpish" and unmasculine. According to Wornian, Justin was in a physical and spiritual crisis.

Dr. Raffle also commented about Dr. Good's report. He noted Justin saying, "We wanted to avoid violence, but we had to sacrifice the few for the greater good."

Dr. Carol Walzer's report was one of the hardest to contend with, for Justin and the defense's viewpoint. She cited no signs of schizophrenia, bipolar disease or signs of delusion or depression in Justin.

At one point, Jewett brought up the condition to Dr. Raffle that Taylor had been faking his mental illness; so it followed that if he wasn't insane, Justin could not share in his insanity. In essence, there could not be a folie à deux, since Taylor was not psychotic. Jewett asked Dr. Raffle, "If Justin's shared delusional disorder is crucial to Taylor's delusional disorder, and you've received all of these reports about Justin knowing of Taylor's faking—why didn't you get Justin's beliefs on that?"

Of these sometimes contentious exchanges, Juley Salkeld said, "The entire exchange between Jewett and Raffle was both frustrating and exhausting, and yet often fascinating. It was as if we were privy to a battle of wits or a chess game with equally matched opponents. Raffle was very deliberate in his answers, as if he was trying to keep his story straight and not give Jewett an inch. Luckily for Jewett, there were plenty of times when Raffle couldn't support his argument."

She also said, "I thought the most important part of the day was when Jewett spent probably forty minutes going through each individual case where a witness testified that Taylor was faking his mental illness to get out of work so he could focus on Impact America. On one occasion, he actually hit himself in the head with a rock so he could go to the doctor and claim he fell during a psychotic episode. The whole point was that shared delusional disorder simply didn't exist if the main psychotic, Taylor, did not have a psychotic disorder."

Jewett even brought in a statement from Justin, where Justin told someone, "Oh, Taylor's faking his mental illness so he doesn't have to work."

Dr. Raffle countered these contentions, by stating that Taylor had been diagnosed as bipolar since 1998. Taylor also experienced a psychotic disorder on February 25, 1999, and was taken by ambulance to Mount Diablo Hospital. Raffle said that Taylor had delusional disorders more than once, heard voices and was not malingering. He added, "He could not separate the voices from reality. He would spend a few minutes on his knees when the angels were calling."

Another point of contention between Jewett and Raffle was Justin's claim that when Annette was cut across the torso, "her organs fell out." Jewett cited Dr. Reiber as saying this was physically impossible. Jewett asked Raffle if Justin was lying. Dr. Raffle replied to this that Justin had been traumatized at the time, and he might have imagined the organs falling out.

* * *

Next on the stand, after a very lengthy stint by Dr. Raffle, was twenty-five-year-old Jennifer Aubrey. She was the daughter of Sherry Matheson, who had directed Harmony in Sacramento. Aubrey was first introduced to Impact in Salt Lake City when she was only eleven years old. She described the experience as very dramatic and very emotional. "Lots of people throwing up, yelling and screaming, degradation and humiliation." The point was to break down the people's barriers and take away their belief systems. She said that the new "trainees" were told to trust the trainer, trust the process and trust the environment.

Her training began on a Wednesday at 6:00 A.M. and went until one or two o'clock the following morning. The same thing happened on Thursday and Friday. On Saturday, it went from ten in the morning until nine-thirty that night, when the graduation ceremony began. During the long days, there was very little food or water, and a person could wait hours to use a rest room, to which they were escorted, there and back. Trash cans, in which people could throw up, were strategically placed around the room.

Aubrey's recollections of Impact were of two large men standing at a double-door entrance and yelling, "Doors open," and then the people walking into a hall, where bright lights were shining and soft mystical music was playing. The temperature in the room was ice cold; the room was soundproofed; there were no windows. If a person showed any resistance to what the facilitator wanted, a screaming match usually ensued. And if the trainee did not eventually break, they were kicked out of the room.

There were many "games," as Aubrey called them, including Lifeboat, which had been in at Harmony, Sacramento. Aubrey's recollection of Lifeboat was pretty much the same as Kelly Lord's. Aubrey recalled that

Justin was a willing participant in everything that happened at Impact. She said, "He was great in training. Very willing. Very engaged. He was really breaking down his walls and finding his inner child. At first, he was very quiet and subdued, but as he progressed, he became more active and involved."

At one time, Justin even asked Aubrey out on a date. She said she would have gone out with him, but she was engaged at the time.

Aubrey's impression of Taylor was very different from her take on Justin. She said, "Taylor was domineering, outspoken and opinionated. In one meeting, he took control of the room. He was very charismatic, very powerful. Around women, he was affectionate and flirtatious. He locked eyes with the woman he was speaking with. He was captivating."

Hoehn asked Aubrey how she felt about Impact now. Tears welled up in her eyes and she related that she had been molested at six years of age. In Impact, she had been taught that even six-year-old victims were responsible for incidents that befell them. Molestation victims were called "daddy's little sluts" and received no sympathy. Aubrey said it wasn't until her late teens that she started coming to grips with her molestation. She was currently in therapy about it.

The next witness was David Sullivan. Sullivan had been Cook's private investigator, and on Cook's instructions, he took two courses of Impact in March and April 2001. He took the courses in Salt Lake City so that they would be the most similar to the ones Justin had taken. Sullivan said that the new trainees were taught that there was no right and wrong and there were no victims. You were not allowed to use words such as "try, hope and need." A key concept was the word "choice." You *chose* to do something and then had to accept it for good or bad. It was posited there that if you got on a plane that crashed, you were not a victim, but had made a conscious choice to take that flight. They even claimed that the Jews were responsible for their own fates in the Holocaust.

There was a "pity party," where people in the group laughed and mocked anyone who tried to elicit sympathy for something that had happened to them. Overweight women were forced to put on cow outfits and wear bells around their necks. They were told that their fates were to be hit by a semitruck.

Trainees were encouraged to spread the word about Impact and its positive results. A phrase was used that it would "transform America." This phrase was not lost on Harold Jewett.

The most incredible incident occurred when Sullivan related his recollections of the game Lifeboat. Sullivan said that the ship you were on sank in shark-infested waters and only four people could climb into a lifeboat and save themselves. All the rest would be dismembered by sharks and killed. Their remains would be picked up later and placed in body bags. All the remains would be intermixed and relatives would have to sort them out later.

Juley Salkeld said, "On cross, Mr. Jewett came unglued. He said, 'Body bags! Ironic, given the facts of this case!'"

Dr. Larry Wornian had many observations of Justin that varied from those of Dr. Raffle. Dr. Wornian was a neuropsychologist and staff psychologist at San Quentin Prison. He had been in more than fifty trials where a sanity phase was at issue. He was court-appointed for Justin's case. He answered to Judge Mary Ann O'Malley, and not Jewett or Cook.

Dr. Wornian, when questioned by Jewett, said that

he'd gone through over one thousand pages of testimony and police reports about Justin. He'd also studied the finding of the other doctors in the case. Picking up the large notebook before him on the stand, he joked, "I hope this doesn't give me a hernia."

In his MCII findings on Justin, he said, "It was one of the most unelevated scales in the whole file. He was an avoidant and shy and retiring person, but not nonfunctional."

Dr. Wornian met with Justin on December 1, 2003, and noted that Justin was tall and thin and wearing a beard at that point. He didn't have any tremors, was oriented to place and time, and seemed coherent. Justin discussed his family, Mormonism and his early years. Wornian noted that Justin had trouble adjusting in school and he thought his older brother, Taylor, was everything he was not—popular with girls, smart and outgoing. Justin told him, "I had a lifelong involvement with the LDS Church until I was twenty-six. Then I felt I was lied to by the Church."

While living with his dad and mom, even in his twenties, he had no girlfriend, little money and few prospects. He said, "I felt imbecilic and simple. I hated that."

He spoke of four women that he had ever loved. One of them was named Emily. She was good to him, but when she moved away to Brigham Young University in Salt Lake City, he said, "I knew there was no chance with her."

It was when Carma went to Impact that Justin really began questioning his faith in the Latter-Day Saints Church. After he went to Impact, he said, "I didn't feel suicidal anymore. It saved my life. I went to the Church and told them I needed an opportunity to sow some wild oats."

Apparently Justin followed through on this and even asked to be formally excommunicated.

As far as his sexuality went, Justin answered one of Dr. Wornian's questions by saying, "Did I have homosexual urges? I tried it once. It wasn't for me."

Justin added, "Taylor and I became spiritual warriors. We had to make a dent in what Satan was doing. Taylor didn't really hear voices. They were thoughts. He could immediately see a person's problems. He was cool to guys, and women loved him.

"We (Justin and Dawn) thought he might be one of the forerunners come to set the Church right. They were wrong about other branches of Christianity. I didn't agree with them about reincarnation. We'd listen to Taylor and say, 'Wow, Taylor is channeling,' and I began to see the truth.

"Over time, I felt that Christ was coming. The Church might protect us, but what about Buddhists? The government was the beast power. You can't trust the government."

Dr. Wornian discovered that Justin had been an adherent of the ultraright-wing Bo Gritz. Like some, Justin believed that the Clinton administration was ushering in the reign of Satan. He said, "We thought the government was trying to enslave the American people."

As far as Taylor scamming Dean Witter, Justin said that the ends justified the means. "You need money to meet with mayors and rich people. We thought that Taylor throwing out ideas was a step closer to success. I had a premortal contract to fulfill. It's an agreement. A contract before I was even born. I was willing to be a martyr. I was at peace with this knowledge."

Justin quoted 1 Nephi 4: vs 10–13:

And it came to pass that I was constrained by the Spirit that I should kill Laban; but I said in my heart: Never at any time have I shed the blood of man. And I shrunk and would that I might not slay him.

And the Spirit said unto me again: Behold the Lord hath delivered him into thy hands. Yea, and I also knew that he had sought to take away mine own life; yea, and he would not hearken unto the commandments of the Lord; and he also had taken away our property.

And it came to pass that the Spirit said unto me again: Slay him, for the Lord hath given him into thy hands.

Behold the Lord slayeth the wicked to bring forth his right-eous purposes. It is better that one man should perish than a nation should dwindle and perish in unbelief.

Justin said, "Nephi didn't want to do it. He killed Laban because God told him to. Robin Hood did it too. Robin Hood fought for the oppressed. He was an archetype, someone to aspire to be like."

Dr. Wornian noted that not only Taylor, but Justin as well, had different plans of how to dispose of bodies. One way that Justin came up with was to pour acid on the remains. Another way was to drop the body parts off a boat at sea. Justin said, "We didn't just wake up one morning and say, 'Let's put them in a duffel bag.'"

As far as the actual killing of Ivan Stineman, Justin said, "I tried to stab him, but the knife kept sticking. There was too much bone. I just wanted to stab him in the heart. Dawn came over and sat on him. I thought this was disgusting. But I never thought this was over the edge. This was for a higher purpose. Like the Twin Towers (on September eleventh). They did it for Allah. They enjoyed killing. I didn't.

"I did not want to go to heaven in shame. I would not back out of this. No way. No way!"

Wornian said of Justin's transformation from wimp to spiritual warrior: "It was intoxicating for him. There was a sense of certainty. An enormous amount of power and certitude. He understood full well that the acts they engaged in were grossly immoral. Justin even said, 'I cried my eyes out' (about Selina's death). It was similar to Ivan. I did use a hammer. We just wanted to get it done. I didn't want her to suffer.'"

As far as chopping up the bodies, Justin said, "It was not a ritual process. It was slimy and it was gross. I had a job to do. A mission to accomplish. I didn't think it was bad. It was a sacrifice. Somebody had to do it."

Dr. Paul Good's assessment of Justin was different from the other two doctors. Dr. Good had done forensic work about people involved in crimes since 1990. He was often a court-appointed psychiatrist. Good saw Justin on three occasions. He also spoke once with Dawn Godman.

Dr. Good administered a Rorschach inkblot test to Justin, and he also read two books on cults and one on Mormonism. Good said, "I've read the complete transcript on Dawn Godman. I've read the transcripts on Keri Furman and Justin's journals from 1998.

"This case is the most disturbing one of my career. It was difficult to read about what happened. The motivations were difficult and complex. I found Justin to be cooperative and genuine in the interviews. And he was not malingering.

"He did believe that Taylor was a prophet who was channeling God. Transform America would be a humanitarian service."

Cook asked Good, "Were they (Dawn and Justin) telling you this was an act of love?"

Good answered, "Yes."

Good also said, "I felt that Justin had feelings and conflicts with what he did at the time of the crime. It was very complex. Justin told me, 'I was convinced they were suffering. I didn't want them to suffer.'"

"I was struck by the amount of feeling that Justin felt. He didn't want to use violence at first. He was upset with Taylor when he revived Ivan and Annette. He even admitted, 'I thought Taylor had a moment of insanity.'"

Justin told Dr. Good that the killings were necessary as a sacrifice. He said, "The words 'right' and 'wrong' never came up."

Good explained, "When I look at the totality of my conclusion, it was more than Justin could tell me. I believe at some level he knew this was wrong."

Cook asked him, "Why would he do it, then?"

Good answered, "Because of religious training. That there were certain characters, certain prophets, who had to kill for God."

Justin had spoken of the sacrifices of Abraham in the Bible and Nephi in the Book of Mormon. Good said, "Justin and Taylor and Dawn were a cultlike group. They were separated from outside influences. Justin became less independent in the group. His family dynamics contributed to that. He was a guy who lost his way.

"I don't think it took him so far that it made him psychotic. He essentially made a big mistake. It was his own mother's suggestion that he attend Harmony. Often a course [like Harmony] can be destructive. It took away his foundations.

"Throughout history, killing for God had been the rule rather than the exception." Good referred to radical Islam in our own time. He said that faith by itself was not delusional. Christians believed in the virgin birth and resurrection of Jesus, while other faiths did not. What seemed like divine intervention by one seemed like a crazy myth to another.

Good said, "Justin was an odd fellow. Believing Taylor was a prophet of God helped him cope. It gave Justin a foundation. It's always a difficult diagnosis when religion is involved. I have to look for other signs of psychosis."

Dr. Good noted that Justin was coherent during the crimes and afterward as well. Justin wrote intelligible letters from jail after he was arrested. As far as a shared delusional disorder went, Good said he had asked to interview Taylor and was refused by Taylor's lawyer.

Another key to Justin's sanity was his own account of how he and Dawn had decided that Taylor was a prophet of God. They thought at first it was the drugs that Taylor was using, and they made him say the things he said. "But then I thought that he might be influenced by an evil spirit," Justin explained. It was by the process of elimination that they came to the conclusion that Taylor was a prophet. Good said, "That process was a rational process."

Then Good told Cook, "Justin retained enough sanity to know right from wrong. The lesson I learned from this case was a decent person can do horrible things."

On cross, Jewett zeroed in on the issue of Justin knowing right from wrong. Dr. Good told him, "Justin said, 'I was totally conscious that people would judge us and condemn us. They wouldn't understand it was a humanitarian act.' Then he added, 'Just because Taylor was indeed a prophet, I wouldn't follow everything he said.'"

Good explained, "Justin was in a weakened state, but I believe he was rational enough to say no."

Dr. Good spoke of a jailhouse letter from Justin to Taylor on August 29, 2000, in which Justin said that he thought he would already be released because authorities would think others had done the crimes. He also gave Taylor advice about how to lie to jailers.

Juley Salkeld was fascinated by the dynamics of the victims' family members and Carma Helzer throughout the testimony of the various doctors. Juley recalled, "Carma arrived late one day and her usual seat was taken by Olga Land, [Jennifer's sister], and their two daughters. While this testimony was going on, the teenage daughters passed notes to each other and played hangman with words like 'psycho.'

"During this entire proceeding, Carma kept her head down and took copious notes. Taylor was the first to be excommunicated from the Church, and it came up in trial that Carma was next, followed by Justin. In talking about Carma's excommunication—Justin had spoken to the doctor about his mother's attitude for doing so, for experimentation purposes. Justin wanted to experiment too. Carma wanted to know if God would still love her if she left the Church and experimented. Justin wanted to try the sinning department. He wanted to see if he became a demonic-possessed person if God would still love him. He felt that he would be forgiven and the Church would take him back, which gave him the 'okay' to sin. His sinning things were things like drinking, drugs, sex, coffee and cigarettes."

Out of the jury's presence, Cook wanted to call Dr. Douglas Tucker to the stand so he could expound on Justin's religious beliefs and drug usage, especially in the summer of 2000. Jewett said that nothing Dr. Tucker might add would be new. He said that Cook had already missed his chance to call him during directs. Jewett said, "This is a serious dose of gamesmanship. He (Cook) chose not to call Dr. Walzer. If he intends to call Dr. Tucker, he needed to inform me. If there's nothing different (than what had already been covered), they can't call him."

Cook: Mr. Jewett has a lot of suspicions.

Jewett: A lot of suspicions.

Cook: The remark about "games playing" is nonsense. My client is fighting for his life. It would be a grave injustice to deny this witness.

Jewett: I implore the court to look at Dr. Worninan's report. Everything he said was in the report.

Cook specifically wanted to get in the case of a man who suffered from religious delusions. The man had somehow decided that God told him to chop down trees in a city park. Even though he felt it was wrong to do so, the man felt that he had no other choice.

Jewett contended that the case was a stretch and very hypothetical at best. Jewett said, "How does this hypothetical [anecdote] help? There is no meaningful basis. I mean, vandalism versus killing people?"

Cook: I'm entitled to bring in about this disorder. It brings clarity to the jury.

O'Malley: Where are you going with this?

Cook: I don't know yet.

O'Malley: You know where you're going, Mr. Cook. Please be honest.

Cook: I'm not going to respond to that. I'm trying to tie this to a religious delusion.

Judge O'Malley was beginning to get irritated, and said, "My reading of it (the pertinent case) is that a theory is allowed within the limits of evidence. It does not allow to ask about a different case study." She denied Cook's motion.

Cook was irritated as well, and Chris Darden noticed that it was the only time that he saw the otherwise polite and conscientious Cook not rise when the jurors filed in.

Dr. Douglas Tucker was allowed on the stand with a limited scope. He could not speak about any religious topics. Judge O'Malley deemed that those had already been fully covered. He could, however, talk about drug use and its effects on Justin. In fact, Judge O'Malley cited *People* v. *Carter* and said that religious beliefs were not rebuttal. She told Cook, "I don't want to hear one thing about religion."

Tucker did talk about meth use and the effects it might have had on Justin in 2000. But his discourse was not a "knockout blow" that the defense needed at this stage.

The sanity phase was key for the defense. In some ways, they had acceded fairly early on that Justin would probably be found guilty of the crimes. Now they wanted to prove that he was too insane when the crimes occurred for him to have made a rational judgment in what he was doing.

Hoehn spoke of how lucky Keri Furman had been. He said, "She got away from Taylor in time. Justin and Dawn didn't."

Hoehn brought up about the wooden staffs with the carved skull and crystal. These items had been sitting at the front of the court near the evidence boxes for weeks on end, in full view of the jury. Hoehn said of these, "Don't let the prosecution fool you with straw men and false items. This person (Justin) deserves justice by the standards of the law. It was not a choice by him to be mentally ill. So what followed from it was not a choice.

"He (Justin) was a true believer and he was deluded. He wanted the love of his brother. A person can lose their moral compass when under the spell of a charismatic, crazy person."

Hoehn spoke of the history of mental illness in the extended Helzer family. He said that Dr. Raffle saw Justin for thirteen hours, while Dr. Wornian and Dr. Walzer only saw Justin for two hours apiece.

Hoehn said, "Use your common sense. What would cause a person who is gentle and loving to do these acts? Don't let Mr. Jewett distance you from your common sense. Do you want to look for the cause, or just seek revenge? This is an American tragedy. Sanity and insanity are the issues.

"You had two wonderful doctors who said he was insane at the time of the crimes. He didn't like what he was doing. He felt that he had to. He was no sadist. He felt he had to do it for his premortal contract. This was a cult, and Taylor was its leader. Justin was one of Taylor's victims."

Hoehn pointed directly at Justin and forcefully said, "This is a diseased person!"

Harold Jewett was just as forceful in his presentation. "I'll talk about something Mr. Hoehn didn't talk about—the law. You looked at those photos. Those killings and dismemberments were done in the name of God, peace and love? Personality and adjustment disorders are not enough for an insanity plea. He knew the nature and quality of his acts!

"We saw a lot in Justin's journal about the idea of choice. The journal shows a logical thought process. They were nothing he got from Taylor.

"Mr. Hoehn brought up what a nice guy Justin was. Remember what he told Sarah Brents? He said, 'I've only been friends with you to see if I could fuck you!'

"Those are the actions of a rude, arrogant and asocial man."

Jewett also brought up about the disturbing and bloody poem that Justin had let Johnette Gray read.

"There was a logic and reason in these crimes," Jewett said. "In respect to the organs [of Annette Stineman], there was something very pagan going on there. There is an undercurrent of a pagan ritual. And those pagan ideas were Justin's. In his own words, Justin said, 'If I become demonic, will God still love me?'"

As to folie à deux, Jewett said sarcastically, "If Joseph Smith was delusional, do we have folie á eleven million?"

Jewett told the jury that Justin was never diagnosed with mental illness before the crimes. He said there were no psych reports in 2000 or 2001. The first evaluation of Justin didn't occur until May 2002, and by then, Jewett contended, Justin was beginning to think about an insanity plea.

Jewett spoke of the doctors who were not called by the defense because their reports would say that Justin was sane. These doctors included a man named O'Reilly and Carol Walzer. Walzer's report, in particular, showed that on the MMPI test, Justin showed no signs of mental illness. He was depressed and socially ill at ease, but not mentally ill.

Dr. Raffle didn't even interview Justin until May 2003, Jewett said, and when he did, Justin told him, "The ends justify the means." Asked if he would kill someone, Justin answered, "If the reason was good enough, yes."

It showed that reason was a part of Justin's mental capacity, according to Jewett. Justin was even cogent enough to tell Dr. Raffle on a question, "I don't want to answer that question. It may lead back to the case."

Jewett brought up the fact that Justin told someone in the mid-1990s: "Even if I sinned, and repented, I would be forgiven." It showed that he made a conscious choice to sin.

Things really propelled Justin to plead insanity, according to Jewett, when Dawn Godman agreed to testify in exchange for a plea bargain. In October 2003, Justin's lawyers entered a plea for him, not guilty by reason of insanity.

Jewett cited Dr. Wornian saying, "Justin Helzer was sane. He had a personality disorder, but not enough to stop him from understanding the nature of his acts. He did understand what was legally right and wrong.

"When you balance all the evidence—there is no mental disease as noted in DSM4. Justin even said, 'I will follow Taylor nine out of ten times.' It shows that he was capable of making a choice."

Unlike the guilt phase, the defense had a last chance to speak in the sanity phase. Hoehn told the jurors, "At the time of the crimes, Justin Helzer was insane. So said Dr. Raffle. So said Dr. Dolgoff. Follow the law according to the doctors, not the words of Mr. Jewett. He (Justin) was crazy! He was out of touch with reality!"

Judge O'Malley then gave the jurors instructions for the sanity phase. They were not to be swayed in reaching their verdict either by sentiment or pity. The only issue before them was sanity or insanity. They were not to think about sentencing. They could consider if Justin knew moral right from wrong. The burden of proof was now on the defense, but unlike the guilty phase, they did not need to go beyond a reasonable doubt. If they were 51 percent sure that Justin was insane at the time of the crime, then they had to vote for insanity.

Chris Darden was in Judge O'Malley's courtroom as Jewett and Cook were discussing some topics with the judge. Around 3:45 P.M. on July 15, Chris noted that a buzzer went off and bailiff Mike Harkelroad announced, "We have a verdict."

"What?" Daniel Cook asked in surprise.

Even Harold Jewett seemed to be surprised by the announcement.

An hour was given for family members and reporters to come to the courtroom. Chris noted that Heather rushed into the court about 4:30 P.M., just as the jurors were filing in. A few minutes later, the verdict in the sanity phase of Justin Alan Helzer was read by court clerk Tom Moyer. The verdict was that Justin had been sane at the time of the crime. He could now face the death penalty.

Chris said, "About three seconds after Tom sat down, Carma rushed in all out of breath. She didn't know what just happened. Heather put her arm around her mother and whispered in her ear. Carma nodded her head and didn't say a thing."

Much of the defense team's hopes had lain with the sanity phase. With those hopes dashed, the sentencing phase truly was a matter of life and death for Justin Helzer. Cook wanted to exclude witnesses who would testify during the victim impact statements from sitting in the gallery during other witnesses' testimony. He told Judge O'Malley, "Their natural humanity may project itself into the trial when it shouldn't."

Judge O'Malley responded, "I'm going to start with an admonition. I will deal with this, incident by incident. There are emotions on both sides. I can understand emotions."

Then she spoke directly to family members. "I cannot

begin to put myself into your situation. As hard as this is, I'm going to ask you to curb your emotions. If you are going to wipe your eyes, lower your head to do it. Everything you have done so far has been outstanding. I would hate the next step to be the removal of witnesses."

On July 21, 2004, Cook was looking at photos of victims and still asking for the exclusion of victim impact statements as being too prejudicial and inflammatory. He was quiet and determined in his arguments. He cited a U.S. Supreme Court case involving an O'Connor decision concerning the Eighth Amendment. He also said that victim impact statements in California were up to interpretation.

Jewett countered with California court and United States court decisions contrary to Cook's allegations. He said, "Emotional testimony is the tenet of this phase. I want to have the jury up personal and real about feelings of the victims' families. Why a person loved another is relevant."

Judge O'Malley took these things into consideration and cited *Tennessee* v. *Price* and *California* v. *Mitchum*. She said these cases allowed such victim impact statements to be heard by a jury. She also noted that the potential victim impact witness list included seventeen people. She said for the number of victims, this was not excessive.

After all the motions, the jury was brought in at 10:00 A.M. Almost immediately, victims' family members grabbed boxes of tissues and passed them around. Because of all the people in the courtroom, Carma Helzer had to sit directly next to Jim Gamble's mother.

As the family members settled in, an incredible thing happened. Justin, who had been quiet and cooperative during the whole trial, began to speak. At first, his voice was so low that people outside of the first two rows could not hear him. But then his words became louder and more persistent. He said, "I want this life to be over. I want to die. I just want to die!"

Momentarily stunned, Judge O'Malley raised her own voice and said, 'No. No. No. This is not the time for this."

Justin continued, calm but determined. "I'm not trying to be rude or anything. I just want to die."

Judge O'Malley's voice became louder and she shook her finger at Justin. "No. No. I'm not going to have this, Mr. Helzer!"

Carma Helzer in the second row began crying quietly. Then as emotion took over, her whole body became racked with sobs. Before long, she was wailing in the courtroom.

Justin would not cease, even as his lawyers tried to calm him down. "I just want to die!" became his mantra. It was a surreal scene; Justin begging for death, Judge O'Malley ordering him to be quiet, and Carma Helzer sobbing.

Judge O'Malley, seeing that she was getting nowhere with Justin, had the courtroom cleared of jury and gallery. One of the last sentences anyone heard as they filed out was "I don't know what possessed you, Mr. Helzer!"

Out in the hallway, it was an incredible scene— jurors bunched together down at one end of the hallway, journalists and gallery milling around in the central alcove, and Carma Helzer, off to the side, crying near the stairs. This situation lasted for nearly fifteen minutes, until everyone was ushered back into the courtroom. As a chastened Justin Helzer sat quietly, Judge O'Malley instructed the jury, "Anything you may have heard, you must disregard and base your decision on evidence." Then the long parade of friends and family of the victims began.

Judy Nemec was first. She spoke of her parents' life and her life with them. Then she described the dark days of August 2000. "I clearly was in a panic," she said. "It was like losing a child at the mall. We were in such shock. Finally I knew we wouldn't find them alive."

Jewett noted that she had been in court almost every day of Justin's trial. He asked her why:

Judy: We'd read the papers for weeks of all the horrible things. We understood that all the evidence had to be presented. [We waited] for some kind of closure.

Jewett: Briefly tell about your time in court.

Judy: All of this is horrible. They were not ready to die—the victims of a harebrained scheme. What pisses me the most, I never got to tell them good-bye. Before trial, I cried every day. I'm fearful of being in public alone. I don't open my doors to strangers. Before, it was my imagination running wild. Now it is more focused.

Nancy Hall also gave a recitation of her parents' lives. Jewett asked her the same question of why she had come to court every day. She answered, "I have to get some kind of closure, though I don't think this will ever be closed. The hardest thing for me is to know that once they'd been taken, what their thoughts must have been for each other. Their last moments."

And so it went, friends and family speaking for Jim Gamble, for Jenny Villarin and for Selina Bishop. Olga Land said of Selina after they knew Jenny was dead, "We knew that Selina would want to curl up in her mommy's bed. But she never came home. I started to realize she would never come home. Selina wouldn't have hurt anybody. I've been here almost every day for four months. Jenny and Selina would have been here for me."

Robert Asuncion added, "I don't take anything for granted anymore." Then he looked right at the jury and said, "Hold your children. Tell them that you love them."

David Villarin was angry and his testimony was potent. He had always been the rock in the family. He said, "I was horrified that somebody could do this. They treated 'em like trash! They dumped their bodies like garbage in the river!"

After the last of the victims' witnesses, it was Cook's turn to present witnesses as to Justin's life and character. Jason Chavez had known Justin at the LDS Third Ward. He attended missionary-school classes with Justin there in 1993. Justin had taught some of the classes. Chavez said, "Justin didn't have a lot of stage presence. But he taught by the Spirit. He was a guy who followed the Spirit. He was the most loving guy I knew. You wanted to be around a guy like Justin. He was a person who lived as he taught.

"Justin was a pure-hearted man who lived the principles of the Gospel. I realize how unpopular this is (speaking up for Justin). That the victims' families are here. But I have to do this. This is the least I could do for the wonderful friend that he was."

Chris Bergez had become acquainted with Justin at the Kaiser Hospital in Concord when Justin worked there. Justin followed Bergez on his rounds, and Bergez taught him how to take care of patients. Justin was always patient and kind and particularly so with the elderly. Bergez said, "We helped people get back on their feet again. Justin was enthusiastic about life. He was a great kid on a way to a good career. He stuck out because he was a kind, intelligent person. I never could have imagined he would do something like this. He does have some redeeming factors."

George Pinney, Justin's old teacher at Sunday school, said, "I saw the Helzer family once a month at home study. This was when Justin was in junior high school. Justin used to baby-sit our kids. I wouldn't have handed over that responsibility to just anyone. He did an excellent job.

"Even at a young age, he was very committed to the Gospel. He would often be ridiculed by other kids for being too 'churchy.' Focusing on God wasn't a top priority for a lot of thirteen- and fourteen-year-olds. Even when he got flak for it, he wasn't ashamed of things he believed in. He wasn't confrontational, but he wouldn't back down.

"Justin had a huge admiration of Taylor. A very strong love and sense of devotion. He kind of worshiped at Taylor's feet. They were very different guys. Taylor was dynamic, even domineering. His eyes were piercing. Justin was quiet, soft-spoken and reserved. He was a follower.

"I remember when I first saw what he was accused of in the news. The Justin I knew would have said stop. It wasn't the Justin I knew. One thing I do know, Justin would have followed Taylor off the face of the earth."

Justin's cousin Charney Hoffman picked up on this theme. He said, "It was impossible to be around Taylor without being deeply influenced by him. The experience of being in Taylor's presence was so profound, I think it would be difficult for someone with Justin's personality. I don't think Justin had a chance."

One of the most powerful spokesmen for Justin was

fifty-four-year-old George Chiu. Chiu was a pharmacist, and in the year 2000 he was convicted of embezelling from the company he worked for. He had to spend six-teen months of his time in the Contra Costa County Jail. It was there that he met Justin at the Bible-study class. Chiu said, "I got to know Justin on a personal level. He was a gentle spirit. He never talked about his crimes. Everyone was afraid of him originally. Every-one shied away from him.

"Justin had a good knowledge of scripture. We were there to learn. It wasn't just an excuse to get out of the pod. It was for inner peace. We looked forward to it every week. We also felt like brothers in the group. To forgive and move on."

Justin even taught Chiu some yoga. Chiu said, "I got a benefit from Justin. Yoga removed me from a tough environment. I read cards that his mom would write. And they were the most beautiful cards. I could imag-ine what his mom was going through.

"I stuck out like a sore thumb in jail. It was a huge range of inmates. Everything from drunk driving to murder. But they were all real human beings. Justin and I wouldn't have been friends on the street, but in there I perceived him as a gentle spirit. A gentle soul. He carried himself well with other people. Always a hard worker. Not just to pass the time, but to make the best of the situation.

"Justin was not prejudiced. He didn't have animos-ity for any group or anyone."

As far as why Chiu thought Justin should live rather than receive the death sentence, he said, "I feel strongly he will help others to come to God. I'm starting a new life. I'm blessed. You learn from your mistakes." In fact, Chiu had flown all the way from the Philippines to speak up for Justin at his trial. He was on a business trip and took a break from it to attend the trial as a witness.

Just as powerful as Chiu, in her own way, was Ann, Taylor Helzer's ex-wife. She said, "It's mind-boggling about Justin's part in this. Justin truly has a heart of gold. He never would have done any of this without Taylor's interaction. Justin was the most sweet, loving and caring guy I knew. We're all terribly sorry. This never should have happened. I can't begin to put myself in the victims' families' shoes."

Then she turned to the jury and implored, "Please spare Justin's life. Please! Justin is a worthwhile person, even if you cannot see that now. People can learn positive things from Justin."

After Ann, Jewett wanted to bring various incident reports into the trial. Outside the presence of the jury, he said there were three in particular. In one instance, Justin had been waiting in line at a Bank of America in Concord when an elderly man cut in front of everyone. When Justin told him that he'd cut into line, the man became belligerent. He even shoved Justin. Justin continued to argue and pushed the man so hard that he fell down. The police were called to the scene.

There were also jailhouse incidents. Justin was in a food line in jail when an argument broke out about who was first in line. Justin began to reach for a sandwich from the sandwich bin when a deputy told him, "Go to the other line."

Instead of following orders, Justin told the deputy, "Chill out."

The deputy asked, "What?"

Justin replied, "You heard me."

In another incident, a deputy was walking by the cells

when he saw Justin and his cellmate punching each other. The deputy told them to stop and they complied. In his report, the deputy did say that he didn't know if they were just playing around or if Justin was defending himself.

A third jailhouse incident occurred when Justin got a new cellmate. The new cellmate complained about Justin's eating habits. He said that Justin had more than forty oranges stuffed into a desk drawer. He also said that he hadn't been in the cell for more than forty-five minutes when Justin started talking about God and the Devil. According to the cellmate, Justin told him, "I believe in the Devil more than in Jesus Christ."

Within two hours of being placed in the cell, the new person wanted to be transferred away from Justin. He said that Justin sat down on the toilet to urinate. The new person concocted a story and told the guards that Justin wanted to kill him. Later, he recanted on the story, but he still did not want to be returned to Justin's cell.

Judge O'Malley ruled that Jewett could tell the jurors about the bank incident, but not about any of the jailhouse incidents. Cook made a request that he be allowed to put Carma Helzer on the stand and ask her only two questions. He wanted to restrict Jewett to only ask her about these two questions as well. But Judge O'Malley would not limit Jewett to those guidelines. According to Chris Darden, "Carma was sitting with her eyes closed and her hands clasped together as if praying for the request to be granted."

Carma's prayers went unanswered. Judge O'Malley denied the request and Carma Helzer did not take the stand in Justin's trial.

Closing arguments in the sentencing phase reverted to the original format, where Jewett spoke first, followed by Cook, and then a short rebuttal by Jewett. Jewett brought in all the aggravating circumstances, from Justin buying a Beretta 9mm pistol, to his use of one in the military, and when he nodded his head at Taylor at the Stinemans' door, indicating "come on." It was a very long list that included killing Ivan Stineman by bashing his head on a bathroom floor and killing Selina with a hammer blow to the head.

Jewettt told the jurors, "Remember the victims' impact statements. Judy having to go down to the Concord Police Department to submit DNA for comparison. Judy receiving the phone call from the Concord police that a torso and right arm had been found in a duffel bag.

"Remember Frances Nelson [Jim Gamble's mother] saying, 'I never got to say good-bye to my son, Hal. I never said good-bye.'

"Remember Olga Land saying how close Selina and Jenny were. Jenny never would have hurt anyone unless they hurt Selina."

Daniel Cook was more emotional now than he had ever been during all the other phases of the trial. He told the jurors, "I gotta say, when you happen to look in your rearview mirror and see Mr. Jewett barreling down on you . . . if you don't think that's trouble, boy, you don't know what trouble is. Last week all of you made the decision that this man is going to die in prison for sure. You've already decided that. Now it's your decision of when."

Cook told them there were eleven circumstances in which the death penalty could be imposed in California. He said it was for the worst of the worst, and Justin did not fall into that category.

Almost crying and angry at Jewett, Cook told the jurors that Justin's military record had to go on the side of mitigating circumstances, not aggravating ones. He said, "This just gets under my skin that the prosecutor would use my client's military and veteran's status as an aggravating factor. My client served his country with honor and dignity!

"This is not a game between the prosecutor and defense attorney. This is not a competition to see who wins. Seek and maintain the moral high ground. You are not grouped together as one. Each of the twelve of you are separate impartial judges. Stand for life. Choose life! Choosing life without parole doesn't mean you're not sensitive to the crimes that happened. Rise up! Choose life!"

Jewett's response during the rebuttal was swift and sarcastic. "Choose life! Justin didn't afford that choice to the five victims! Ivan's murder alone is punishable by the death penalty."

Then Jewett played a short audiotape retrieved from a new phone machine the Stinemans had bought. They were having trouble with the machine and Ivan's voice could be heard saying, "Just buy a new one."

Annette responded, "I'd hate to do that because what'll we do with this one? It'll just end up out in the garage like everything else."

At that moment, one of the Stinemans' cats wandered in, and everyone in court heard Annette say, "Goochy-goochy-goo" to the cat.

The courtroom erupted into laughter, including the jurors and Judge O'Malley. But it was laughter tinged with sadness. They all knew that those voices would be stilled on August 2, 2000.

The court regulars were stumped about how this verdict would turn out. Usually in unanimity on the outcomes, they were divided now. Chris Darden said, "I'm completely lost on what the verdict will be. Something I never was on the other phases. Juror number five—she was already struggling with the verdict on the other phases. I think she doesn't want to put Justin to death, but she also loves the Stinemans."

The jurors decided not to congregate on Friday, July 30, 2004, in the deliberation room. They gathered again on Monday, August 2, 2004, at 9:37 A.M. and deliberated all through the day.

One of the courtroom regulars, Chris, was sitting on a bench out in the hallway in front of Judge O'Malley's courtroom when he saw the jurors coming. He said, "As the jurors were walking to the stairwell, Mike the bailiff turned around, looked at me and said, 'Don't leave.'

"Mike came out of O'Malley's courtroom, walked over to me and said, 'There's been a verdict! It's going to be read tomorrow morning at nine A.M.' I was completely shocked and caught off guard."

Then Chris, note taker that he always was, jotted down what he thought the verdict would be. He wrote, "Three death penalties—Ivan Stineman, Annette Stineman and Selina Bishop." He did admit later that this was just a guess and he really didn't know how things would turn out.

Chris also jotted down, "Tomorrow when the verdict is read, it will be four years to the day when Jennifer and James were killed."

On the morning of Tuesday, August 3, 2004, the courtroom was packed as the jurors filed in. As soon as they sat down, they all held each other's hands throughout the reading of the verdict. Tom Moyer, the court clerk, read the jurors' decision. He began, "We the jury recommend Justin Alan Helzer be put to death. . . ."

As soon as Tom said "death," according to Chris, juror number five began sobbing uncontrollably. She doubled over in her seat, still holding hands with jurors four and six. Other jurors were crying softly as well. Justin Helzer sat passively and seemed to stare at nothing in particular. Chris Darden's prediction from the day before came true—Justin received the death penalty for the murders of Ivan, Annette and Selina. He got life without the possibility of parole for Jennifer and James.

Daniel Cook had the jurors polled individually on all the death penalty counts. Tom Moyer made his way from juror to juror, asking them if death was their true verdict. Each of them answered yes until juror number five. She was crying uncontrollably by now and could not speak. Tom stood patiently, waiting for her to calm down.

According to Chris, "Judge O'Malley looked at juror number five with compassionate eyes, patiently awaiting her answer as well. Finally after about thirty seconds or more of silence and waiting, juror number five, while sobbing, mustered up the word yes, which was barely audible.

"Instead of the usual five bailiffs on a verdict announcement, they had eight bailiffs in the courtroom. Judge O'Malley started crying while she was thanking the jury. She told them, 'We have placed a heavy burden on all of you. This county will be indebted to you all.'

"Then, while the jury was excused, five bailiffs went over to the jury box step and formed a tight wall so the jury could exit through the side door. The press and media cameras could not come inside O'Malley's courtroom. So every time someone would open up the double doors to exit, there were three photographers snapping pictures of every single person coming out, connected to the case or not.

"All the television cameras were at the exit door and bombarded the Stineman daughters and all the Bishop, Villarin and Gamble families with their bright lights and microphones in their faces.

"The press and media were all outside the courtroom in the lobby of the second floor. I had my back against the courtroom double doors, and Carma and Heather happened to walk up to their usual spots next to the courtroom doors. The press and media started snapping still pictures of us from about five different cameras. There were cameras being held up high in the air, outstretched by the photographers' arms, and then other photographers going underneath my armpit to snap pictures of Carma and Heather. All this time, I held up papers to cover the side of my face.

"I had Heather hide on the opposite side of me and I used my body as a shield, since she was facing the cameras head-on. And I had Carma stand directly in front of me and face me, so her back was to the cameras. It was bad! A very uncomfortable situation."

After the chaos of the courtroom hallway, the victims' family members went to different locales to hold impromptu memorial services.

A reporter for the *Contra Costa Times* was in Marin County and spoke with an employee at the Paper Mill Creek Saloon. The employee said, "I just wish he'd (Justin) say he was ready for execution now. But he won't because he's a selfish pig. He's not a man."

Down the road at a memorial in Forest Knolls, friends, relatives and family members of Selina Bishop, Jennifer Villarin and James Gamble held hands in a circle. Robert Asuncion said, "We thank God for our family and for keeping us together. If it wasn't for the strength of this family, it would be tough right now. If it wasn't for the strength of our friends, it would be tough right now."

David Villarin added, "For the loss we've had, we are rich in memories and rich in the love we have for each other. It's a relief today. It's not a celebration. It will never be a celebration."

Jenny's sister Olga Land summed it up for many by saying, "It's not a baseball game. We didn't win. Nobody won."

The trial for Justin Alan Helzer was over. The trial for Glenn Taylor Helzer was just beginning.

CHAPTER 15

The End of Days

In the back of many people's minds for Taylor's trial was the thought "When will the fireworks begin?" If Justin was mildly disruptive with his "I want to die," statements, many believed that was nothing compared to what Taylor might say while in court. One reporter even told Chris Darden that he would be going to the trial in expectation of Taylor blowing up at some point.

At first, before jury selection began, those predictions seemed to come true. Taylor and the lawyers had a hearing on September 17, 2004, to discuss issues while Suzanne Chapot was asking once more for a change of venue. During the proceedings, Ray and Mabel Carberry were in the gallery, as were Chris Darden and Nancy Hall. Chris said later, "Taylor was laughing loudly during some parts of the hearing. He was smiling and really interacting with his two attorneys. He seemed to be having a very, very good time at the defense table. He was talking so loud that everyone was listening to him talk to his attorneys.

"Taylor then turned around and looked into the gallery. He saw a young, very tall attorney in the gallery. Taylor gave a huge smile to the young attorney. Then he wrote a half-page letter, handed it to Ms. Chapot, who got up from the defense table, walked back to the gallery and gave the letter to the young attorney. That attorney wrote back to Taylor and then walked up to the defense table and started talking to Taylor. Taylor was laughing and smiling. It almost looked like he was hanging out with a buddy of his. Clearly having a great time."

Chris noticed one more thing. After Taylor was escorted away for the day, Judge O'Malley made eye contact with Chris Darden and Ray and Mabel Carberry. She smiled and said, "It's good to see everyone again."

If Taylor was having fun in the courtroom, the 650 prospective jurors were not. Brought in seventy-five at a time, many looked for ways to get out of jury duty any way they could. They cited financial hardships, vacations, illness and child-care concerns. One woman even said that she mostly spoke Mandarin and did not understand English very well. About people with vacations, Judge O'Malley smiled and said, "We take vacations very, very seriously around here."

The biggest laugh during jury selection was when O'Malley asked a person if she had any dependents. The woman answered, "Just my parrot."

If Justin's trial got off to a rocky start with the Associated Press reporter, it didn't take long for Taylor's trial to be heading in the same direction on October 28, 2004. One potential juror was a Mormon, and Judge O'Malley asked if she could put that aside. The woman said that she could, but she wondered if she could tell her husband about aspects of the case as it went along. O'Malley informed her that she wouldn't be able to speak about the case with anyone until the trial was over. The woman acknowledged this and said that she understood.

Less than an hour later, the same woman was out in the hall during a break and phoned her husband on her cell phone. Someone overheard her talk about Taylor's case on the phone and it sounded like the woman was indeed talking to her husband, because of the nature of the conversation.

Incredibly, the woman with the cell phone had a husband who was a Mormon who had done his mission in Brazil, just like Taylor. The woman's conversation had even included the phrases "That's what I thought. I thought you did yours in Brazil. I told the judge that you did, and I got a look from everyone in the courtroom."

Another comment by the woman, according to the person who overheard the conversation, was "The prosecutor—I'm not sure about yet. But that defense woman, I don't care for her!"

The person who overheard the conversation went up to bailiff Mike Harkelroad and asked, "Would Judge O'Malley want to know about this?" Mike said that she would.

Harkelroad, Judge O'Malley, Harold Jewett, Suzanne Chapot and Gordon Scott (also a lawyer for Taylor) all went into chambers and discussed the problem. A short time later, Judge O'Malley in open court said, "We're on the record to discuss the matter that has been brought to the attention of the court. A potential juror who was overheard discussing the case after having been admonished several times not to do so and specifically admonished not to talk about the case to her husband—that potential juror assured the court that she would not discuss the case with her husband. It has become very clear that she was indeed speaking to her husband when asking if it was Brazil where he did his mission, as well as making some remark as to her feelings toward some of the attorneys in this case. I feel I have a problem with this person. Do any of the attorneys have any objection to the court itself removing her?"

Then she added, "Neither side will lose any of their peremptory challenges. This one will be on the court."

Neither side did object, and the juror was sent packing.

If Taylor Helzer had been all smiles and good cheer on September 17, that was not the case on November 5, 2004. A professional photographer, Don Wilson, was allowed by the court to take photos of Taylor sitting with his attorneys. As Wilson set up his camera in the front of the courtroom, Taylor snapped, "Can you give us a minute? This isn't a circus! This is serious business! Hold on. I said, hold on!"

Wilson ignored Taylor's outburst and quietly went about his business. He did snap several shots of Taylor sitting with Suzanne Chapot and Gordon Scott.

One person who was sitting in the gallery commented later, "Well, we just saw the real Taylor Helzer."

Chris Darden commented later, "I'll bet he (Taylor) was that way with the Stinemans. Demanding and abrupt. Can you imagine how scary that must have been for them?"

The jury was all selected by November 5, and Tom Moyer, the court clerk, read all eighteen charges and thirty-nine overt acts. The reading took almost a half hour to complete.

On November 8, 2004, opening statements began in *The People of California* v. *Glenn Taylor Helzer*. Harold Jewett told the jurors, "There is a tremendous amount of information in this case. Where does all the evidence fit into the big picture? And there is a big picture. This trial is the end of an investigation that began on August

3, 2000. And it all started with a nine-one-one call in Marin County."

Jewett said that over time, fifty investigators interviewed 450 witnesses. There were stacks of boxes of evidence in the courtroom, and they were only a small percentage of the total. Many more items were kept in a storage room and took up two whole walls.

Jewett declared, "The investigation is not over yet. This case is not over until you say it's over!"

Once again, he gave a recitation of the lives of the victims: Ivan and Annette Stineman, Selina Bishop, Jenny Villarin and James Gamble. Then he recited about the lives and crimes of Taylor Helzer, Justin Helzer and Dawn Godman before Children of Thunder. Jewett said, "Selina was necessary as a middle person. They needed a patsy. From the day the defendant met Selina, she was marked for death."

Jewett recounted, day by day, the carnage that had been dealt out starting on Sunday, July 30, 2000. Unlike at Justin's trial, the story did not end with the initial arrests at Saddlewood Court on August 7. The story took off again, as Taylor had, when he jumped out the window of Detective Inskip's vehicle. It followed him as he ran down his neighborhood streets and confronted William Sharp and Mary Mozzochi.

Jewett summed it all up by saying, "At the end of this case, we want one thing—justice!"

Suzanne Chapot, on the other hand, told the jury that Taylor had already pleaded guilty on all charges and was remorseful. He would be locked up for life, no matter what happened now. She said, "You are human. You have feelings of outrage. But you must restrain your emotions.

"Taylor was a friend, a husband and a devoted father. What made him do this? We will present evidence of a life spinning out of control. Only a sick person would do it. This doesn't minimize Taylor's responsibility, but we are asking for life.

"The prosecution wants you to focus on a single period of time. [But] there is mental illness in his family. Both sides of the family are Mormons, and his grandfather on his mother's side claimed that he once saw Jesus Christ in his front yard. He was there for hours.

"Taylor was ordained at twelve, became a teacher at eighteen and was called to the priesthood. He had a blessing from a bishop saying how special he was. Taylor's first experience away from home was in the National Guard. There was evil that he saw there in Texas. He had discussions about premarital sex with others in his unit and even made some converts. He was determined to fight evil and he had the scriptures to fall back on.

"Taylor trained for his mission in Utah. He was one of the star trainees and he knew many of the scriptures better than the teachers.

"It was in Brazil that he began to argue about the LDS Church's doctrine. He even argued with the mission president in Brazil."

Then Chapot said that when Taylor married Ann, it opened up a whole new world for him—a world he had no contact with before. He could now watch television programs he was not allowed to watch at home while living with his parents. He could go to movies. As far as sex was concerned, Chapot said, "He was like a kid in a candy store. Everything was new. It was overwhelming.

"It was a combination of his extreme views on scripture, mental illness and Introspect that tipped Taylor over the edge. He combined Introspect with Mormonism. He thought he could transform the world. He saw governments within governments that affected us."

Then Chapot spoke of Taylor being committed to a mental ward in 1999. She claimed that he never thought he was crazy, so he made up a tale about faking mental illness to his friends so that he could cover up his real mental illness. He was afraid and ashamed of being mentally ill and did everything he could to hide it, even by saying that he was just faking it. He made them believe he was scamming the government. Chapot said that Taylor began taking meds and meth to make the voices stop.

As Taylor went to raves, sold ecstasy and recruited Justin and Dawn, Chapot said, "His world became smaller and smaller. His inner voices became more prevalent. Dawn and Justin and Taylor fed on their own neurosis."

Many of the witnesses on the stand were the same as in Justin's trial and much of their testimony touched the same areas. Every so often, however, a new and unheard wrinkle would be added. Nancy Hall summed up the aftermath of the first week of August 2000 by saying, "I think of my life as a spinning plate on a stick. When you break the stick, the plate falls. That's how I felt. I was numb most of the time. The news was always worse. Our cornerstone was gone. Then you have to figure out how you're going to live the rest of your life. We know that if we do anything to disgrace ourselves, it hurts our mother and father."

George Calhoun spoke of trying to snap Taylor out of his New Age philosophy, or "New Age bullshit," as Calhoun put it. He said, "We started getting complaints from clients. I told him, 'You're going to screw up a good job, your life and family.' Taylor was getting off track. I tried to get him grounded and back to business. I tried to steer him away from that philosophy."

Kelly Lord expanded on her previous testimony in Justin's trial. She said of Taylor, "At first, I thought his energy was terrific. He was somebody fun. Somebody cool. He had so much hair. It was almost like a disguise. I thought, 'Hooray! Somebody who is alive and wants to go do God's work.'"

Lord also told of going to a Wicca meeting with Taylor, Justin and Keri. She said, "It was a group of people sitting around talking about energy. They were talking about emotions and primal screams. Primal screams was where you released energy by screaming as loud as you can. Keri, Justin and Taylor all screamed. I didn't."

Lord also expounded on the incident with Taylor at a Carl's Jr. restaurant. He asked her, "If we could rob a small place like this, would you be up for it?"

She thought it was just one more of his rhetorical questions, a chance to see how loyal she was to him and his ideas. Then he said, "If I did something that the newspapers said was criminal, but I didn't do it, would you come and get me?"

She answered, "Absolutely."

Looking back at the incident, she said, "If a newspaper said he did something wrong, then it could be proven later he was already legally insane."

Lord spoke of the incident in Marin County where Taylor told her, "If Kelly gets in my way, she's fucked!" She looked over at him now, sitting at the defense table and said, "That's not the Taylor I knew. He never wore glasses. He was more stylish. New Age. He had a lot of energy. I've never seen Taylor sit this still or be this quiet for so long."

Chapot asked Kelly Lord how Taylor was when he changed. She said, "I found out he was just regurgitating others' beliefs. They weren't original ideas. I'd found out that they weren't his quotes. He was full of crap.

"He became very curt and condescending. I felt so betrayed after learning about the drugs. After the drugs, it was a real cutoff point for me.

"One of the things was, he tried to hug me on that

last night. I said no. I knew I had a victory over him that night. Otherwise, I could have been Dawn (Godman)."

Dawn Kirkland said on the stand that Taylor's testimony at the Third Ward had been bizarre. She said, "He made some comments about not going to church for a while, but God had wanted him to come back. He asked, 'Do you know what it's like to live without sin?' He said he lived without sin for a period of time."

Rosanne Lusk Urban and Tony Micelli testified again. There were always motions outside the presence of the jury as well. Suzanne Chapot had concerns about several potential witnesses. She said that a woman named Robin, whom Jewett wanted to call, had supposedly been involved in a scam Taylor wanted to pull on Dean Witter in 1998. Chapot said that Robin and Taylor had been boyfriend and girlfriend for a very brief time in 1996, but they were out of touch by 1998.

Jewett responded that Taylor had been coherent enough in 1998 to plan the scam, when he was claiming to be mentally ill to Kaiser Hospital psychologists. He added, "Taylor was perfectly capable of using his mental processes to buy and sell stock."

Judge Mary Ann O'Malley, however, would not let this evidence in.

Bishop Halversen once again took the stand and spoke of Mormon doctrine and Taylor's deviation from it. He said that there was no passage in the Book of Mormon that advocated by doing evil, one could hasten the Second Coming of Christ. Halversen also said that Taylor's testimony at the Third Ward had been "disturbing and bizarre." Halversen said, "Taylor shared his feelings from the pulpit. The things he shared were not coherent to me. After two or three minutes, I asked that he be excused so that the next person could testify."

Halversen claimed that the aftermath of the situation

was not confrontational. He said, "I met him that day and shook hands with him after the meeting. There was no acrimony."

At a second meeting with Taylor about three weeks later, Halversen said they had about a five-minute discussion. Halversen wanted to welcome him to the ward and asked if there was anything he could do for Taylor. Halversen would not discuss directly what Taylor talked about. To do so would have been to abuse confidentiality, much like a Roman Catholic priest not speaking of what's said in confession. But Halversen noted some things in general that Taylor had touched on.

Taylor at some point spoke of John 3:5 from the Bible:

> *Truly, truly, I say to you, unless one is born of water and the Spirit, he cannot enter the Kingdom of God.*

This tied in with Taylor's preoccupation with Spirit and voices from Spirit.

Halversen also spoke of Taylor's concern with Article 10 of the Mormon faith about the restoration of the tribes of Israel and the Second Coming of Christ. There was a concept of millennialism in Mormonism and many Protestant sects of Christianity.

Jewett asked about a note found at Saddlewood concerning 2 Nephi 2:22 and 2:27. In part Halversen spoke of it:

> *And now, behold, if Adam had not transgressed, he would not have fallen, but he would have remained in the Garden of Eden.*
>
> *And all things which were created must have remained in the same state in which they were after they were created; and they must have remained forever, and had no end.*

Wherefore, men are free according to the flesh; and all things are given them, which are expedient unto man.

And they are free to choose liberty and eternal life, through the great Mediator of all men, or to choose captivity and power of the devil.

Halversen said that Taylor did know good from evil, right from wrong. He said, "We have an intuitive knowledge about whether we are heading toward the light or darkness."

Jewett asked, "Anything in the Book of Mormon that speaks of killing someone and dismembering them and feeding their flesh to a dog?"

Halversen responded, "I'm not aware of anything in the writing."

A witness who hadn't been heard from in Justin's trial was Robin Stewart. She had met Taylor in 1996 at a birthday party. They became friends and were soon intimate. She said, "Initially we got along very well. We got involved very quickly. What was so attractive about him was that he was so positive. You are wonderful. I'm wonderful. Life is wonderful.

"He experimented with things that were taboo. This included sex. He was into pornography and trying sexual things out of the mainstream. I was uncomfortable with that. He wanted to embrace all of life's experiences and not be afraid of pain. He thought that all human beings had the potential to become God. He wanted to eliminate fear. He said that he had a pre-knowledge of life. It was like reincarnation.

"None of his behavior ever mortified him. He was very self-aware of what he wanted to do with his life. It never occurred to me that he might be mentally ill."

Like many others, Stewart went river rafting with Taylor. It was in the early summer of 1998 when the water was swift and treacherous in the mountain rivers. Stewart, with some others, was in a raft guided by Taylor. Only after they were through did he tell them that he'd been up all night, the night before, partying. Stewart said, "That was very upsetting for me. It can be dangerous in those rivers."

That was the last time Robin Stewart saw Taylor.

Another new witness on the stand was Tyler Bergland. He moved from North Dakota to an apartment on Victory Lane in Concord in November 1997. It was at those apartments that he met Taylor and became friends with him. Bergland recalled, "Taylor said he wanted to scam the system. He didn't want to work. He said that he was pretending to act crazy so they'd have to pay him. I never saw him acting crazy.

"He was very charismatic. Very open. He could get you to explore different ways of thought. I think I'm the one who introduced him to raves. He spoke to me about selling marijuana. Later, ecstasy and cocaine. He had brought a large sheet of paper with rules about how it would happen if it did happen (meaning the sale of drugs)."

Bergland spoke of meeting Taylor again at the Willows Shopping Center in Concord in late July 2000. Indications are that it was a few days before the abduction of the Stinemans. Taylor was with his kids and Bergland said that, "he seemed normal."

One person who had definitely been at Justin's trial was Keri Furman Mendoza. She was back on the stand again, wearing a green sweater and dark sunglasses. She looked like a Hollywood starlet. If many in the gallery expected another round of fireworks between her and Deputy DA Jewett, they were disappointed. Keri, this time, was soft-spoken, demure and straightforward. She added a few more things to the record that were not presented in Justin's trial.

Keri said, "Taylor and I became friends after meeting him at the Peppermill Restaurant. We'd talk after I got off my shift. There were no actual dates for a while."

When she moved in with him at the apartments on Victory Lane, she said, "He was very professional. He showed a lot of responsibility. He got up very early. Dressed nicely.

"He talked a lot about Impact and how it served him well in life. I was very intrigued and interested. I wanted to go. I couldn't understand how he could be so positive. He was full of life and love. I had a difficult life growing up. I aspired to be like Taylor. I loved him."

As for mental illness and his possible faking of it, Keri recalled, "He talked of having a breakdown. He wouldn't shower for a couple of days. Taylor would practice how he would act before going to a doctor."

Of raves and drugs, she said, "There was one rave at the old Home Depot in Oakland. I helped him by looking out for security during his ecstasy sales. He could gross a thousand dollars in a night. He wore black leather pants and flashy shirts.

"Once I started working for the Gold Club, he wanted me to influence other dancers. There would be a party to have men in a room with dancers. The purpose behind the parties was to make money. The men would pay a lump sum up front. It was just talk, though. It never got that far. It never evolved. It was in part from the movie *Eyes Wide Shut.*"

As far as In To Me See went, Keri recalled, "It would be Taylor sharing himself and how he looked at things and viewed relationships. Taylor did counsel his mom and her boyfriend, Donald, who was an instructor with Harmony. The questionnaire was actually brought to Donald's house at one point. I thought the questionnaire was funny. I just attended the counseling group there. People could see I was Taylor's girlfriend and they too could have true happiness and love."

Jewett asked her about the "it depends" questions on the questionnaire:

Lying is wrong: T F It depends
Stealing is wrong: T F It depends.
Breaking the law is wrong: T F It depends.
Murder is wrong: T F It depends.

Keri said she didn't remember the "it depends" questions. She thought the questionnaire may have evolved through several versions. She may have been right about this—Dawn Godman spoke of helping Taylor on a version of the questionnaire.

Keri stated, "Taylor always said things were a choice. As an example, you don't have to clean the cat box. But if you have a cat, and you don't want the house to smell, it would be a good idea to clean the cat box."

Keri said that she did help him create the In To Me See cards. On them were written things such as, "Do you enjoy love? Passion? Communication? Openness?"

It had the name Jordan Andrew Taylor on the card, along with a phone number. The last line read, "Are you ready for a change?"

Keri said that by the time they moved out of the Oak Grove house to Martinez, she and Taylor were distant from each other. In February 2000, she moved away from Taylor back down to southern California. She only visited him in northern California one more time. She thought that was either in May or June 2000. This visit may or may not have led to Rosanne Lusk Urban sighting her silver Mitsubishi in Woodacre. If the car was there, Taylor may have borrowed it and Keri was not there. There is no official record that Keri and Selina Bishop ever met.

Taylor did call Keri several times during spring 2000. She said, "We mostly argued. He wouldn't answer some of my questions. We were supposed to meet in San Luis Obispo, about halfway between where we lived. He didn't come. He did loan me money for my Mitsubishi. But I felt it wasn't really a loan. I felt like he owed me that money. I had supported him for years."

Keri told Jewett about a phone call she made to Taylor on Wednesday, August 2, 2000. Indications are that she called him from Dallas, Texas, where she was on a promotional tour. Keri said, "Taylor told me, 'Don't call me again unless you're dying or seriously injured!'"

Of course, on August 2, 2000, Taylor was luring Selina to her death at Saddlewood.

Keri also testified that Taylor wrote her a few letters from jail after he was arrested. In one, he told her to remember who he was and not believe newspaper reports and television news about what he had supposedly done. He claimed that the police had planted evidence at Saddlewood and that he was innocent.

Dawn Godman also had a few new things to say from the stand. One was: "One time, Taylor was sitting in the back of the church surreptitiously holding hands during a service. It was with Keri."

Dawn also said, "Taylor believed everything could be filtered through the Twelve Principles of Magic. Spirit knows everything that is going on around you. It was a way to live your life more in alignment with God. I began to accept the Twelve Principles of Magic. I believed that Taylor and Jesus Christ were brothers.

"When I first heard of Children of Thunder, I felt

unsure. But I never felt it was wrong. By then I was so wrapped up in Taylor, I would have followed any idea."

Dawn also spoke of a half-baked plan that Taylor came up with to get young girls from the "Burning Man Festival" and turn them into sex slaves. She didn't elaborate if they were supposed to be Taylor's harem or sell their bodies for money. Like many of Taylor's ideas, this one did not get off the ground.

Dawn said that just before Children of Thunder went into effect, "We asked God to protect us by beams of light and his angels. During the time we were deciding who these people [to be killed] would be, we prayed for God to lead them to us. We believed that they would give up their lives, whether they knew it or not. The only thing I felt in 2000 that was evil, was Satan."

Asked by Jewett if she still felt that way, Dawn answered, "Now I don't have an answer to that question."

Detective Erin Inskip presented emotional testimony of Taylor's flight from her vehicle. She said, "I heard a terrible thud. He threw himself through the window. I lost sight of him and got on the phone with Sergeant Heying to set up a perimeter. Concord PD responded."

There was testimony by William Sharp. Asked what he was doing on the morning of Monday, August 7, 2000, he responded, "Bathroom, kitchen and coffee."

Jewett asked what he thought of Taylor and his demands. Sharp replied, "I thought, 'This guy's screwy.'"

Mozzochi spoke, as well as Patrol Officer Kathy Watson, Detective Mike Warnock and Ron Mingas. Detective Mingas said, "The evidence you see in the court is only a small percentage of the total."

Other people had spoken of Impact and Harmony, but when Neil Fisher got on the stand, he gave insights into what it was like to head a self-awareness group. Fisher was the creator and organizer of Introspect. Originally he had gone to Impact in 1990 and gone on to became a trainer and enrollment director for that group. Even though Fisher enjoyed Impact, he eventually left because he was often not paid on time for his services. He said in court, "I had a terrific experience with Impact. It was life-changing. But I thought I could run a business better. My fundamental philosophy was the celebration of life. Love yourself and love your neighbor.

"Introspect was set up for people to notice things that limited them. Anything that impeded aliveness. The role of the trainer was to confront a person about their belief systems. In Impact, it could be harsh and confrontational. Introspect was gentler and kinder. I hired two trainers from Impact, who left for the same reason I did. Introspect was similar to Impact, but more spiritual in nature. You got to know people on a more intimate basis."

Fisher said of Introspect that it was less rigid. It was a "shift in the way to experience life." As for love, he said the Greeks had many words for it, so perceptions of the word "love" in English depended upon a person's outlook. Fisher recalled that he met Taylor in 1992 or 1993. He said, "Taylor loved the workshops. He helped people to love life. He asked to come and work for me. He was very sensitive and very kind. He got along with everyone in the group. He was a seeker. He wanted to live a full and happy life."

Jewett: "No talk from him about the end of the world?

Fisher: No.

Jewett: Any talk about the Garden of Eden? A perfect environment?

Fisher: No.

Jewett: Did it come up, if a tree falls in the forest, and no one is there, does it make a sound?

Fisher: (laughing) I really don't know.

Something new was introduced to court outside the presence of the jury by Harold Jewett. He wanted to get into evidence the matter of Taylor making a forty-foot rope out of shredded bedsheets and T-shirts in August 2002. And even more than that, he wanted to introduce some evidence no one had heard up until that point.

According to Harold Jewett, on February 7, 2004, Taylor was talking to a fellow inmate at the county jail named Danny Ramirez. Ramirez was there on a court matter—his usual place of confinement was the maximum-security prison of Pelican Bay. Knowing that both Ramirez and Helzer had committed violent crimes, a jail deputy flipped a switch and listened in on their conversation.

Taylor, at one point, asked Ramirez, "Once I'm transferred to a state prison, what level is the best level to escape from?"

Taylor also wanted to know where guard towers were located at various state prisons. Ramirez told Taylor that for $100,000 he could set up a prison break. He would have a helicopter fly in with "SWAT-type stuff." He said he'd need $25,000 each for four participants in the escape.

Taylor wondered if he could be freed while riding on a prison bus to one of his regular psychiatric meetings in Martinez. Ramirez told him it would be difficult because the bus was bulletproof and the guards had a lot of firepower.

Taylor also spoke with inmate Adam Gardner that day and discussed the possibility of escaping while en route to the doctor's office. Gardner told him it would be possible to put a sniper on the roof of a building on Alhambra Avenue, near the high school. This person would take out the driver while "some dudes blast the other three guards."

The next day, Carma Helzer visited Taylor in the jail. A jail deputy was listening in on the intercom because of the previous day's discussion of an escape. The guard heard Taylor tell his mom that he needed $100,000. He also said he wanted nothing to do with Justin's trial because it would make his own escape harder to accomplish. Then he said that if he was on death row, it would be very hard to escape.

Just how serious the escape attempt was became a matter of debate now. Later, Gardner and Ramirez would say that they were only trying to bilk Taylor Helzer out of $100,000. They even called him re-tarded.

According to Chris Darden, "Taylor was able to get Carma to take $10,000 out of her bank account, since she was not able to raise $100,000. The next part isn't really clear. She either put $10,000 into some stranger's mailbox in the middle of the night, or her husband, Gerry, stopped her from doing it before it went that far."

Even the local newspapers were intrigued by this new angle. The *Contra Costa Times* headline of December 3, 2004, was DETAILS OF HELZER ESCAPE PLOT TOLD:

> Lt. Joe Caruso said Helzer asked his mother, Carma, to raise at least $100,000. Carma refused to respond to Taylor's strange request, but she later placed $10,000 cash into an unknown person's mailbox, prosecutor Harold Jewett said.

Jewett did tell the court, "Whether or not Carma Helzer knew what the purpose of the money was, it's certainly more than just a coincidence."

As to why Carma Helzer had not been charged with anything was never brought up in court by Jewett or anyone else.

Jewett definitely wanted all these escape plans to be presented before the jury. More than anything, he said it would refute the contention that Taylor was now a model prisoner who no longer was a threat to anyone and was remorseful for what he had done. Jewett said it proved that less than a year before, Taylor was willing to kill guards. Jewett said, "It shows he understands the depths and wrongfulness of his crimes, and was not under the influence of meth at the time."

Chapot contended, "This consciousness of guilt is irrelevant. Taylor has already pled guilty. This cannot be brought out in the penalty phase.

"Those were idiotic ideas. There is no evidence of an overt act. It was just jail talk."

Jewett countered, "Before July 30, 2000, people might have thought that killing five people to bring peace and love to the world was idiotic. But it happened."

Judge O'Malley pondered the matter and said, "Getting down to the nitty-gritty of it, is it sufficient to go to the jury?"

The next day, O'Malley ruled that it couldn't come in under Factor A—that was closed off because they were past the guilt phase. She left open the possibility that it could come in through Factor B. As far as that went, she would have to do more research on the matter.

That a door was still open seemed to satisfy Jewett. He withdrew his request to have the jury hear about Taylor's escape plans, with a proviso. Jewett said to the judge, "I hope the court keeps a good ear open during all of these doctors that defense brings in, giving their testimony about his mental illness and how bad he is, for when that door is open."

Chris Darden said, "I took it that since the doctors will say Taylor was so mentally ill and on meth, he can't understand the nature of his crimes when they occurred, but Jewett will counter that he is still thinking how to commit crimes. And Taylor has been in a controlled environment for the past four years and has had no access to meth and is still thinking of how to kill multiple people."

By December 6, 2004, the defense began to call a parade of psychologists and psychiatrists once again. In fact, not unlike Justin's trial, Taylor's fate in many ways hinged upon whether the jury decided he was insane at the time of the crimes. Dr. Richard Foster was a clinical psychologist with a Ph.D. His specialty was working with young men who had mental problems. In 1995, Foster saw Taylor Helzer at a Kaiser Hospital clinic.

Dr. Foster said that in that year Taylor came to see him about sexual problems within his marriage. He claimed he was dissatisfied in that area because his wife would not do sexual things he wanted to do. From the way Taylor talked and the things he spoke about, Foster came up with a diagnosis of "narcissistic features with grandiosity and self-inflation."

Taylor complained that he could influence all the events in his life—except sexual satisfaction with his wife, Ann. Foster said, "Taylor felt as if his wife had somehow tricked him about being more sexually open. Taylor felt, 'I deserve this.' He had a lack of ability to put himself in the shoes of his wife. He felt he was being deprived. He wanted a wife to give him what he saw in pornographic films."

On top of this, Taylor told Dr. Foster, "Man is becoming like the 'Father in Heaven.' I have the ability to reform society, but I can't get the kind of sex I want from my own wife!"

At Dr. Foster and Taylor's second meeting, Taylor showed him a detailed plan about what he wanted sexually. Taylor was scheming to put ads in Brazilian newspapers for eighty to 120 women applicants. They had to want sex on a daily basis. He would whittle down the list to thirty-five women and then meet them. They would have to sign a two-year contract to satisfy him sexually whenever he wanted. Supposedly he would do all of this while still married to Ann.

Foster noted that Taylor craved the approval of everyone around him. He couldn't stand it if someone thought ill of him. It was a classic case of narcissism, as far as Dr. Foster was concerned.

The next doctor on the stand was Dr. Jeffrey Kaye. In 1998, he was working at the Kaiser Intensive Outpatient facility (IOP) in Martinez. Many patients who came to the IOP had been hospitalized for a short while for mental problems. In fact, in 1998, a doctor named Pollock told Dr. Kaye, "Taylor Helzer is a perfect candidate for IOP."

Dr. Kaye said, "He (Taylor) was coming to see me because he was not able to function in his job and didn't understand what was happening to him. He was in a manic phase. He was all over the map. His movements were jerky, and he had pressured speech. He was under obvious distress."

In fact, Dr. Pollock's reports had noted, "This person is falling apart. It's a cry for help."

On September 1, 1998, Dr. Kaye noted that Taylor couldn't concentrate and was angry at inappropriate times. He complained that people could see right through him. There was a rapid shift of moods and he was constantly on the verge of tears.

On his first visit with Taylor, Dr. Kaye diagnosed him

with a bipolar disorder type I with manic/psychotic features. He also noted ecstasy abuse and marijuana abuse.

According to Dr. Kaye, Taylor couldn't tolerate being around a group of people in a therapy setting. Jewett, on the other hand, pointed out that this was at the same time that Taylor was mixing with lots of people at raves and seemed to enjoy company.

Dr. Kaye talked to Keri Furman about Taylor and she seemed genuinely concerned for his welfare. On September 29, 1998, Taylor came in with Keri and began to talk about spirits. About Keri, Dr. Kaye said, "I thought hers were authentic concerns. She seemed both loving and concerned. She seemed to be a young woman way in over her head. I believe Keri was in love with him. She was scared for him."

Dr. Kaye said that he wanted Keri to contact the Alliance for the Mentally Ill. This was a support group for family and friends of mentally ill people. Kaye recalled, "I felt Keri was supportive of this with Taylor."

Dr. Kaye thought that Taylor should voluntarily place himself in a mental hospital for treatment. On December 10, 1998, Taylor was full of mixed moods and Keri was so frustrated with him that she said she would leave him if he didn't take his meds. It was also around this time, at least according to Taylor, that he picked up a hitchhiker in his car. Then, in an irrational gesture of trust, he let the hitchhiker "borrow" his car. He never got it back.

On December 22, Taylor had a full-fledged panic attack in front of Dr. Kaye. He was hyperventilating, sweating and supposedly filled with intense fear. A week later, he showed up wearing a bizarre outfit. Dr. Kaye said, "He looked like a strange cartoon character."

On January 13, 1999, Taylor told the doctor that he was walking in the street when a voice told him to walk up to a man with a motorcycle. If he did so, he would come into a great deal of money. Taylor walked up to the motorcyclist, but no money came his way.

Taylor also said, "God has great plans for me. Like being president. The voices told me not to take my meds."

February 25 was either a bravura performance by Taylor, or a genuine nervous breakdown. Keri had to take him to Mount Diablo Hospital. Taylor hid in the bushes until attendants got him. He was transferred by ambulance to a Kaiser Hospital. He was kept under observation for a couple of days, under a 5150 hold (meaning they could hold him for 72 hours).

Dr. Kaye saw Taylor again on March 9. Taylor spoke of spirits and hallucinations. On March 24, he complained of erectile problems. Two weeks later, Taylor looked and acted more coherent, and said maybe he really wasn't a prophet.

Dr. Kaye's last meeting with Taylor occurred on April 23, 1999. Instead of looking unkempt and acting crazy, Taylor once again looked like a stockbroker with a clean-cut appearance and pleasant manners. He did, however, relate a strange story about sleepwalking. It wasn't clear if during the sleepwalk, he intended to hurt himself or someone else.

Dr. Douglas Tucker had a return appearance to court in Taylor's trial. He interviewed Taylor in jail for three hours on December 5, 2004, as Taylor's trial was ongoing. Tucker's diagnosis of Taylor was acute mania that bordered on the psychotic. Taylor claimed, "The whole world is crazy, so who's to say I'm not a prophet of God? I'm naturally more evolved than the rest of humanity. That's why I can hear God. We are all in a dream state. I am not Taylor. I am a manifestation of God's consciousness. He created the illusion of individuality. We are all aspects of God."

Dr. Tucker described Taylor's flitting from one subject to another as "tangentiality." He said, "You just go off into the ozone. It is difficult to fake mania. Unless you're a psychiatrist, you wouldn't know the symptoms, especially the nonverbal parts. It's almost impossible to keep it up for hours. It's too exhausting."

As to the crimes, Taylor told Dr. Tucker, "Maybe I failed because I didn't hear God correctly. I wanted to free humanity from sexual slavery and other horrific things. I could end war and sexual slavery. Right and wrong are statistical and illusions, but good and evil are deeper and eternal traits. I regret what I did. I feel bad about the people who died. I was guilty as charged, but my purpose was right and good. I could have avoided all this by being selfish and enjoying the paradise of my life. But some die, so many can live. The idea was beautiful and right. The drugs might have confused me."

Dr. Tucker said, "He's a guy who wants to do right. His orientation is to helping people. He is not antisocial."

The testimony of doctors Foster, Kaye and Tucker were only a prelude to psychiatrist Dr. Robert Chamberlain. He had seen Taylor more than all the others, from February to September 2004, and they often based some of their conclusions on what Dr. Chamberlain already had written. In a grueling one-and-a-half day struggle, Jewett covered almost every point that Chamberlain had made. He covered all of Chamberlain's thirty-one-page report that had only been finished on November 19, 2004. Jewett seemed to wear down Chamberlain, the jury, the gallery and even himself in the lengthy questioning.

It might have seemed unnecessary to some, but this was the crux of the matter. Was Taylor sane or insane at the time of the crimes? Whether he got life without parole or the death penalty depended on this.

Dr. Chamberlain's testimony went clear back to when Taylor was on his mission in Brazil. Chamberlain noted, "Taylor would write in his journal at three and four in the morning. He couldn't sleep. His relationship with God became more intense. His speech patterns were littered with scripture. A very stilted language. He would link disparate ideas. A person struggling with mental illness will often say they are faking it. It is to mask their shame of really being mentally ill. There was an illogic in his schemes. A flamboyant mania."

Chamberlain's diagnosis of Taylor was one of an individual with schizo-affective disorder and possibly bipolar as well. A schizo-affective disorder could be effected by a family history of mental illness, something that seemed to be prevalent on Carma's side of the family.

As far as religious aspects and grandiosity went, Jewett had Dr. Chamberlain admit that he had not consulted with any experts in Mormon religion or doctrine. Chamberlain was basing most of what he knew by layman's input. His diagnosis of Taylor also came from personal observation, and by speaking with Taylor, Carma and Taylor's cousins and friends.

Jewett talked on at length and sometimes became somewhat agitated himself. He drew a laugh at one point by stating, "Let me slow down. I'm becoming manic myself."

Many in the gallery wondered if Jewett would get in testimony about Taylor's escape attempts from jail. This seemed like a real possibility when Jewett asked Chamberlain if he'd heard that Taylor had forty feet of hand-made rope in his cell. Taylor's claim was that he was going to use it to commit suicide. Chamberlain admitted, "It seems longer than necessary." That's as far as any testimony of jail breaks went.

Jewett also zeroed in about Taylor's sanity at the time of the Stinemans' murders. Taylor supposedly said later, "We decided to bang their heads on the bathroom floor until they were dead. A gunshot would have been too loud." This statement indicated that Taylor knew what he was doing and took steps not to be caught in an act that he knew to be illegal and wrong.

Heather took the stand for Taylor, as she had done for Justin during his trial. She was also once again almost breathless and crying as she answered questions. Even members of the victims' families in the gallery felt sorry for her.

Heather was the historian of the family and told of various members, especially on her mother's side, who had suffered from mental illness. She spoke of Grandpa Doyle Sorenson seeing Jesus Christ standing in his front yard for hours. She recalled, "Taylor was interested in spiritual things, since I can remember. He was wonderful. A good brother. When Taylor came back from his mission, he was still good and motivated. He met and married Ann, and that was a good thing. Everything was great in 1993. In 1994, I saw changes in Taylor. I saw him sad about his marriage and his job."

As the changes grew with Taylor and her mother, Carma, Heather moved about as far away from them as she could. She went to college in Alaska. When her mother was excommunicated, she thought that Taylor should be as well. He had deviated far from the mainline Mormon doctrine.

Heather said, "By 1997, Taylor had thrown away his

religion. He seemed so callous. It was hard to listen to him. He was confrontational. He wanted to argue with me about God and the Church. We argued a lot on the phone. He had a different philosophy. He wanted me to see my religion as false. He wanted me to see a greater truth. I was very disillusioned by all the New Age ideas of my parents."

Heather got married and moved with her husband to Utah. She saw Taylor only once in 1998 and twice in 1999. She said, "He was actually better in 1999. We didn't fight. There was a safe topic about our chil-dren."

Asked how she felt now, Heather cried, "I can't tell you how we've all felt. I can't explain how awful we feel."

She apologized to the family members in the gallery for what her brother had done.

Chapot asked her, "Do you want your brother to die?"

Heather practically wailed, "No!"

Even Harold Jewett could see her sincerity and pain. He didn't cross-examine her.

Ann Helzer took the stand as well. She was somewhat more restrained than she had been about Justin in pleading for his life. But she said, "Taylor writes to our girls and sees them in jail. His girls love their father. It would be catastrophic to my girls if he was put to death. This is their dad."

Closing arguments began on December 14, 2004. Jewett started by showing a collage of photographs on an overhead screen. Each photo showed a pair of people; Annette and Ivan, Jenny and Selina, Jim and his mom, Frances. Jewett asked, "Is this case about the service of God or is it about power and greed?" He answered his own question by saying, "It is about cru-elty. It is In To Me See, not In To God See. It was all about promoting Taylor.

"Greed is a selfish desire for power and money. Cruelty—it's a willingness to hurt. A savageness and inhumanity. Ends justifying the means. The defendant is a psychopath, but that does not make him mentally ill.

"The defendant cited Samuel 15: 'And Saul said to Samuel, "I have sinned, for I have transgressed the commandment of the Lord.'"

"It's Samuel's retribution. It's ironic the defendant chose that passage."

Jewett pointed to the Bill of Rights on the wall of the courtroom and the Fourth Amendment; these dealt with due process and life, liberty and property. He said that Taylor had taken property, liberty and life from others illegally. "This is not revenge—this is retribution. Follow the law whether you agree with it or not. You don't want to leave this courtroom with a sense of regret. Reach a just verdict. This has all been about justice."

Jewett read through a series of aggravating circumstances. For Factor A, he said, "It can be things like feeding a tattoo to a dog or slitting Annette Stineman's throat while her husband's head is being beaten on the floor." For Factor D, mental disturbance, he said, "this case was not in the heat of passion. It was cold-blooded and premeditated." And for Factor F, moral justification, Jewett said, "Doing it for God—wasn't that his Star Trekkian philosophy?"

Jewett showed a gym bag to the jury and said that he'd done them a favor by not showing one of the real bags that Taylor had used. Jewett said that he spared them the blood and stench of the real bags. The smell of death. He said, "This bag was to hide the bodies. Taylor appreciated the criminality. There was a reason Jenny and Jim were killed."

And then very passionately Jewett related, "Each photograph has two people in it. The ties that bind." Jewett started up the electrical reciprocating saw and its noise filled the courtroom. Jewett thundered, "Taylor cut the ties that bind! You have to see that bathroom in your mind's eye. The sights, sounds and smells. There was blood everywhere. He did it with extreme cruelty.

"In your mind's eye, look inside that house on Saddlewood, the living room lit only by a fire. All the lights are out and Selina's effects are burning. Then he (Taylor) had to fish through the bags of body parts to slice off her tattoo. The tattoo, he cut it off because he understood the criminality of his actions. I hope you see the reality of this. What does feeding a tattoo to a dog have to do with love? With God? That's as evil as it gets!"

Jewett took the jurors back through the case, witness by witness, statement by statement. One of Taylor's self-incriminating statements was to Debra McClanahan. She had asked him about one crazy scheme, "Aren't you afraid you'll be caught?"

Taylor answered, "I've been talking to God. Who would believe I'm guilty? I won't be held responsible."

Another damning statement was from Taylor to his aunt Marsha Helzer. He said, "Since I can't be perfect, I have to get all of the evil out of me in this life."

Jewett declared, "Taylor said that there had to be darkness at the Apocalypse. There was darkness and Apocalypse at Saddlewood Court!"

Jewett told the jury to look at all the items and evidence, even the small evidence that was found in Selina's car. He said, "If I wasted your time, I'm sorry. But sometimes these things are the last vestiges of our lives. Hell was brought to earth that week! It's been four years, but don't think the memories have diminished by the passage of time for the family members. Justice is what this trial is about. You have to look at the degree of enormity. Justice is the imposition of the death penalty."

Jewett's entire argument had gone from 9:00 A.M. to 4:10 P.M. on December 14.

Suzanne Chapot began her closing arguments on December 15. By contrast, her remarks were sober and measured. She told the jurors, "Each of you, look into your hearts and your minds. Ultimately you must answer to your own conscience. You can never shift the responsibility to another. It must be your individual act."

As for mitigation, she said, "This is a human calculation, not a mathematical calculation. A single factor to vote for life is enough. There is nothing in our laws that say you must return a verdict of death. It doesn't mean you're forgiving Taylor. Life without parole is hardly a tolerant act.

"Mercy is the better part of justice. For all the days of his life, all his actions will be circumscribed by stone walls."

She quoted a poem by James Joyce that spoke of the horrors of prison life.

"Right and wrong, good and evil, these are concepts you've heard all through this trial, but they are not the law. As his mental illness took hold, he began to lose his place in society. Mental illness comes to different people in different ways."

She spoke of three cousins of Taylor who were mentally ill. She asked, "Was that a choice for them? None of them was faking their mental illness. And Taylor was not faking his either. He could not fool all of the doctors, all of the time. Taylor had no choice in his mental illness.

"'That's not the Taylor I know.' You heard that from a lot of people. How do you judge this man? Taylor was sweet, loving and gentle. If one aspect can be singled out about Taylor, it was to help other people. Mormons don't believe they can bring the Second Coming of Christ. These were delusional thoughts. Even in his darkest hours, he believed he was acting for the greater good.

"In Brazil, he began to struggle with his demons. Later, he became obsessed with Impact. He began drinking and using drugs, not uncommon for someone with mental illness. In his twisted mind, Taylor believed he had a special mission. Everyone expected great things of him, but he lost his battle with mental illness and his world turned upside down.

"Safely locked in prison, he will have to live with the horror of what he did, all the days of his life. The prosecutor said he was rational. What is rational about Children of Thunder? Extreme mental illness is mitigation. What does death for Taylor accomplish? It offers the illusion that taking a life preserves life. An exercise of mercy is one of the more noble human traits. You must look at Taylor's life as a whole. This man is a complex mixture of love, compassion, mental illness and remorse.

"What good will it accomplish by putting Taylor to death? What good will it do those five people? Taylor's death will solve nothing."

Chapot showed the jurors a large photo of Taylor and his children. She said, "You will decide what kind of society we live in. I am pleading with you that we overcome hatred with compassion."

CHAPTER 16

What shifting films of distance fold you, blind you,
This windy eve of dreams, I cannot tell.
I know they grope through some strange mist to find you,
My hands that give you Greeting and Farewell.

Nora May French, 1906

Ave Atque Vale

After the final arguments, it was a matter of waiting for the decision of the jury. They were escorted into the deliberation room by the bailiff Mike Harkelroad. The victims' family members went to a downtown restaurant, as they had been doing since the previous May during Justin's trial. Over lunch, they tried to fathom Taylor's jury and how they might decide. Many agreed that they had a harder time reading the "poker faces" of this jury than those of Justin's jury.

On December 16, the jurors came back into the courtroom to ask some specific questions. One question was whether in the summer of 2000, Taylor was delusional with schizo-affective disorder. There were also questions about one of the psychologists' reports about Taylor's mental illness, or lack thereof, when he was on mission in Brazil. After the questions were addressed, the jurors filed back to the deliberation room. Jewett discussed these matters with victims' family members, and Chapot spoke with Taylor. Then the victims' family members spent the rest of the day hanging around in the hallway outside of court, reading, chatting and contemplating.

On December 17, 2000, family and friends of Ivan, Annette, Selina, Jenny and James were still camped out in the hallway on the second floor of the Bray Building in Martinez. Some played cards on the floor, while others talked or tried to catch a nap. Then, unexpectedly, at 9:40 A.M., Bailiff Harkelroad walked out into the hallway and announced, "There's been a verdict."

An hour was given so that the defendant's family, print reporters and television crews could arrive. Carma and Heather, who had not been at the Bray Building, rushed to the scene. Everywhere around the doorway of Courtroom 4, there was a sense of anticipation and finality. What had begun in July and August 2000 was finally coming to a close.

The courtroom doors were opened at 10:30 A.M., and a crowd of family members, friends, court observers and the merely curious filed in, taking every seat in the gallery. Among these were Chris Darden, Ray and Mabel Carberry, Juley Salkeld and Roger Riddle, who had begun their observations seven months before. In the intervening months, Courtroom 4 had practically become their home away from home.

Taylor Helzer was escorted to the defense table, wearing his usual blue shirt and sweater. The jurors soon followed and took their assigned seating in the jury box. Asked if they had reached a decision, the jury foreman announced that they had. A form was passed to Tom Moyer.

In a steady voice, the court clerk began the reading of the verdict. On the count of first-degree murder in the death of Selina Bishop, the jury found that Glenn Taylor Helzer should be put to death. Friends and family of the victims hugged and cried as the first sentence was delivered, followed by four more sentences of death for the murders of Ivan, Annette, Jennifer and James.

Taylor smiled at the jurors and thanked them then turned and mouthed the words to his mom, Carma, "It's okay."

When he was escorted away, Taylor kept a bemused smile on his face. He didn't appear to be upset or agitated.

Outside the courtroom was a battery of television news cameras and still cameras of photojournalists. Suzanne Chapot only had a short statement for them. "The death of any person is sad. Society hasn't reached a place where they don't realize that killing people who kill people doesn't serve a purpose."

Carma Helzer was equally brief. She said, "I just want to say I'm sorry for all the trauma that the victims and their families have had to go through."

Heather was somewhat more talkative. She said, "California should have a better way of treating mentally ill criminals, like my brothers. But in some ways, I think death is the kinder sentence."

Harold Jewett said to the reporters, "The jury's decision shows how valuable life is, not a sense of callousness. This decision is a reflection of how truly precious life is. He (Taylor) obviously values his life. That's why he put up a defense. The jury's verdict speaks to his disability claim."

In a news conference after the verdict, jury foreman Bernie Rose, who was an attorney from San Ramon, spoke of how difficult the decision had been. He told reporters, "It is always difficult deciding to deliver death, regardless of what has been done. But we couldn't find anything lesser. We tried to find any mitigating factors, but were unable to. I believe the death penalty is ultimately state-sanctioned revenge. The question in the end is how much does it heal wounds. But we took an oath. We couldn't find anything lesser than death."

To the point of death versus life for Taylor, Olga Land told a roomful of reporters, "Taylor needs to face Selina. He needs to face Jenny, and Mr. Gamble, and Mr. and Mrs. Stineman. He needs to face God. He was not the Second Coming of Jesus Christ. He was the Second Coming of Manson."

The victims' family members sat at a long table answering questions of news reporters. They insisted that Concord PD detective Judy Elo and Marin County detective Erin Inskip sit with them. Through most of the conference, they all held hands.

Jenny's sister-in-law Donna Futch said, "We can start to recover from this. Every day in court was like ripping the wound open again."

Nancy Hall explained, "Taylor befriended my parents and then he did this to them. It's very hard to believe that there's a human being on this planet who could do something like this to such sweet old people."

Except for Justin's one outburst in the courtroom during his penalty phase, he had been silent while sitting at a defense table. All of that changed on February 5, 2005, however. According to Chris Darden, who was sitting in the gallery, along with Nancy Hall, "Justin walked into the courtroom with a full, scraggly beard. He was essentially acting as his own attorney at this point, with Mr. Cook and Mr. Hoehn at his side. Starting at nine-twenty A.M., Justin started speaking to the court. The reason Justin was speaking was that he had received two law books in the jail and wanted to represent himself.

"Justin claimed prosecutorial misconduct on Mr. Jewett's part. He claimed that Jewett continued slamming the hammer down on his file repeatedly in front of the jury at least three times.

"Mr. Jewett replied, 'Actually, I believe that was Justin remembering himself doing that to Selina! I only hit my file once.'

"Justin went so far as to want the transcript to be read back, to prove his point. And Justin wanted to know why, if it wasn't in the transcript, the reason it was missing.

"Justin said, 'Who's to say Mr. Jewett's memory is to be believed more than my memory? Why take Mr. Jewett's memory about the hammer being slammed down once, over my memory of it being slammed down at least three times, but no more than five times, if it is not in the transcript at all?

"Then Justin added, 'Mr. Jewett is an experienced, skillful prosecutor and should have known Mr. Cook or Mr. Hoehn would object to him slamming the hammer down on the files, and therefore should have given them the opportunity to raise objections. But he chose to be deceitful about letting anyone know he was going to do that in front of the jury, so as not to risk being ordered by the court not to slam the hammer down. Then, after doing so, Mr. Jewett was not even admonished by the court or given a slap on the wrist.'

"To emphasize this point, Justin slapped himself on the wrist, and said angrily, 'Mr. Jewett got off scot-free!'

"As Justin glared down past Mr. Cook, at Mr. Jewett,

Jewett refused to turn away from Justin's sassy looks. He continued to glare back at Justin.

"Then Justin said that Jewett had misled the jury about the AK-47 he was supposed to own. Justin said, 'Mr. Jewett would just have the jury believe that I was walking around the city blasting an AK-47 at everyone!'

"Justin said that Jewett had implied that Justin was not just a follower of Taylor, but acted on his own. At that point, Justin started verbally going berserk and mouthing off as he leaned behind Mr. Cook's back toward Mr. Jewett. And Justin mouthed off to the judge as well, stating his notions and repeating analogies three or four times. His analogy would come full circle, but right when you thought it was over, he would lead into another analogy. To me, it seemed like pent-up anger that Justin had been holding back for so long.

"While he was rambling on, he said, 'I'm not the same person I was four-and-a-half years ago. I've grown since I've been in jail. You have to grow in jail or you'll die. It's sink or swim in there—so, of course, I'm not a follower now!

"'No, I don't think Taylor is a prophet anymore. I haven't been around Taylor since I've been in jail, so I've been able to grow to be assertive and in people's faces. If you're not, you'll die there. So when Mr. Jewett is comparing me to what I was like four-and-a-half years ago, it's like comparing apples to oranges.

"'And why, oh why, folks? Well, let me tell you why! Mr. Jewett is a liar and a hypocrite. I don't know which is worse! But I would think being a hypocrite is worse.'

"At this point, the court reporter said, 'Justin! Justin! Can you slow down some? I just want to be sure that I get everything you're saying.'

"Mr. Cook whispered to Justin in a very forceful manner, 'Calm down!'

"Justin looked over at Mr. Cook with his cocky half-smile, as if to show Cook that he no longer was under Mr. Cook's counsel, nor taking his advice.

"Then Justin asked Judge Mary Ann O'Malley to 'recant' herself. He probably meant to say recuse herself. He said, 'Your Honor, before we get started on the motion of the court recanting herself, I would like another judge to decide that motion, since it's just like Mr. Jewett deciding his own matter on prosecutorial misconduct.'

"Judge O'Malley nodded her acknowledgment at Justin's request and continued on with Justin's motions.

"Justin said that Judge O'Malley allowed the jury pool to grow too large during the screening process. And he disagreed with specific rulings throughout the trial. He implied that Judge O'Malley made her rulings based on emotions and personal feelings, rather than based on law. Justin said he would take any judge to rule on his objections except from Judge O'Malley's husband, who was also a Contra Costa County judge.

"Of this, he said, 'I understand your husband is a judge. So I wouldn't want your husband to be appointed to my case, since you're married to him.'

"Then Justin directed his arguments toward his counsel Mr. Cook. He said that Cook refused to subpoena a lot of people Justin requested. These included neighbors at Pacheco Manor with whom he had a very good relationship while growing up. He had also requested the Phister family, who had spoken at Taylor's trial, and several Sorenson relatives. Justin's reasoning for the Sorenson family, however, didn't make a lot of sense. He said, 'The information is out there in the Sorenson family. If Gail Kissam (a defense investigator) was not able to get the information from them, it was because the right questions were not asked. The Sorensons won't talk to Carma, or have anything to do with her. Carma calls up the Sorensons and all she gets is, "You're the Devil and your son is a murderer!" And then the phone clicks. The right approach was not taken. It's because if the right approach was taken, and if the court would have ordered a writ or a mandate, or something to order these people to tell the truth, under oath, under penalty of perjury, here in front of people, then I think there would have been a different result. The Sorensons don't believe in mental illness. They think if you murder someone, then the murderer should be executed. They don't believe mental illness might have played a part in it.'

"When it came time to rule on Justin's motions, Judge O'Malley reminded Justin that Mr. Jewett hit his file with the hammer one time to show the jury a person's intent to kill Selina Bishop. Since the hammer blow came during the guilt phase, it was allowed as evidence.

"Judge O'Malley refused to recuse herself and said she had made all of her decisions during the trials based upon the law. O'Malley stood fast that no inappropriate actions had occurred on her bench during the trial or at any time thereafter, and therefore she would remain the presiding judge in his case."

Simon Read, of the *Tri Valley Herald*, was also there and wrote of Justin's antics: "As he (Justin) explained his concerns with the prosecutor's case, Helzer often looked directly at Jewett and spoke as if scolding a child. Helzer castigated his defense team for not calling additional witnesses on his behalf. Among those he wanted called were his former neighbors for whom he had baked cookies."

By February 2005, Justin Helzer's cookie baking

days were over. In that month he awaited Judge O'Malley's formal declaration of his sentence, as did Taylor Helzer. The formal sentencing finally arrived on March 11, 2005. One of those allowed to speak for the families was Judy Nemec, the Stinemans' daughter. She said, "I've had four and a half years to compose this. I'm the youngest daughter of Ivan and Annette Stineman. My parents did the right things in life. They worked full time, paid their bills and taxes and provided a secure home life for my sister and me. As they raised their family, they invested in company stock with an eye toward retirement. They weren't wealthy, but they sacrificed to save for their retirement years. Once retired, they entrusted their savings to what they perceived to be a reputable trading company.

"My mom and dad were not ready to die. They were not terminally ill. They still had their faculties and were extremely active. They were members in several clubs, volunteers at the senior center, traveled frequently and enjoyed their pets, family and friends. They were the stereotypical elderly couple in their sunset years, living simply to assure their retirement money would see them through their lives.

"My parents didn't pass away. The Lord didn't call them home. And their time on earth was not up. Someone they knew, trusted and cared for handcuffed and shackled them and abducted them from the safety and security of their home. They were then drugged and forced to write checks for a large portion of the nest egg they worked so hard for.

"I still am haunted by the fact my parents were held hostage for a period of time. I don't care how smooth the perpetrators thought they were. I know my mother and dad. It doesn't matter that they were told they would be released in three days. The fact that they were handcuffed and guarded led them to suspect otherwise.

"It sickens me to know the last faces my parents saw were those of evil, uncaring people who were so greedy for my parents' retirement money that they were willing to kill for it. I am still dumbfounded that an impersonator can request your investments be liquidated by phone and it is done without question as long as the right information is provided.

"These murders go beyond cruel, based on Dawn Godman's testimony. After my parents were drugged and carried into the bathroom, they were awakened to say good-bye. Did the murderers need to see the panic and fear in my parents' eyes to know what it was like to kill?

"After unsuccessfully trying to smother my struggling parents, Justin Helzer beat my father to death, hammering his head on the bathroom floor again and again until his heart gave out. Daddy's autopsy report also indicated contusions to his upper chest and abdomen. These cowards found pleasure in beating a drugged, defenseless and arthritic eighty-five-year-old man.

"Glenn Taylor Helzer slit my mother's throat. Mama's right orbit bone fractured and she was stabbed more than twenty times, some wounds occurring before death according to the medical examiners. These gentle people spent their last hours on earth as terrified captives who were cruelly and brutally slain by evil personified for their retirement money. I can not think of anything more cowardly than to target helpless people to satisfy selfish greed.

"It would seem that learning my parents were captive, beaten, drugged, stabbed, dismembered, and my mother eviscerated and thrown out like garbage would be the hardest part of coping with this horror. It is not. Not finding them or knowing what happened to them was far worse. If nature hadn't intervened, the murderers would have been successful in their plan to hide what they had done.

"Mama and Daddy should have died with dignity. Instead, we laid our murdered and dismembered parents to rest on their 55th wedding anniversary. The mortician leading us throughout the early days of this horror, explained that the coroner was trying to assure that the right parts went to the right family. When we discussed the mortuary's involvement in my parents' preparation for burial, we were told that very little could be done other than to add a disinfectant to keep the smell down.

"My mother had an unnatural fear of water. Because of this, she and daddy arranged for a mausoleum crypt so she wouldn't be laid to rest in the wet ground. To know she was left in a watery grave haunts me to this day. There is no penalty in our judicial system to adequately compensate these people for their acts against these two sweet, trusting, elderly people. If the world were fair, the same amount of compassion would be shown the Helzers as they showed my parents. But the world is not fair.

"The impact of my parents' murders have [sic] had on my life a huge impact. After hearing the testimony, with four and a half years to adjust, I still have trouble believing the acts these three people carefully planned out. I know my mom and dad are gone, but the brutality of their deaths is still too horrific to accept. I'm confused, distracted, fearful, depressed, lost and alone. My life is a little too complicated for my long-time friends. I have suffered financially, since I am self-employed.

"My parents' ordeal was not an episode of *Law and Order*, in which fictional characters meet an untimely death and there is an arrest and trial in an hour. Ivan and Annette Stineman were living, kind, gentle and happy people. These two lovely people have always been a source of love and support in my life. They taught me that things happen for a reason, but there is no good reason for what happened to them.

"I will forever be haunted by the events that began on July 30, 2000. My sister and I knew something serious had happened to my mom and dad. I can only imagine how frightened they were before they were murdered. Due to the fact my mother's internal organs were removed, I'll never know if she was beaten, raped or whatever motivated these evil people to eviscerate her. It's not that I think of these things occasionally. Even with the passage of this incredible amount of time, I think of them constantly. Every day, every hour of my life.

"My parents were my best friends. Birthdays, Mother's Day, Father's Day and Thanksgiving are times when the grief is overwhelming. Christmas used to be a holiday our family looked forward to with food, family, friends and gifts. Now my husband, sister, aunt and I spend Christmas at the movies. I feel cheated and realize what I am feeling is nothing like the betrayal that Mama and Daddy must have felt.

"Throughout the Helzer trials, I have heard repeatedly the plan to bring unconditional love to the world. I found it ironic that the first comment I made when my parents' remains were recovered from the Delta was that my unconditional love was gone. I didn't appreciate it for what it was until it was taken away.

"Thankfully, I spent some quality time with Mama and Daddy two months to the day before they were murdered. I can still see them at the airport with their arms around each other, waving as I boarded my plane for home. My love for them is still as strong as it was the last time that we hugged good-bye."

After Judy Nemec, Justin Helzer spoke briefly. "I hope to see the day when globally all spiritual truths are fully and voluntarily embraced in our collective spiritual beings, the awareness in every mind great and small. And violence is never necessary, that love joy and peace are the only eternal constants so that confusion, fear and suffering no longer exist amongst us. That day's birth is in process, and though at times, the process is painful, when that day arrives, all will rejoice together. Thank you. That's all."

A few more matters were discussed between the judge and Justin's lawyers, and it almost went unnoticed that Carma Helzer wanted to speak from the gallery until Daniel Cook said, "Before you impose sentence in the remaining counts, would you please give the opportunity for my client's mother to be heard?"

With a soft, kind voice Judge Mary Ann O'Malley responded, "Absolutely. Ms. Helzer, go ahead."

In a voice, very much akin to Heather's voice on the stand, Carma said through tears, almost gasping for breath, "First of all, I would like to express my gratitude for the makers of the Constitution of the United States who attempted to the best of their ability to provide each of us as citizens to [sic] have a fair trial. I have never seen the system in action before and I thank all those who formed it and all those who are doing their best to implement the intention of giving us a fair trial.

"I want to express my gratitude to all of you who took part in this and did your very best. I know that everyone in this room . . . well, I feel that those who took part in this are doing their best to create a safe place for us to live in comfort and peace. And I do not take this as a personal vendetta against anyone in particular. This (case) has moved through with a desire and intention for peace and safety for all.

"I want to acknowledge the tremendous amount of suffering that has been experienced because of all of this and I also acknowledge the natural tendency to blame families and mothers and parents for people who they believe committed the crime. Everybody who does blame me, I don't blame you for blaming me. And those who blame Justin, I don't blame you for blaming him. And I understand all the reasons for it.

"I want to thank you, Judge O'Malley, today, publicly, for your efforts in creating a safe place for us to live. I want to thank you, Mr. Jewett, publicly today, for doing what you think is right in creating a safe place for us to live. And I want to thank the juries publicly and all the people, the time and sacrifice that they made in following through on their duties as citizens. And I know how hard . . . well, I don't know how hard it must have been, because I wasn't there, but I can imagine it.

"And I want to thank Justin's attorneys for doing their best.

"I want to thank my son, for being my son, and for all the blessings he's brought into my life and to many other people in his life before these events occurred. I know, Justin, that you are not the sum of what you've been convicted of, but you are far more than that. All of us are far more than just one event in our lives and one stupid mistake.

"Thank you for letting me speak."

Once again in a thoughtful voice, Judge O'Malley said, "You're welcome, Mrs. Helzer."

Now it was time. Judge O'Malley read through the various counts and said, "Therefore, this is to command you, the Sheriff of said Contra Costa County, as provided in said judgement, to take Justin Alan Helzer to the State Prison at San Quentin, California, and deliver him into the custody of the warden of the State Prison.

"Further, this is to command you, the warden of the State Prison at San Quentin, California, to hold in your custody the said Justin Alan Helzer pending the decision of this cause on appeal, and upon this judgement becoming final, to carry into effect the judgement of said Court at a time and on a date to be hereafter fixed by order of this Court within the State Prison and at which time and place you shall then and there put to death said Justin Alan Helzer, in the manner and means prescribed by law.

"In witness thereof, I have hereunto set my hand as Judge of said Superior Court and have caused the seal of the said Court to be affixed hereto, in open court this day of March 11, 2005."

Then in the absolutely silent courtroom, she wrote her name on the document, and everyone could hear the sound of the pen as it moved along the paper.

That same afternoon, it was Taylor's turn. Robert Asuncion once again spoke for his side of the family and former Detective Erin Inskip spoke of what the tragedy had done to her personally. She said in part, "In the thirteen years I was in law enforcement, I have to say this, in the courtroom when I entered here, I was scared to death. I thank you Mr. Jewett and his team for every sacrifice that they made. It makes me really sad to know that Mr. Helzer took out five beautiful people in a very brutal fashion."

Turning directly toward Taylor she said, "You profoundly affected my life, and I mean it affected every aspect of my life. It still does today. Unfortunately, I lost my career as a result of this. During a conversation in the jail (with Taylor) he said, that he was afraid. That's why he jumped out of the car and took off running. And said that he was sorry that he had done that. He hoped that he hadn't hurt my career.

"You know, I think that at times, people have an expectation of law enforcement, that we're strong and that we have to be in order to do our job. Without going into great detail, what I witnessed was awful. It was absolutely awful, and to know that it happened to a person . . . well, they weren't strangers to Mr. Helzer. They trusted him and allowed him into their lives.

"I'll never be able to understand how a person can do that to another person. It just makes no sense. I'm not the only one who struggles with that. I will always struggle with that.

"As I reflect on the initial part of our investigation . . . Selina was a smart cookie. Her intuition told her that something was not right. And she put the pen to paper and put her thoughts down on paper. And she left her pager behind. Nobody will know why she did that. I think she had a sixth sense. I think she knew that something wrong was happening. And as an investigator I'm so glad we had that information, because it took us to the right place in a very short period of time."

(Pointing to the Stineman daughters and Selina's relatives) "I have an extended family now. More brothers and sisters. I love each and everyone of you. And God bless you. I am so, so sorry."

Ms. Chapot spoke briefly on Taylor's behalf, saying there was more to him than just a murderer. "Taylor is not all evil. There is a wonderful, wonderful part of Taylor. A fascinating, interesting, good part of Taylor. That I was not able to show that sufficiently in court is a burden that I have to bear for the rest of my life."

Finally it was the turn of the mastermind of everything that had happened in the Days of Thunder in

2000. A hush fell over the court room as Taylor Helzer stood and began to address the gallery.

He told the people in the packed gallery that he felt like he risked giving offense by speaking or keeping silent, and he apologized if his words did give offense. He acknowledged that even his presence might give offense. He said that his hope was that his words might speed the healing process for them. And then he said that he realized that his actions had been "unspeakably horrific," and that he was very, very sorry. Taylor said that at the time, his actions were not meant to be horrific. He turned toward Detective Erin Inskip and said that he had been doing a good thing.

Taylor explained that if he was purely evil, he would delight in their misery. Then he added, this was not the case, and to continue hating him was to give him power. He said, "I cannot conceive of suggesting that you forgive. I suggest that if you choose not to forgive, that you consider me less than dirt on your shoes, and do whatever you can to forget me. If your peace of mind depends on my execution, you give my life and my choices continuous power over you and your lives."

Taylor said that evil had no value, and that he hoped their memories of him would fade when he was executed. If they obtained joy from his death, then he was for that. He asked why they should even taint their thoughts with him, and he understood why they, and society, would want to execute him. From here, however, his words veered in a different direction. Taylor spoke of children who were mentally, emotionally, sexually and physically addicted to drugs and dangerous behavior. They turned to crime to support their habits. He said these things led to murder, but could the people in the courtroom, say in all honesty, that the murderers should not have time to repent and change their ways?

He announced that a trial often hund in the balance between two unequal actors (in a reference to Mr. Jewett and Ms. Chapot). He said that in America, a great deal of time and money was placed in a capital case to try and enforce fairness. Then he added that governments less noble than America's used capital punishment for political ends. He called it legalized, state-sanctioned murder.

At this point, Mr. Jewett became incensed at the direction that Taylor's speech was going. Jewett said to Judge O'Malley, "Could I request if the defendant is going to talk about the government, he be admonished to contain his comments to the Court and not the gallery, please?"

Taylor replied, "If you want me to, I will."

Judge O'Malley said, "If you're talking about policy on the death pentalty, address those comments to me. If you're apolgizing to the victims' families, you may make your comments to the audience. Thank you."

Taylor replied, "Thank you. And thank you, Mr. Jewett." He then faced Judge O'Malley and said that governments less noble than that of the United States murdered thousands of innocent people with the specific intent to keep themselves in power. He added, that by having the death penalty in the United States, the government lost whatever moral high ground they sought to obtain within the whole community. Then he said he was done talking about the death penalty, and turned once more toward the gallery, and Detective Inskip in particular.

Then Taylor turned once more to the gallery. "Ms. Inskip brought such a sense of openness and honesty and such pain with the statement that she didn't understand. I have felt until I saw it per you that what I did was inexplicable. And forgive me and I'm sorry if I offend anybody else by this explanation. For one person, I'm going to try to explain. And you can believe it or not, but this is the truth.

"This is the explanation if anybody wants to know how. For those of you who don't, again, I'm sorry. I care so much about people. Worldwide. I feel like we're a selective unit. I feel like we're all spirit beings having a human experience, trying to progress."

Now Taylor became very emotional and on the verge of tears. "Hundreds of thousands of people live in absolute abject poverty. Sexual slavery. Little boys are raped and sold as slaves. In the *Contra Costa Times* there are articles on slavery.

"There's so much pain on a global scale in this world and the division of wealth is abhorrently concentrated in the small concentration of people. Murders, rape, thefts, terrorism, wars . . . and we don't care. The wealth is in this country and we don't care if it's not our family and if it's not our friends. We don't care.

"We go along in our materialistic desire to pursue short-term happiness and as long as our loved ones are fine, who cares about the millions starving, dying, being raped, enslaved economically, physically and sexually. It just doesn't matter.

"I reached a point where I was so blessed in my life, that I got fixated. I couldn't sleep at night with the hypocrisy I found in myself, enjoying the absolute beauty of life while millions of people suffered. And I had a vision in my head what I could do to solve it if I cared enough, to follow God as much as Nephi, as much as Abraham, the prophets, through the ages.

"I saw clearly, accurate, inaccurate, who cares, how it could occur with $200,000. And people were getting in my way . . . well, whatever. I think you get the point.

"If anybody thinks this is justification, it is not justification. It is no attempt to justify my actions. There is no way I would do that. In pure idiocy, I did a coldhearted calculation. I thought, be a hypocrite. Enjoy your life to the utmost and fullness and let the world suffer for a finite amount or save millions. And that's your answer how."

Outraged that Taylor considered Selina to be a finite number and not a real human being, Roseanne Lusk Urban sitting in the second row of the gallery waved a small photo of Selina Bishop at him in anger. Taylor noticed her action and mouthed the words, "I see it."

Despite his words, despite his detailed explanation of what had motivated him in those Days of Thunder, Judge Mary Ann O'Malley stressed the same points as she had done with Justin Helzer, only hours before. She commanded that Glenn Taylor Helzer be taken to San Quentin Prison and suffer the death penalty for his crimes against Ivan Stineman, Annette Stineman, Selina Bishop, Jenny Villarin and James Gamble.

EPILOGUE

In March 2005, Taylor and Justin's sister, Heather, tried to make sense of how things had gone so terribly wrong. She began to write her thoughts down on paper beginning with their youth.

Childhood

Taylor and Justin were best friends from childhood. I remember them riding their big-wheels (and later bicycles) off to grand adventures, making elaborate set-ups with their plastic toy soldiers, and running off to play too fast for me to catch up with them. I remember them being super-heroes, wrestling, and stick-fighting each other. We did occasionally play together. I remember Go Fish, Candyland, and Chutes and Ladders. Taylor and Justin were unusually nice brothers. For example, they never hit me which would have actually been normal sibling behavior. As for fighting, neither of them ever started a fight with other children. I remember Justin coming home from elementary school after losing a fight though. It made the world seem scary but Taylor stepped in the next day and Justin didn't get another bully lesson. I don't remember Taylor ever getting into a physical fight. All Taylor's fights were verbal and he always seemed to win them. When Taylor was twelve and Justin was ten, they both shared a paper route for a couple of years. I remember that Taylor spent all of his money and that Justin saved almost all of his. Justin bought the bicycle he had wanted and being content, quit the paper route. I believe all three of us were more self-reliant than average children since once mother hit her late teens she found that she was "ill" about half the time. If she could be induced to see a psychologist, I am confident that she would be diagnosed as psychosomatic. Probably like Taylor and Justin, I was about ten when I realized that she actually wasn't dying and that although her "sick" days represented some challenges caring for ourselves, they were also opportunities to do whatever we wanted. Please note that half the time our mother was very present in our lives, playing, teaching, hugging, listening, etc. It is just that half the time she wasn't and since our father held so firmly to the idea that women were to take care of children, and men were to earn the money, he didn't bother to notice the situation.

Adolescence

Taylor was able to make friends and girlfriends easily, and since Justin didn't make friends easily, Justin was more than willing to make do with being "Taylor's brother." Interestingly, despite their close ages, they never attended high school together. Justin was home-schooled for eighth grade and his Freshman year. When Justin began his Sophomore year at Ygnacio

Valley High, Taylor had decided to test out of high school and begin college a year early. Taylor lasted a semester at college. As for Justin at high school, he became a self-styled nerd. He might have been labeled such anyway, but he played it like it was his Oscar role. He actually sought out hazing and ridicule and his classmates willingly gave it. Justin's social behavior was outrageous and he was shunned except for two other boys who did not speak English well and had their own troubles being accepted. As his sister, I was angry with him for being "super-geek" when I knew how nice he was at home. Like many teenagers though, I thought my friends were supposed to be the focus of my life and beyond privately telling Justin that I thought he was being dumb, left him to himself. My parents never knew how high school was going for Justin. However, adolescence was the time our family did more things together because our father noticed that we were not children anymore and therefore more enjoyable. As a family we watched movies, went camping, played video games, went to the library, and occasionally ate dinner together as I had finally learned to cook.

River Rafting

In the summer of 1991 my father, thankfully, skipped the "mid-life crisis" many men go through and instead found a hobby he couldn't do without, in river rafting. Not only that, by the time we reached young adulthood, Dad had realized that Taylor, Justin and I were some of his favorite people, that he absolutely loved us, and that he was willing to tell us so. By the summer of 1992, Dad had gone to guide school, had all the equipment, and was rafting every Saturday. Since our whole family enjoyed rafting, we joined him much of the time. River rafting was definitely our family thing. Our river of choice was the American. Some days we'd do the upper fork, some days the lower fork, some days we'd do both. After going through "Troublemaker," the biggest rapid on the upper fork, we'd pull the rafts over, climb onto the rocks, and have lunch while we watched other rafts go through it. There were plenty of jump off spots to use to cool us off without getting in the paths of rafts that weren't stopping, so it was a great time for water play. And of course, the scenery was fantastic. River rafting was a part of my family's life heavily in the early 1990's, frequently in the later 1990's, but virtually stopped after 2000.

How did this happen?

In short, the answer would be Taylor. The complete answer includes five factors, where if any had not been present, I doubt murder would have happened.

The first ingredient was Taylor's natural charismatic personality. To date, I have never met anyone like him. He was certainly the most interesting person in our family and we willingly gave him center stage. He could talk so convincingly, had genuinely great ideas, and had a talent for making anyone feel special. All of us expected him to do great things in his life and he expected to do so as well.

The second ingredient was the history of mental illness on our mother's side of the family. Our grandmother was suicidal, our grandmother's sister was institutionalized much of her life and had children who were likewise institutionalized. We have had several close relatives (aunts, uncles, cousins) who have been institutionalized or diagnosed as mentally disabled. Out of the nine children of my maternal grandparents that reached adulthood, many, including my mother, find it challenging to care for themselves and function in roles such as "employee" or "parent" or "spouse."

The third ingredient was our family religion. The Church of Christ of Latter Day Saints. We were a very religious family and Taylor and Justin definitely used the teachings, which ranged from being honest and giving service, to no sex before marriage and no alcohol, as the foundation of their morality. When they lost that foundation by leaving their religion (Taylor in 1995 and Justin in 1996), they began a process of establishing new principals to live by and appeared to be stagnating in life in terms of education, careers and relationships. However, Taylor and Justin still held to some of the concepts of our religion which included Jesus Christ's establishing a church while on earth, that there was a falling away from the truths that He taught, that a prophet was called to restore those truths, that we have a prophet today, and that Jesus Christ will return to earth someday amid great turbulence. These concepts of course were to become the core of their delusion with Taylor being a restorer of God's truth.

The fourth ingredient was LGAP's (Large Group Awareness Programs). These are low-level, live-out cults and our family became involved in one called IMPACT in 1991. For a substantial profit they make you feel horrible and then super special using some truth, group psychological tactics, late hours, and hypnosis. Then there is nothing left for you to do but bring all your friends. This we faithfully did and our family phased out of IMPACT after the appropriate year of so span of time that LGAP's plan on keeping you. Unfortunately, and unusually so, Taylor felt drawn back to IMPACT in 1994, two years after having gotten out. He led my mother, father, and Justin back into other LGAP's called Introspect and Harmony. For Taylor and Justin, LGAP's were a part of their lives through the late 1990's. One LGAP teaching that stands out under the circumstances is, "There is no right or wrong, only what works." That seems like a particularly dangerous idea to put into a mentally fragile mind. Normally LGAP's teach people how to follow cult leaders and Justin (and Dawn as well), became well trained at doing so by attending LGAP's. On the other hand, Taylor, being the unique person that he is, learned somethng different. Taylor learned how to *be* a cult leader and he apparently created the more destructive, live-in kind.

The fifth ingredient was drugs. This is a very common component in crime today. Methamphetamine makes everyone psychotic eventually and it turns out Taylor had been using for several years rather than giving them up in 1999, like I thought.

I see these five factors coming together as the cause for the tragic deaths of so many people. Everyone knows that drugs are bad, but few people know how to recognize signs of mental illness in their loved ones and the times of life they usually show up. Fewer still are aware of the destructiveness of cults, how common they are, and how they solicit and ensnare.

Please notice that I do not consider my parents' moderate failings worth rating as a factor in the murderous events of August 2000. I mention their failings so as to bury any hypothesis that might exaggerate them. I know it is quite popular for children, parents themselves, and the public in general to blame parents for failings of their children. However, if one was to give it more than a moment's thought they would be compelled to admit that many children have had

a somewhat distant parent and/or one that was divided between their love for their child and their
own "issues" and yet proceeded to turn out fine. In
fact, having a mother and father without moderately
flawed parenting skills is a rare thing.

So there it was in a nutshell. In some ways, Heather
had analyzed her family dynamics and the personality
traits and outside factors that influenced Taylor and
Justin, as well as more learned psychiatrists and psychologists. Some of the things she had witnessed in the
1990's, especially the spell of IMPACT, and Harmony,
frightened her, and she fled to distant regions to escape
its influence. She fled beyond Taylor's influence to
drag her down as it had others in his orbit.

The last of the sentencings for the Children of
Thunder was on Monday May 2, 2005, for Dawn
Godman. By that point, court observer Chris Darden
pondered Taylor Helzer's last ride from his home
county of Contra Costa to San Quentin in Marin
County, after his being sentenced to death in March.
Taylor's ride in a prison van, crossed over the Rich-
mond/San Rafael Bridge beneath the shadows of
Mount Tamalpais. Chris said, "I wondered if Taylor
would recall the early morning hours of August 3,
2000, when he and Dawn had driven the exact same
route to kill Jennifer Villarin, and by extension, James
Gamble. It was these last two murders that had been
Taylor's and the Children of Thunder's undoing.

"Until the Marin County Sheriff's Office got
involved, and especially Detective Steve Nash, the
Stinemans and Selina were just missing persons.
Once Taylor had pumped those 9 mm bullets into

Jenny and James, the bullets would lead in a long chain back through Selina's pager and other items to the Helzers. It was the murders in Marin County that started tying everything together. It was so typical. Taylor never knew when to quit. His meth use, his aggression and his narcissism, did him in, in the end. Unfortunately, he brought so many people down with him."